About This Book

This book demonstrates that a handful of companies have gained an alarming level of control over the food chain through the industrialisation of agriculture, the forces of globalisation, and the vertical and horizontal integration of business. These corporations are deeply involved in the current push for genetic engineering in agriculture. Industry argues that genetic engineering is the technology of the next industrial revolution and that it can help resolve the problem of hunger. This book shows that the way the technology is being applied is instead a continuation and intensification of an industrial agriculture model that has failed to live up to its expectations and promises. Rather than offer new solutions, genetic engineering will advance a stronger, already established trend towards the social, political and economic reorganisation of our communities according to the interests of the world's largest corporations, with little regard for environmental and social impacts. In this context, genetic engineering is not merely a new technology, but a means to gain power over people and resources.

After looking at how biotechnology was introduced in the name of solving the hunger problem, the book surveys the green revolution and then explores the growth of the corporation, its acquisition of rights and its gradual shedding of liability for and limitations on its activities. We touch on the various elements that are key to the success of transnational corporations (TNCs): the liberalisation of financial markets, the extension of patents on living organisms and their parts, and the appropriation of research. We then focus on the institutions the TNCs create, shape, hire or manipulate for their purposes: public relations companies, biotech trade organisations, think tanks, the World Bank, UN institutions, universities and research bodies, governments, the World Trade Organisation. Finally, we look at how the activities of TNCs are now being directed at developing countries, and how the small farmers and regions that escaped the impacts of the green revolution, such as Africa, are a particular target.

The authors have selected examples to indicate patterns and trends. Detailed references are included to show where further information can be found. Change will continue to be rapid. The aim of this book is to show how the corporate promotion of GM crops has proceeded to date, in order to provide the basis for developing an accurate analysis of events as they unfold in the future. The book can be read straight through, dipped into or kept as a reference. The aim is to make the information in it as accessible as possible. The Econexus and PAN–AP websites offer further information.

Hungry Corporations
Transnational Biotech Companies Colonise the Food Chain

Helena Paul and Ricarda Steinbrecher

with Devlin Kuyek and Lucy Michaels

In association with Econexus and the Pesticide Action
Network Asia–Pacific (PAN–AP)

Zed Books

LONDON & NEW YORK

Hungry Corporations was first published in 2003 by
Zed Books Ltd, 7 Cynthia Street, London N1 9JF, UK and
Room 400, 175 Fifth Avenue, New York, NY 10010, USA

www.zedbooks.co.uk

in association with

Econexus and the Pesticide Action
Network Asia–Pacific (PAN–AP)

Cover designed by Andrew Corbett
Designed and set in 10/12 pt MT Bembo
by Long House, Cumbria, UK
Printed and bound in Malta by Gutenberg Ltd

Distributed in the USA exclusively by Palgrave, a division
of St. Martin's Press, LLC, 175 Fifth Avenue, New York 10010

A catalogue record for this book is available from the British Library
US CIP data is available from the Library of Congress

ISBN 1 84277 300 3 cased
ISBN 1 84277 301 1 limp

Contents

List of Tables and Boxes   vii
List of Abbreviations   ix
About the Authors and Organisations   xii
Acknowledgements   xiv

1 In the Name of Hunger:
   Paving the Road to Biotech Agriculture   **1**
   Prologue   1
   The green revolution   4
   From green revolution to gene revolution   13
   Economic globalisation and debt creation   15
   Free trade and its inconsistencies   17

2 Corporations: from Royal Charters to
   Biotech Gold Rush   **21**
   A brief history of the corporation   21
   Factors in the growth of the biotechnology industry   24
   The extension of patents to genes, cells and organisms   28
   'Independent' research companies   36
   A new gold rush: the run on genes and genomes   38

3 Image Control: Manipulation and Public Relations   **45**
   Growth and consolidation of the public relations industry   46
   Cleaning the corporate image   47
   Corporate mind control   52
   Helping hands   62

4 Consolidation, Contamination and
   Loss of Diversity: the Biotech Dream Takes Hold   **78**
   The life science concept   78
   Consolidation in the agrochemical industries   82

Consolidation in the seed industry 83
Loss of agricultural diversity: Seminis and Savia 87
GM contamination: plot or blunder? 88

5 The Main International Players and Corporate Influence **101**
The World Bank 102
The Consultative Group for International Agricultural
    Research (CGIAR) 108
International foundations 122
International organisations promoting biotechnology 124
Universities and research institutes 130

6 Corporate Influence on International Regulatory Bodies **147**
Corporate influence at the World Trade Organisation (WTO) 147
Transatlantic Business Dialogue (TABD) 149
The Food and Agriculture Organisation (FAO) 151
Codex Alimentarius: UN body for food standards 152
The Convention on Biological Diversity (CBD) 154

7 Government Legislation and Corporate Influence **161**
Exerting influence worldwide 162
US legislation 164
European Union legislation 171
Central and Eastern Europe: a corporate paradise 173

8 Opening Up the South **184**
GM crops worldwide 186
Agricultural research and development 186
Promoting technology to farmers 189
Micro-credit agencies 196
Binding the farmer to the corporation 199
Lack of choice for farmers 202
Argentina: the cost of complying with US pressure 203
Preparing the ground for GM 206
The struggle for Africa's agriculture 210
Resistance in the South 214
ConTill: Monsanto's brand of sustainable development 217

9 Conclusion: Summing Up and Moving On **226**

Index 233

Tables and Boxes

Tables

3.1 Examples of biotech proponents, their websites and
anti-environmentalist views 68
4.1 World crop protection 84
4.2 Global ranking 2001 by sector: agrochemicals, seeds and
pharmaceuticals, based on revenues in 2000 84
4.3 The world's top ten seed corporations 86
5.1 How the World Bank finances G7 pesticide producers 106
6.1. Revenues of largest TNCs compared with country GNPs 148
8.1 Countries planting GM crops in 2001 and 2002 187
8.2 GM crop areas and percentages (of total crop and of total GM
planted globally) in 2001 and 2002 187
8.3 Traits expressed by GM crops planted worldwide for 2001 and
2002, as areas and percentages 187
8.4 SG 2000 collaborators 195

Boxes

Sketch of an anti-revolutionary 7
Living soil: the importance of a healthy soil food web 10
From war chemicals to agrochemicals 13
Benefiting the colonial powers 22
British Biotech misleads investors 27
Myriad, Syngenta and the rice genome 39
Contaminated seed 89
Contamination through food aid 95
Partnerships with agribusiness 107
Creeping contradictions: IPRs and the CGIAR system 115
True breeding lines versus F1 hybrids 120

Bt treasure trove 122
Monsanto and the ISAAA 126
Other current programmes of the CNFA 129
Corporate funding of US universities and patents 132
The John Innes Centre (JIC), UK 134
An example of appropriate use of the precautionary principle
    from 150 years ago 157
Threatening Sri Lanka with the WTO 162
Teamwork to put pressure on Ireland 163
Pulling strings in Pakistan 163
GM foods: not approval – just acknowledgement 168
ConTill in Costa Rica 220

Abbreviations

ABUCO	Association of Burundi Consumers	BIA	BioIndustry Association
ACDI/ VOCA	Agricultural Cooperative Development International	BIO	Biotechnology Industry Organisation
ACI	Advance Chemical Industries Ltd	BIOTHAI	Biodiversity and Community Rights Action, Thailand
ACRE	Advisory Committee on Releases to the Environment	BRAC	Bangladesh Rural Advancement Committee
ACSH	American Council on Science and Health	BSE	Bovine spongiform encephalopathy
ADM	Archer Daniels Midland (GM grain company)	Bt	*Bacillus thuringiensis*
AEBC	Agriculture and Environment Biotechnology Commission	CABIO	Collaborative Agricultural Biotechnology Initiative
AFRC	Agriculture and Food Research Council	CBD	Convention on Biological Diversity
Agbiotech	Agricultural biotechnology	CBI	Council for Biotechnology Information
AGOA	African Growth and Opportunity Act	CCPR	Codex Committee on Pesticide Residues
AIA	Advance Informed Agreement	CDMT	Change Design and Management Team (CGIAR)
AIBA	All India Biotech Association	CEE	Central and Eastern Europe
AICHA	Agricultural Initiative to Cut Hunger in Africa	CEI	Competitive Enterprise Institute
ANPED	Northern Alliance for Sustainability	CEO	Chief executive officer
APEC	Asia–Pacific Economic Cooperation	CEPR	Centre for Economic and Policy Research
APHIS	Animal and Plant Health Inspection Service (of USDA)	CGIAR	Consultative Group for International Agricultural Research
APSA	Asia Pacific Seed Association		
ASEAN	Association of South-East Asian Nations	CIAT	Centre for Tropical Agriculture
ASSINSEL	International Association of Plant Breeders for the Protection of Plant Varieties	CIDA	Canadian International Development Agency
		CIMMYT	International Maize and Wheat Improvement Centre (Mexico)
BBSRC	Biotechnology and Biological Science Research Centre	CIP	International Potato Centre
		CNAA	Citizens' Network Agribusiness Alliance
BCSD	Business Council for Sustainable Development	CNFA	Citizens' Network for Foreign Affairs

CRRI	Central Rice Research Institute	IDA	International Development Association
CSD	Cotton Seed Distributors		
CSIRO	Commonwealth Scientific and Industrial Research Organisation	IDEA	Investment in Developing Export Agriculture
CTNBio	National Technical Biosafety Commission	IDEC	Brazilian Consumer Defence Institute
EPA	Environmental Protection Agency	IEA	Institute of Economic Affairs
		IFAD	International Fund for Agricultural Development
ESEF	European Science and Environment Forum	IFC	International Finance Corporation
ETC	Action Group on Erosion Technology and Concentration	IFPRI	International Food Policy Research Institute
EU	European Union		
FACTT	Familiarisation with and Acceptance of Crops Incorporating Transgenic Technology in Modern Agriculture	IFVC	Institute for Food and Vegetable Crops
		IGAU	Indira Gandhi Agricultural University
		IITA	International Institute of Tropical Agriculture
FAO	Food and Agriculture Organisation	ILRI	International Livestock Research Institute
FDA	Food and Drug Administration	IMF	International Monetary Fund
FTAA	Free Trade Area of the Americas	IP	Intellectual property
GATT	General Agreement on Tariffs and Trade	IPM	Integrated pest management
		IPR(s)	Intellectual property right(s)
GE	Genetic engineering	IRGSP	International Rice Sequencing Group
GEAC	Genetic Engineering Approval Committee	IRMA	Insect-Resistant Maize for Africa
GENET	European NGO Network on Genetic Engineering	IRRI	International Rice Research Institute
GFAR	Global Forum on Agricultural Research	ISAAA	International Service for the Acquisition of Agri-Biotech Applications
GM	Genetic modification, genetically modified	ISNAR	International Service for National Agricultural Research
GMO	Genetically modified organism	ISSSA	Initiative on Seed Supply in Sub-Saharan Africa
GRAIN	Genetic Resources Action International	ITDG	Intermediate Technology Development Group
GRAS	Generally regarded as safe	JIC	John Innes Centre
GURT	Genetic use restriction technology	KARI	Kenyan Agricultural Research Institute
ha	Hectare		
HIPC	Heavily indebted poor countries	KMP	Kilusang Magbubukid ng Pilipinas (Peasant Movement of the Philippines)
HRV	High response varieties		
HYV	High-yielding varieties		
IARC	International agricultural research centre	LMO	Living modified organism
		LSBC	Large Scale Biology Corporation
ICARDA	International Centre for Agricultural Research in Dry Areas	Mahyco	Maharashtra Hybrid Seed Company
ICIPE	International Centre of Insect Physiology and Ecology	MAI	Multilateral Agreement on Investment
ICRISAT	International Crops Research Institute for Semi-Arid Tropics		
ICSID	International Centre for Settlement of Investment Disputes		

MASIPAG	Farmer–Scientist Partnership for Development		International
MEA	Multilateral environmental agreement	RIAD	Red Interamericana de Democracia (Interamerican Network on Democracy)
MIGA	Multilateral Investment Guarantee Agency	SAA	Sasakawa Africa Association
MPRRI	Madhya Pradesh Rice Research Institute	SAP	Structural adjustment programme
MRL	Maximum residue limit	SDPI	Sustainable Policy Development Unit, Pakistan
mt	Metric tons	SEC	Securities and Exchange Commission
MTA	Material Transfer Agreement		
NADII	Novartis Agricultural Discovery Institute Inc.	SERC	Science and Engineering Research Council
NAFTA	North American Free Trade Agreement	SG 2000	Sasakawa–Global 2000 Programme
NARS	National agricultural research system	SIBAT	Wellspring of Science Technology
NCBI	National Center for Biotechnology Information	SPLT	Substantive Patent Law Treaty
		SPS	Sanitary and Phytosanitary
NFSD	Novartis Foundation for Sustainable Development	TABD	Transatlantic Business Dialogue
NGIN	Norfolk Genetic Information Network	TAC	Technical Advisory Committee (CGIAR)
NGO	Non-governmental organisation	TASSC	The Advancement of Sound Science Coalition
NIS	Newly Independent States (of the former USSR)	TBT	Technical Barriers to Trade
		TNC	Transnational corporations
NRC	National Research Council	TRIPs	Trade-related Intellectual Property Rights
OECD	Organisation for Economic Cooperation and Development	TWN	Third World Network
ONFARM	On-Farm Agricultural Resources Management	UBINIG	Policy Research for Development Alternatives
OPEC	Organisation of Petroleum Exporting Countries	UK	United Kingdom
		UN	United Nations
PA	Precautionary Approach	UNDP	United Nations Development Programme
PANNA	Pesticide Action Network North America	UNEP	United Nations Environment Programme
PAN–AP	Pesticide Action Network Asia–Pacific	UPOV	Union for the Protection of New Varieties of Plants
PASAD	Provincial Advocates for Sustainable Development	US	United States (of America)
PBRs	Plant breeders' rights	USDA	US Department of Agriculture
PCB	Polychlorinated biphenyl	USSR	Union of Soviet Socialist Republics
PCT	Patent Cooperation Treaty		
PEACE	Pesticide Efficacy Advisory Centres	VAD	Vitamin A deficiency
		WBCSD	World Business Council for Sustainable Development
PEM	Protein energy malnutrition		
PGS	Plant Genetics Systems	WFP	World Food Programme
PP	Precautionary Principle	WHO	World Health Organisation
PR	Public relations	WIPO	World Intellectual Property Organisation
PRSV	Papaya ring spot virus		
R	Real (Brazilian currency)	WPP	Wire and Plastic Products
R&D	Research and development	WTO	World Trade Organisation
RAFI	Rural Advancement Foundation		

About the Authors and Organisations

Helena Paul worked with the Gaia Foundation on indigenous rights, the protection of rainforests, patents on life, and genetic engineering. She was the European representative on the International Committee of Oilwatch International and an active co-founder and participant in the UK Forest Network, the No Patents on Life Coalition and the Genetic Engineering Network. She was a co-founder and chair of the UK Five Year Freeze on Genetic Engineering in Food and Farming. She is now an independent consultant and member of Econexus, and also works with the Programme on Corporations Law and Democracy in the United States.

Lucy Michaels has campaigned both locally and nationally in the UK to raise awareness about genetic engineering and industrial agriculture. She has worked with the Women's Environmental Network in London and as a guest researcher for Econexus, and is currently the food and agriculture researcher at CorporateWatch UK – a small radical research and publishing group based in Oxford.

Devlin Kuyek is an activist researcher who spent nearly three years with PAN–AP (see below), leading its Pesticide Industry Programme and organising the launch of the International Alliance Against Agrochemical TNCs. Since leaving PAN–AP, he has conducted research for international networks of peasant movements, farmers' organisations and NGOs in Asia and Africa into the impacts of emerging trends in agricultural research and development on small farmers, and published a study of the development of Canadian biotechnology policy in 2002. He is a member of the Groupe de Recherche de Technosciences du Vivant et Société at the University of Quebec in Montreal and of the recently formed Union Paysanne. He joined the staff of GRAIN in 2003.

Ricarda Steinbrecher, a biologist and genetic scientist, is Director of Econexus. She is a critic of gene patenting and genetic engineering in food and farming, and has worked closely with NGOs and grassroots groups on these issues since 1994. She is an adviser to many national and international NGOs and works in collaboration with researchers at universities in the United Kingdom, the United States and Asia on issues of genetic engineering, toxicity and gene ecology. For four years she acted as adviser and advocate at the negotiations for the Cartagena Protocol on Biosafety – part of the UN Convention on Biological Diversity – which concluded in January 2000. She has taken part in numerous government consultations on British and European legislation to regulate genetically modified organisms (GMOs) and patents, as well as on the repercussions of experimental trials and the commercialisation of GMOs in the UK.

Econexus is a non-profit research organisation and watchdog investigating the impacts of modern technologies, especially genetic engineering, on the environment, health and society. More recently it has been examining corporate involvement in development issues and science.

Econexus, PO Box 3279, Brighton BN1 1UR, UK
E-mail: contact@econexus.info
http://www.econexus.info

Pesticide Action Network (PAN) Asia–Pacific is part of an international network formed to protect people and the environment from pesticide use and genetic engineering and to promote alternatives, especially people-centred, pro-women development through sustainable agriculture.

PAN Asia–Pacific, PO Box 1170, 10850 Penang, Malaysia
Telephone: (604) 657 0271/656 0381
E-mail: panap@panap.net
http://www.panap.net

Acknowledgements

We would like to express our gratitude to the many people who have helped us with advice and information at different times. Among them we would particularly like to thank Iza Kruszewska, Brewster and Kathleen Kneen, Brian Tokar, Jennifer Mourin, Hartmut Meyer, Devinder Sharma, Rowan Tilly, Jose Lutzenberger, Elizabeth Bravo, Tewolde Egziabher and Sue Edwards, Hope Shand, Liz Hosken, David Hathaway, Beth Burrows, Michael Hansen, Patrick Mulvany, Clem Davis, Claire Watson, Jonathan Matthews, Bob Evans, Robert Vint, Antje Lorch, Florianne Koechlin, Joyce Hambling, Angela Cordeiro, Moyra Bremner, Farida Akhter and Elfrieda Pschorn-Strauss.

We would like to thank the Polden-Puckham Charitable Foundation, Tracy Worcester, Edward Goldsmith and Hivos (The Hague) for providing funds to distribute free copies of this book in the global south and in Eastern Europe.

1

In the Name of Hunger:
Paving the Road to Biotech Agriculture

Food has long been a political tool in US foreign policy. Twenty-five years ago USDA Secretary Earl Butz told the 1974 World Food Conference in Rome that food was a weapon, calling it 'one of the principal tools in our negotiating kit'. As far back as 1957 US Vice-President Hubert Humphrey told a US audience, 'If you are looking for a way to get people to lean on you and to be dependent on you in terms of their cooperation with you, it seems to me that food dependence would be terrific.'

Rafael V. Mariano, chairperson of the Peasant Movement
of the Philippines, 2000[1]

Prologue

At the 1974 UN World Food Conference in Rome governments adopted the Universal Declaration on the Eradication of Hunger and Malnutrition, proclaiming that 'every man, woman and child has the inalienable right to be free from hunger and malnutrition in order to develop their physical and mental faculties'.[2] The goal was to eradicate hunger, food insecurity and malnutrition within the next decade, and emphasis was placed on increasing food production, mainly by technical means and especially those developed as part of the 'green revolution'.

The global community failed to achieve its goal and, when governments reconvened in Rome in 1996 for the World Food Summit, 800 million people faced hunger and malnutrition. A Plan of Action that accommodated the interests of all participating countries was agreed and governments renewed their resolve: 'We pledge our political will and our common and national commitment to achieving food security for all and to an ongoing effort to eradicate hunger in all countries, with an immediate view to reducing the number of undernourished people to half their present level no later than 2015.'

1

At the same time governments stressed that the Summit was 'not a pledging conference' where governments come prepared to make actual financial commitments. It was instead a conference of non-binding commitments. Many NGO participants criticised the lack of positive undertakings and political will, and the failure to evaluate previous programmes and approaches. Furthermore, NGOs reported a growing bias towards solutions involving genetic engineering, predominantly led by US initiatives and backed by the public relations campaigns of the biotech industry. The Summit was an early target of the protests involving direct action that have since become a hallmark of the public response to genetically engineered food.

Five years later, the Rome-based Food and Agriculture Organisation (FAO) of the United Nations, recognising that the number of hungry people had remained the same and that the 1996 targets were not going to be met, decided to host yet another World Food Summit in 2002.[3] This time biotechnology was formally endorsed as a way to address hunger, not least because 'the US had been heavily pushing biotechnology as a solution to world hunger'.[4] Patrick Mulvany of the UK's Intermediate Technology Development Group (ITDG), an NGO participant, reported:

> The US say they left the Food Summit happy: they had achieved acceptance of the term 'biotechnology' in the final declaration, with no reference to biosafety, the Cartagena Protocol or the Precautionary Principle; had deleted any reference to an international legally-binding Code of Conduct on the Right to Food; and had watered down the call to ratify the new International Seed Treaty … to something for countries 'to consider'.[5]

The declaration – prepared in long negotiations prior to the Summit and adopted in Rome by 180 countries – says: 'We are committed to study, share and facilitate the responsible use of biotechnology in addressing development needs.' Paragraph 25 further reads:

> We call on the FAO, in conjunction with the CGIAR [Consultative Group for International Agricultural Research] and other international research institutes, to advance agricultural research and research into new technologies, including biotechnology. The introduction of tried and tested new technologies including biotechnology should be accomplished in a safe manner and adapted to local conditions to help improve agricultural productivity in developing countries.[6]

During the six years between 1996 and 2002 the biotech industry had wasted no time in pushing genetically engineered food on to the market. To its bemusement, it had met with success in the US but opposition in Europe, and this setback had forced it to turn to advertising and public relations.

During the summer of 1998, the British media was treated to a £1 million advertising campaign from Monsanto, genetic engineering's most vocal proponent. This campaign was later criticised by the UK's Advertising Standards Authority, which ruled in July 1999 that Monsanto had used 'confusing' and 'misleading' claims. The public were told by Monsanto that 'worrying about starving future generations won't feed them' and 'slowing its [genetic engineering's] acceptance is a luxury our hungry world cannot afford'. The response from the FAO's African delegates was swift and damning. Calling on the corporations to 'Let Nature's Harvest Continue', they stated:

> We strongly object that the image of the poor and hungry from our countries is being used by giant multinational corporations to push a technology that is neither safe, environmentally friendly, nor economically beneficial to us. We do not believe that such companies or gene technologies will help our farmers to produce the food that is needed in the twenty-first century. On the contrary, we think it will destroy the diversity, the local knowledge and the sustainable agricultural systems that our farmers have developed for millennia and that it will undermine our capacity to feed ourselves. (FAO statement by 24 delegates from 18 African countries, 1998)

Underlying this debate are two very different approaches to world hunger. The first focuses narrowly on the seed and its genes – seeking to develop a few varieties that will provide high yields under monoculture conditions over vast areas. Such varieties are often called high-response varieties (HRVs), because in order to prosper they require inputs of pesticide, fertiliser and, often, irrigation. Such seeds are not adapted to local conditions but instead require conditions to be adapted to their own growing requirements. The only values considered are yields; the costs and impact of pesticides and fertilisers on soil, water, biological and agricultural diversity, and human health are discounted or externalised. The other approach considers that food insecurity is highly complex and requires careful analysis of the problems and possible solutions. Issues such as poverty, lack of access to land, water, seed and food, poor infrastructure and distribution, unsustainable farming practices, national debt, or wild fluctuations and inequalities in the world market are seen as more fundamental. They need political solutions rather than technical fixes, and approaches to research that see the farm as a complex ecological system. Crop yields are only a small part of the solution. Enough food is produced for everyone now, yet 800 million people are hungry, thus indicating that production levels are not the real problem.

Those who support the second view believe that genetic engineering will do nothing to address the underlying structural causes of hunger but could instead do much to exacerbate them. There are shades of grey between these two positions. Some commentators argue that genetic engineering of crops could be part of the solution if its agenda was not set by the corporations and limited by corporate control of patents. Gradually, corporate executives have begun to reflect this argument in their rhetoric, if not necessarily in their research and development (R&D) projects. They have toned down their claims from insisting that genetic modification (GM) is the solution to hunger, to presenting it as just one of the tools that can be used. For example, Steve Smith of Novartis Seeds (UK) made the following statement at a public meeting in Norfolk in March 2000:

If anyone tells you that GM is going to feed the world, tell them that it is not ....To feed the world takes political and financial will, it's not about production and distribution. It is not the single answer; it is one of many areas that is being investigated. It may produce more for less and create more food but it won't feed the world.

Yet the reality is that the proponents of GM technology are still pushing GM crops as if they were the single answer to many problems. Moreover, opponents of GM point out that contamination problems alone may mean that in many areas coexistence between GM and non-GM agriculture will prove impossible, ruling GM out as part of a diverse approach. Proponents counter by claiming that 'technology protection systems' such as 'genetic use restriction technologies' or GURTs, otherwise known as Terminator and Traitor technologies (see Chapter 8), can prevent contamination. Opponents point to the implications of saved seed which is sterile – and the arguments continue.

The green revolution

The green revolution myth goes like this: the miracle seeds of the green revolution increase grain yields and therefore are a key to ending world hunger. Higher yields mean more income for poor farmers, helping them to climb out of poverty, and more food means less hunger. Dealing with the root causes of poverty that contribute to hunger takes a very long time and people are starving now. So we must do what we can – increase production.

Rosset *et al.*, 'Lessons from the Green Revolution', 2000[7]

The green revolution was a transformation of agriculture practice developed for the South by scientists, governments and donor agencies from the North. Essentially it involved the development of varieties of certain major crops – such as wheat, rice, and maize – that would, in response to higher inputs, produce higher yields. The Food and Agriculture Organisation itself admits: 'The green revolution of the 1960s and 1970s depended on applications of fertilisers, pesticides and irrigation to create conditions in which high-yielding modern varieties could thrive.'[8]

The first international agricultural research centres (IARCs), such as the International Rice Research Institute (IRRI) in the Philippines and the

International Maize and Wheat Improvement Centre (CIMMYT) in Mexico, were established in the early 1960s with the help of the Ford and Rockefeller foundations (see Chapter 5). They promoted the idea that these new, uniform, high-response varieties (HRVs) could flourish anywhere, irrespective of local differences in conditions. This approach was also favoured by Robert S. McNamara, who moved from being president of the Ford Motor Company to become US Secretary of Defense and Vietnam War hawk, and who left the US administration to be president of the World Bank for 13 years (1968–81).[9] In 1971, the World Bank, the US and the FAO established the CGIAR, an informal group of Northern donors aiming to support a network of international agricultural research centres based in the South (see Chapter 5).

The green revolution was heralded both as the miracle path for economic development and as a necessity to meet the needs of the 'ever-growing' populations of the South. It was also quietly promoted as a means to stem the potential threat of communism[10] in South-east Asia and Central America, since persistent poverty and hunger were considered fertile ground for revolution.[11] Once the new HRVs (also called high-yielding varieties or HYVs) had been developed by the IARCs, a plethora of governments, extension workers, aid agencies and corporations specialising in chemicals and machinery gave incentives to small-scale and subsistence farmers to adopt this 'revolution' in agriculture. They were encouraged with free starter supplies of seeds, fertilisers or pesticides. Irrigation facilities were built, and loans and credit schemes were employed to encourage farmers to use the new hybrid seeds, pesticides and machinery. It was intended that the higher yields would give these farmers a surplus to sell, thus incorporating 'subsistence' farmers into the market economy.

To promote green revolution practices, governments designed their own measures, of which the following are just a sample:

- In the Philippines up to 1981, government loans were given solely to farmers who agreed to plant one of the ten government-approved HRVs.

- The Kenyan government forbids outreach workers to teach local farmers how to compost, and rather promotes the use of chemical fertilisers.[12]

- In Iran during the 1970s large landowners who mechanised their farms were exempt from a land reform act.[13]

Impacts of the green revolution

[I]t is also argued that the Indian peasants in Chiapas, Mexico … are backward, they produce only two tons of maize per hectare as against six on modern Mexican plantations.

But this is only part of the picture – the modern plantation produces six tons per hectare and that's it. But the Indian grows a mixed crop – among his corn stalks, that also serve as support for climbing beans, he grows squash and pumpkins, sweet potatoes, tomatoes and all sorts of vegetables, fruit and medicinal herbs. From the same hectare he also feeds his cattle and chickens. He easily produces more than fifteen tons of food per hectare and all without commercial fertilizers or pesticides and no assistance from banks or governments or transnational corporations.

José A. Lutzenberger and Melissa Holloway, 1998[14]

The conclusions of Lutzenberger and Holloway contrast with findings reported by the FAO. In a document ('Towards a New Green Revolution') produced for the 1996 World Food Summit, the FAO claims that

The gains in production were dramatic: world cereal yields jumped from 1.4 tonnes per hectare in the early 1960s to 2.7 tonnes per hectare in 1989–91. Over the past 30 years, the volume of world agricultural production has doubled and world agricultural trade has increased threefold.[15]

However, the same report records that

In order to reap the potential of the new seeds, farmers also rapidly increased their use of mineral fertilisers, pesticides and irrigation. Between 1970 and 1990, fertiliser applications in developing countries shot up by 360 per cent while pesticide use increased by 7 to 8 per cent per year. The amount of land under irrigation increased by one-third.

Although it undoubtedly increased yields of certain crop grains for a number of years, the green revolution had a wide range of negative impacts which, like the impacts of other new technologies, often did not appear until later. These included introducing hybrids at the expense of locally adapted 'farmer varieties', removing farmers from their land, forcing changes in practice and creating dependence on pesticides, fertilisers, petroleum and machinery. The costs of farming increased. Land was concentrated in the hands of fewer and fewer farmers. Water resources were depleted, while increased irrigation led to greater salinity and left large amounts of land unusable. Water, land and people's health were damaged by fertiliser and pesticide use.[16] Nutrient levels in soils and crops declined. Moreover pests and diseases, far from being eliminated, often increased. Finally, the green revolution helped transform agriculture into agribusiness, so paving the way for the entry of the corporations and their products.

The green revolution also transformed traditional farming cultures. Farmers, mostly women, have for thousands of years selected and saved seed to create literally thousands of 'farmer varieties' of food crops adapted to local conditions and preferences. As the green revolution spread across the South, the diversity that these farmers had nurtured was eroded. Farmer varieties could only survive in interaction with people and disappeared if not

Sketch of an anti-revolutionary

R. H. Richharia, a famous Indian rice scientist, made a collection of more than 19,000 rice cultivars and examples of wild rice in the 1970s, which is now held at the Indira Gandhi Agricultural University (IGAU) in Raipur. He wrote lovingly about the diversity of varieties in Madhya Pradesh, and noted that many were high-yielding and resistant to pests. There is little irrigation in the region, which is often affected by drought.

He was director of the Central Rice Research Institute (CRRI), Cuttack, India as well as of the Madhya Pradesh Rice Research Institute (MPRRI). As Meena Menon noted in her article on rice varieties, 'He was removed from the CRRI as he opposed the dwarf varieties which were being brought into the country in 1966, as he felt they were highly susceptible to pests.'[17]

Later, at a conference in Malaysia in 1986, 'Dr Richharia in a paper said "pressure was brought about by the World Bank to close the activities of this Institute [MPRRI] in lieu of offering a substantial financial assistance as I had refused to pass on the entire rice germplasm to IRRI without studying it"'.

In 2002, Syngenta failed in a bid to enter into an agreement with the IGAU to use the collection as raw material for developing its own products.[18]

saved and planted. In the Indian state of Andhra Pradesh, one study found that the incursion of the green revolution led to a loss of 95 per cent of traditional rice varieties without their collection or documentation.[19] The FAO calculates that 75 per cent of India's rice production may now be planted with just 12 varieties. Communities also lost traditional sources of essential micro-nutrients and vitamins, such as vitamin A, in the form of plants that were considered weeds under the new regime and had to be eliminated.

The costs of farming increased, with serious impacts on smaller farmers. The need for expensive inputs and machinery gave bigger farmers an advantage, since either they could afford the required inputs or they found it easier to obtain credit. As large operators, they also benefited from economies of scale and were better able to survive profit squeezes brought about by increased costs or any fall in price for their products. This meant that smaller farmers were often driven off their land into the burgeoning cities of the South, so that instead of producing food, they swelled the numbers of people who depended on being able to purchase it – though often having scant means to do so. The bigger farmers therefore increased their landholdings and their strength, while the overall number of farmers fell.

However, the promised yields of the new varieties of crop were not always forthcoming. In order to try to emulate the high yields achieved at research stations, farmers sought to replicate the field-test conditions where the varieties were developed. In the words of one scientist from the IRRI, the new green revolution varieties led to 'sharp increases in the use of fertilisers and pesticides needed to ensure bumper harvests'.[20] However, from the outset farmers planting these varieties were unable to achieve the promised yields, lacking either the specific ecological conditions, the inputs or the varieties needed to grow these crops properly. In Asia, where IRRI claims that its green revolution rice varieties can achieve yields of 10 mt/ha (metric tons per hectare) at the research stations, in practice most farmers only get around 3–6 mt/ha, depending on the country.[21]

PESTS AND DISEASES

By planting genetically uniform varieties over large areas under monoculture conditions, the green revolution increased disease and pest population pressures. Once a pathogen or pest has adapted to the defences of one plant, the defence barriers of all the neighbouring genetically uniform plants fall with it. Pests or disease can overrun crops with the same genetic make-up as rapidly as an epidemic:

> In 1973–4 the Philippines rice crop was almost wiped out by tungro, a virus disease carried by the brown plant-hopper – an insect pest which keeps developing new biotypes resistant to the latest crop strain's immunity to it. In 1975 Indonesian farmers lost half a million acres of rice to damage caused by the rice hopper.[22]

Diseases began to break out in places where they had never before been a problem. Genetic diversity is the best protection against pathogens and pests. Monocultures represent a serious loss of biodiversity, thus creating an artificial ecosystem that depends on constant human intervention, mostly in the form of agrochemical inputs. Many scientists agree that monocultures and overuse of agrochemicals have increased outbreaks of disease. Pesticides also kill so-called 'friendly insects' – crucial predators on pests or disease vectors – and fertilisers too can have a very harmful effect on vital soil organisms. The massive use of pesticides helped resistance to develop rapidly among pests. Just using variety mixes can fend off diseases like rice blast.[23]

INCREASED USE OF PESTICIDES

Where they had lost the traditional varieties that were often more resistant to pests than the new hybrids, farmers had little choice but to return to their suppliers for new chemical pesticides. The green revolution breeders, for their part, began to search through their collections of landraces or farmers' variety seeds to identify resistance traits/genes that they could crossbreed into their high-yielding varieties. But it may take as little as two years for diseases and pests to overcome the resistance of each new variety that the breeders develop. The result has been perpetual crisis for farmers and a constant race between the breeders and the pests and diseases, which the breeder is guaranteed to lose as the gene pool dwindles, thanks in large part to the loss of on-farm diversity that the green revolution has exacerbated.[24]

The impact of all this fertiliser and pesticide has been extremely serious, causing contamination of the environment and seriously affecting human health. The World Health Organisation (WHO) estimated in 1989 that 3 million people a year suffer acute pesticide poisoning, and that there are many more unreported cases resulting in conditions such as dermatitis. These may result in 20,000 unintentional deaths, a figure that rises to 220,000 when suicides carried out with the aid of pesticide are included.[25] These figures remain the best estimate made so far of the scale of the problem.

SOIL AND WATER DEPLETION

Perhaps one of the most serious long-term impacts has been on soil and water resources. Green revolution methods do not maintain the natural fertility of the soil, so farmers need to use more and more fertiliser in order to maintain yields. Treating the soil as a passive medium, where only external inputs are important, means ignoring the complex life of the soil and undermining it for the future (see Box, p. 10: 'Living soil'). The impact of both fertilisers and pesticides on the soil has been little researched, yet food production ultimately depends on soil quality. The green revolution extended Northern industrial practices of depleting the soil rather than maintaining it to vast regions of the South, with the result that soil quality worldwide is seriously compromised. This may be one of the major causes of the decline of green revolution yields and micro-nutrient levels in food.

> Other intensive farming practices, particularly with wheat and rice, have virtually mined nutrients from the soil. When fertilisers are added to a crop, a plant absorbs not only the extra nitrogen, phosphorus and potassium from the fertiliser, but also proportionately increased levels of micronutrients from the soil, including zinc, iron and copper. Over time – about 10 years in this case – the soil becomes deficient in these micronutrients. Lack of them also inhibits a plant's capacity to absorb nitrogen, phosphorus and potassium.[26]

The green revolution also required large increases in the use of water, including a huge extension of irrigation facilities. This has reduced reserves of groundwater and lowered water tables in regions such as the Indian states of Punjab and Haryana.

> Irrigation made growing rice possible, and it was introduced as a cash crop and cultivated alongside wheat. Now, however, it has begun to suck the land dry. Excessive pumping during the rice-growing season has led to a drop in the groundwater table of an average of half a metre a year. In some areas, levels have

fallen well below the reach of the deep tube wells used by farmers, or the water has become saline.[27]

It has also rendered large areas of land unusable due to waterlogging and a build-up of salt in the soil, while water resources have been heavily polluted by fertiliser and pesticide run-off.

Living soil: the importance of a healthy soil food web

A key factor for crop health is a healthy soil food web, as this determines the fertility of soil and its capacity to break down organic and inorganic substances such as herbicides, as well as to drain or to hold water. The soil food web is a complex, interactive and interdependent system of mutually beneficial soil organisms made up of micro-organisms such as bacteria, fungi, algae and protozoa as well as insects, nematodes and earthworms. A teaspoonful (or one gram) of soil can contain 1–600 million micro-organisms from 5–25,000 different species, with conventional agricultural soil often lying in the lower range. In addition, soil is also made up of minerals, nutrients, air pockets, roots and decaying matter.

Scientific research into the soil food web has been underfunded and neglected within agricultural research. Despite this, the knowledge obtained so far shows that soil organisms are vital to plant and soil health, structure and water-retaining properties, to nutrient cycling, and to the accessibility and transport of nutrients to plants. In exchange, plants excrete nutrients such as sugars from their roots as extra food for the micro-organisms.

Mycorrhizae – or root fungi – are particularly important because they link plants with the soil. Through symbiotic relationships they extend the root systems of plants, improving their capacity to take up water and nutrients, and to resist drought, pathogens or toxins. They also modify the structure of the soil in a beneficial manner, reducing the need for fertilisers and pesticides. However, industrial agricultural practices such as fertiliser and pesticide application, irrigation and compaction of the soil all have a detrimental effect on mycorrhizae, and most crop plants now lack them as a consequence.

Herbicides and other pesticides alter the balance of soil ecosystems with often detrimental effects on beneficial soil organisms such as earthworms, antagonists to pathogens, fungi (including mycorrhizae) and bacteria.[28] Loss of soil organisms leads to nutrient deficiencies and unhealthy plants.

HIDDEN HUNGER

The green revolution has been blamed for causing reduced levels of essential micro-nutrients (certain essential vitamins, trace elements and minerals) in food crops. This has occurred for a number of reasons. Green revolution methods and inputs have depleted and degraded soils and killed off many of the micro-organisms that make micronutrients available to plants. Chemical fertilisers are no substitute for organic matter and cannot replace these vital interrelationships or the essential micronutrients in either the soil or the plant. In the search for higher yields, breeders have selected varieties for bulk rather than nutritional value. This has had negative impacts on food quality and human physical and mental health:

> Today, more than 2 billion people consume diets that are less diverse than 30 years ago, leading to deficiencies in micronutrients, especially iron, vitamin A, iodine, zinc and selenium. The green revolution, with its increased global caloric output, is said to have contributed to micronutrient malnutrition afflicting more than 40 per cent of the world population, and it continues to take its toll in developing countries.[29]

Such micronutrient malnutrition can lead to intellectual deficits as well as chronic ill health, affecting the capacity of whole populations:

> Malnutrition has been an accepted cause of intellectual decline since the 1970s. More recent research concerning protein energy malnutrition (PEM), and inter-related social factors, provides better understandings of 'sub-clinical' problems resulting from poor quality food. High-yield 'green revolution' crops were introduced in poorer countries in the 1960s to overcome famine. But these are now blamed for causing intellectual deficits because they do not take up essential micronutrients. They have also displaced other nutritious indigenous food sources.[30]

The FAO has confirmed that micronutrient deficiencies have a serious impact on human health, learning ability and productivity, which has high costs in terms of lost human potential and well-being with serious socio-economic consequences.[31]

In the UK, the average content of the main minerals in British-grown fruits and vegetables declined by 46 per cent from 1946 to 1991. Comparison of the 1946 and 1991 McCance and Widdowson reports for the UK government on the composition of foods revealed that across all vegetables measured, mineral content in 1946 was 45 per cent higher in magnesium, 46 per cent in calcium, 49 per cent in sodium and 75 per cent in copper.[32] Geologist David Thomas published detailed comparisons between these reports and commented:

> Intensive farming methods during the past 50 years, plus acid rain and overuse of artificial fertilisers, have reduced the absorption of minerals such as selenium and zinc into our fruits, vegetables and grains.... Mass-produced fertilisers generally contain only three minerals, but there are more than 36 known minerals, 21 of which are vital. If they're not in our soil, they're not going to make it into our foods. This imbalance is having a big impact on our health.[33]

A CLOSER LOOK AT THE FIGURES

In addition to the problems discussed above, it now appears that claims made for the positive impact of the green revolution on the numbers of hungry people require closer examination. Figures suggesting that the number of the world's hungry dropped during the green revolution (942 million to 786 million, a 16 per cent drop in 1970–90) look rather different when China is removed from the equation. China used green revolution methods and is often cited as a triumph, in that crop yields rose by 4.1 per cent a year from 1978 to 1984. What is less often mentioned, however, is that during this same period, China introduced what has been called its third land revolution, the 'household responsibility system', which gave farmers decision-making powers about land use that they had not been allowed under collectivisation.[34] The increases in production correspond with the introduction of household responsibility. Without China, figures show that the number of hungry people in the world actually increased by 11 per cent during the period, from 536 to 597 million.[35]

Thus, in spite of increased amounts of food produced, which have kept pace with population increases, the poor are having more difficulty in accessing food or the means of producing it: land and seed. The green revolution (except possibly in China) did not change existing power structures that led to inequity but actually exacerbated them. It did nothing to improve the distribution of land and resources. Finally, the green revolution is not maintaining its promise. It first showed signs of failure in the very region where it had been most enthusiastically adopted: in Luzon and Laguna, in the Philippines. There, long-term investigations conducted by IRRI show that yields peaked in the 1980s, then levelled off and are now falling steadily. Evidence is now emerging of similar patterns throughout Asia. A major part of the problem is the degradation of the soil through irrigation, impaction of the soil through the use of heavy machinery, and the inputs used, which are likely to have had serious impacts on the soil food web. Since little was known about this web before the damage was done, and little research has been done on damaged soils since then, ignorance of the actual nature of the impacts remains almost complete.

However, even if the gains are not maintained, the green revolution opened up the world's agriculture to agrochemical corporations, as the new seeds were dependent on fertilisers, pesticides and farm machinery. According to Lester Brown of the WorldWatch Institute, corporations had a vested interest in the green revolution:

> Fertiliser is in the package of new inputs which farmers need in order to realise the full potential of new seed. Once it becomes profitable to use modern technology, the demand for all kinds of farm inputs increases rapidly. And so, only agribusiness firms can supply these new inputs sufficiently.[36]

This impact may be extremely hard to reverse; these corporations have maintained their grip on agriculture and genetic engineering may simply intensify it.[37]

From war chemicals to agrochemicals

The history of chemical farming inputs, technology initially developed for military use during the twentieth century, illustrates a close relationship between war and the agrochemical industry. As José A. Lutzenberger explains:

Commercial fertilisers became big business after World War I. Right at the beginning of the war the Allied blockade cut the Germans off from Chilean nitrate, essential for the production of explosives. The Haber-Bosch process for the fixation of nitrogen from the air was known but had not been exploited commercially yet. So the Germans set up enormous production capacities and managed to fight for four years.... When the war was over, there were enormous stocks and production capacities but there was no more market for explosives. Industry then decided to push nitrogen fertilisers onto agriculture.

The Second World War gave a big push to a small, almost insignificant pesticide industry, and really got it started on a big scale. During the Second World War, no poison gases were applied in battle, but a lot of research was conducted. Bayer, among others, were in this game. They developed the phosphoric acid esters. After the war they had large production capacities and stocks and they decided that what kills people should also kill insects. They made new formulations of the stuff and sold it as insecticide.

Shortly before the end of the war in the Pacific, an American freighter was on its way to Manila with a load of potent plant killers of the 2,4-D and 2,4,5-T group. The intention was to starve the Japanese by destroying their crops by spraying the plant poison from the air. It was too late. The boat was ordered back before it arrived. Another group of Americans had dropped the atom bombs.... Same story: large production capacities, enormous stocks with no buyer. The stuff was reformulated as 'herbicide' and unloaded on the farmers.[38]

Thus the processes and chemicals created in the war effort were turned into fertilisers, insecticides and herbicides and formed the basis of the green revolution.

From green revolution to gene revolution

We lost our own seeds when company people and government officers told us that Irri dhan *[HYV] was good. Believing them we not only lost our seeds, but we lost our fish because of pesticide, lost our livestock because the fodder was reduced and the quality was bad, and most importantly we lost our health. It took more than 10 years of hard work to reintroduce our varieties and we are far better than before. Now the companies are talking about new types of seed produced by bizarre manipulation [biotechnology] to cheat us again.*

Rekha Begum, Village Kandapara, Delduar, Tangail, Bangladesh[39]

Although it increased production levels for a few key crops, the green revolution did not actually tackle the problem of food insecurity. As Fowler and Mooney conclude:

> The green revolution failed to live up to its promise of solving the problem of world hunger. It failed because the problem was not simply one of too little food and could not be solved simply by producing more. The problem was and is one of maldistribution and ultimately lack of power and opportunity amongst the hungry in Third World countries to participate in the process of food production and consumption.[40]

Groups in the South are also challenging the green revolution's conception of food security and bringing to light the importance of non-cultivated crops, which were neglected and jeopardised by green revolution development, to the food security of the rural poor. According to Policy Research for Development Alternatives (UBINIG) of Bangladesh:

> The notion of 'wild' food is misleading because it implies the absence of human influence and management. In reality, there is no clear divide between 'domesti-cated' and 'wild' species: rather, it is a continuum resulting from co-evolutionary relationship between humans and their environment. Species that have long been considered wild are actually carefully nurtured by people.[41]

Most importantly, the green revolution did not respond to the farmer's needs. It did not explore or support local solutions to food security issues based on local knowledge and related to the specific local conditions. By promising tantalising yields and profits to the handful of farmers able to afford the seeds and inputs on a long-term basis, 'it in fact concentrated rural wealth and power in the hands of a few – exacerbating the very process that had helped create so much hunger in the first place'.[42]

A major weakness of the green revolution was its narrow focus on the seed. It failed to see the farm as a complex system, where the seed is only one element that contributes to overall productivity. As a result, whole areas of research into soil fertility, mixed cropping, water management and other sustainable practices, which can easily double yields, were overlooked as scientists focused on finding the perfect genetic combination, an approach with major limitations. But instead of looking upon the experience of the green revolution as a clear indication that a fundamental change is needed in the way scientists approach agricultural research, proponents of genetic engineering are looking for new ways to expand the search for genes – going beyond the confines of a single species to search for genes across species and even kingdoms. Seen in this way, genetic engineering is merely a means to perpetuate an agricultural model that is long overdue for a profound transformation.

Economic globalisation and debt creation

The green revolution grew out of a political, social and economic context specific to the post-Second World War period. The end of the Cold War and the growth of corporate globalisation have modified the global landscape and neoliberalism dominates public policy in many countries. Neoliberalism generally involves a belief in unfettered market forces, promoting freedom of movement for capital, goods and services, and the removal of government controls over private enterprise. It breaks links to particular localities and seeks to remove regulation because this distorts markets. It dismantles community networks of care for the weakest members of society, believing they should be replaced by individual responsibility. Often, therefore, it entails budget cuts for health, education and social security programmes and the reduction of workers' rights. Imposed by the global financial institutions throughout the world, and actively embraced by many Northern governments and some Southern ones, its impact has been enormous. The emergence of biotechnology and genetic engineering cannot be divorced from this context of neoliberal globalisation.

The oil shock

In 1973 the Organisation of Petroleum Exporting Countries (OPEC) more than doubled oil prices, gaining some OPEC countries vast sums of money in a very short time and funnelling large amounts of this oil money into banks in the US, Europe and Japan. This led to lower interest rates and made banks keen to lend money. The increase in oil prices also caused oil-importing, low-income countries to be short of funds. This combination of factors fuelled an orgy of loans. Southern countries took advantage of the low interest rates – offered by private banks, multilateral lending institutions and Northern governments flooded with money from OPEC countries – to borrow heavily. Many used the loans to enrich élite segments of the population. Some – encouraged by the North – invested in transforming their agricultural sectors to take advantage of a buoyant market for tropical cash crops such as bananas, cocoa, coffee and palm oil. Many World Bank client countries became accustomed to supplementing their foreign exchange earnings with loans and using both to consume imported goods rather than investing them in public services. At the same time the increased production and export of natural resources and agricultural cash crops led to falling commodity prices for the indebted countries, necessitating further loans.

Commodity price crashes

When the second OPEC oil price rise occurred in 1979, Northern govern-ments drastically increased interest rates in an effort to curb inflation. The oil price increase tipped the industrialised Northern countries into a deep recession which in turn led to reduced purchase of imports, including pro-ducts from the South. Southern countries had already found that prices for their raw materials – such as copper, coffee, tea, cotton and cocoa – were falling, and now demand was sharply cut. With higher interest rates and reduced income, the long-term external debt of Southern countries soared: massive defaults looked imminent, threatening the global financial system.

Enter structural adjustment

At this point the World Bank and International Monetary Fund (IMF) began to impose stringent conditions for further loans, known as structural adjustment programmes (SAPs). The programmes aimed to facilitate debt repayment by increasing export earnings and foreign investment through the restructuring of national economies and social systems. They also opened up national industries and natural resources to foreign corporations. This brought heavy social and environmental costs as countries were forced to cut their education and health programmes, reduce workforces, and deregulate environmental controls. Yet most countries still did not succeed in actually repaying their debts and many ended up on a treadmill of further borrowing in order to service existing debts. Many countries have now paid the original amount borrowed many times over in debt service charges, but have never managed to pay off the principal and regain their independence. Some would say that this has been a deliberate policy of control on the part of the wealthiest nations. International indebtedness of low-income countries increased from $134 billion in 1980 to $473 billion in 1992, while their excess of imports over exports increased from $6.4 billion to $34.7 billion.[43] The financial institutions have used their stranglehold over Southern governments to dictate terms favourable for the entry of the transnationals. Even debt forgiveness, campaigned for over many years, is being made conditional on countries putting World Bank- and IMF-approved economic reforms in place, through the Heavily Indebted Poor Countries (HIPC) Initiative.[44]

Adjusting the food trade?

As has been pointed out by many researchers, food production and consumption were local until market economies emerged, which in turn drove the growth of global food trade. In order to pay back their debt, countries are still being encouraged to switch from agricultural production for their own local and national needs to the export of cash crops. This is leading to local and national food insecurity, with countries being urged to continue to export food, even when threatened by national shortages (Ireland and Ethiopia during famines, and Malawi in 2002–3). Holding of food stocks is discouraged by the international finance institutions, who advocate selling them off to repay debts. For a country to seek self-reliance or self-sufficiency in food is now derided as out of date in a world of international trade. This further increases dependence amongst countries.

Free trade and its inconsistencies

SAPs are part of a wider philosophy of free trade that has been gaining momentum since the 1980s. This philosophy is promoted by transnational corporations (TNCs) in the World Trade Organisation (WTO) and supported by many Northern governments. It not only proposes that national economies should be opened up to foreign competition and investment, but also that state intervention in the economy should be discouraged, especially measures designed to protect the country's own production and resources. Meanwhile the US and the EU continue to subsidise their agricultural sectors both directly and indirectly, which makes it impossible for farmers in Southern countries to compete in domestic or global markets. However, this does not mean that Northern farmers are prospering. In fact, small farmers – and, increasingly, medium-sized farmers – are being forced to quit by low farm-gate prices and heavy debts. Hundreds of thousands of farmers have left the land in Europe (200,000 farmers and 60,000 beef producers in 1999) and the US (235,000 farms failed during the mid-1980s farm crisis).[45] The beneficiaries are the largest farmers, national and international supermarket chains, and the food and agribusiness TNCs.

State intervention in the form of national regulation and international treaties protecting human rights, animal rights and the environment, are also being challenged through the WTO, as free trade philosophy considers them barriers to trade. Proponents of free trade theory believe that corporations will regulate themselves and do not need state or multilateral regulation.

Furthermore, free trade is supposed to encourage competition between corporations leading to greater efficiency and higher productivity, but in fact TNCs around the world operate virtual monopolies. Two-thirds of international trade is handled by global corporations and a third of all trade is intra-TNC transactions.[46] TNCs also control around 80 per cent of all foreign investment.[47] Fewer than five companies control 90 per cent of the export market for each of wheat, corn, coffee, tea, pineapple, cotton, tobacco, jute, and forest products.[48] This kind of consolidation is especially evident in genetic engineering, where, even by 2000, just five companies controlled nearly 100 per cent of GM seeds:

> The American Corn Growers Association noticed that the five 'gene giants', Syngenta, AstraZeneca, Aventis, DuPont [owns Pioneer Hi-Bred] and Monsanto [owns DeKalb], control virtually 100 per cent of the genetically modified seed business. The top 10 consolidated seed companies now control 33 per cent of the $23 billion world seed trade and the top ten agrochemical companies control 91 per cent of the $31 billion agrochemical market. Vertical integration means these companies have some form of control over all aspects of a commodity, through holding patents on the technology, owning the seed production and sales process, enforcing provisions in farmer contracts and manufacturing and distribution of the processed foods marketed to the consumer.[49]

In 2002 consolidation continued, when DuPont and Monsanto agreed to share their proprietary agricultural biotechnologies with each other.[50]

Notes

1 Rafael V. Mariano, '"Genetic Imperialism" and "Bio-serfdom": the Implications of Genetic Engineering for Farmers and Agriculture', keynote speech at the Citizens Protecting Health and the Environment Regional Workshop on Genetic Engineering, 30 March–1 April 2000; the quotation from Earl Butz was taken from an interview with *Time* magazine, 11 November 1974.

2 Universal Declaration on the Eradication of Hunger and Malnutrition, adopted by the World Food Conference, Rome, UN Doc. E/CONF. 65/20, at 1 (1974).

3 'World Food Summit – Five Years Later' (WFS–FYL), Rome, 10–13 June 2002.

4 '"Right to Food" Pushes FAO Closer to Trade Debate', *BRIDGES Weekly Trade News Digest*, 12 June 2002, Volume 6.
http://www.ictsd.org/weekly/02-06-12/story2.htm

5 Patrick Mulvany, Intermediate Technology Development Group (ITDG), 'Hunger a Gnawing Shame: Report from World Food Summit – Five Years Later', 19 June 2002. Patrick_Mulvany@compuserve.com

6 Declaration of the World Food Summit – Five Years Later, International Alliance against Hunger, Rome, 2002.
http://www.fao.org/DOCREP/MEETING/005/Y7106E/Y7106E09.htm

7 P. Rosset *et al.* (2000) 'Lessons from the Green Revolution: Do We Need New Technology to End Hunger?', *Tikkun*, 15, 2 (March/April 2000): 52–6.
http://www.twnside.org.sg/title/twr118c.htm

8 FAO, 'Towards A New Green Revolution', document for the World Food Summit, Rome, 13–17 November 1996. <http://www.fao.org> or <gopher.fao.org>

9 http://www.defenselink.mil/specials/secdef_histories/bios/mcnamara.htm

10 Cary Fowler and Pat Mooney, *The Threatened Gene*, Cambridge: Lutterworth Press, 1991.

11 *Ibid.*

12 Wangari Maathai, Royal Africa Society Memorial Lecture, School of Oriental and African Studies (SOAS), London, June 1998.

13 Fowler and Mooney, *The Threatened Gene*.

14 José A. Lutzenberger and Melissa Holloway, 'The Absurdity of Modern Agriculture: from Chemical Fertilisers and Agropoisons to Biotechnology', Fundação Gaia/Gaia Foundation, Brazil, April 1998. <www.fgaia.org.br> or <www.vida-e.com.br>

15 FAO, 'Towards A New Green Revolution'.

16 *Ibid.*

17 Meena Menon, 'Rice Varieties', Business Line (India), 2 July 2001. cats@bol.net.in

18 'Syngenta Pulls out of Research Collaboration with IGAU', PTI/Outlook India, 10 December 2002. http://www.outlookindia.com/pti_news.asp?id=103244

19 Ashish Kothari, 'Agricultural Biodiversity: Luxury or Necessity?', *Seminar* (Indian monthly magazine), 418 (1994).

20 'A Successful Alternative Way to Control Rice Blast', *Agriculture Magazine* (Manila Bulletin Publishing Corporation), 4, 12 (December 2000): 30.

21 International Rice Commission, *Country Rice Facts*, FAO, December 1999. See also Bernhard Glaeser (ed.), *The Green Revolution Revisited: Critique and Alternatives*, London: Allen and Unwin, 1987.

22 Keith Addison, 'Nutrient Starved Soils Lead to Nutrient Starved People', *acres* (US), June 1983; *Asian Business*, February 1983. http://journeytoforever.org/keith_phsoil.html

23 Zhu, Y. *et al.* 'Genetic Diversity and Disease Control in Rice' *Nature*, 406 (2000): 718–22.

24 For case study see Devlin Kuyek, 'BB Rice: IRRI's First Transgenic Field Test', published by GRAIN with Biothai, KMP, MASIPAG, PAN Indonesia, Philippine Greens, UBINIG, Romeo Quijano and Oscar B. Zamora, May 2000. http://www.grain.org/publications/bbrice-en.cfm

25 WHO/UNEP, *Public Health Impact of Pesticides Used in Agriculture*, WHO in collaboration with UN Environment Programme, Geneva, 1990.

26 Devinder Sharma: 'Green Revolution Turns Sour', *New Scientist*, 8 July 2000.

27 *Ibid.*

28 D. Pimentel *et al.*, 'Environmental and economic costs of pesticide use', *Bioscience* 42 (10), 1992, cited in Chapter 3 ('Adverse Impacts') of the report 'Risky Business: Invasive Species Management on National Forests – a Review and Summary of Needed Changes in Current Plans, Policies and Programs', February 2001. http://www.kettlerange.org/weeds/Chapter-3.html

29 Genetic Resources Action International (GRAIN): 'Engineering Solutions to Malnutrition', March 2000. http://www.grain.org/publications/reports/malnutrition.htm

30 Christopher Williams, *Terminus Brain: the Environmental Threats to Human Intelligence*, London: Cassell, 1997.

31 FAO/ILSI, *Preventing Micronutrient Malnutrition: a Guide to Food-based Approaches – a Manual for Policy Makers and Programme Planners*, prepared by the FAO and the International Life Sciences Institute, 1997. http://www.fao.org/docrep/X5244E/X5244e00.htm

32 D. Thomas, 'Mineral Depletion in Foods over the Period 1940 to 1991'. *The Nutrition Practitioner*, 2, 1 (2001): 27–9 ; Matthew Engel, 'Broccoli Is Beginning to Worry Me – Carrots and Runner Beans Are Looking Pretty Dodgy Too', *Guardian*, 20 February 2001.
   http://www.guardian.co.uk/ comment/story/0,3604,440263,00.html
33 http://www.cookingisfun.ie/letters/mayandjune%202001/foodfor15May2001.htm
34 Fu Chen, Luming Wang and John Davis, 'Land Reform in Rural China Since the Mid-1980s', Part 1, posted September 1999.
   www.fao.org/sd/Ltdirect/ Ltan0031.htm
35 Rosset *et al.*, 'Lessons from the Green Revolution'.
36 Quoted in 'Forty Years of Unfulfilled Promises', article in *SUHAY*, the newsletter of MASIPAG, special edition, Los Banos Laguna, Phillipines, 2000.
37 R. S. Anderson, E. Levy and B. M. Morrison, *Rice Science and Development Politics: Research Strategies and IRRI's Technologies Confront Asian Diversity (1950–1980)*, Oxford: Clarendon Press, 1991; Bernhard Glaeser (ed.), *The Green Revolution Revisited: Critique and Alternatives*, London: Allen and Unwin, 1987.
38 Lutzenberger and Holloway, 'The Absurdity of Modern Agriculture'.
39 Devlin Kuyek, 'ISAAA in Asia: Promoting Corporate Profits in the Name of the Poor', www.grain.org/publications/isaaa-en.cfm/, GRAIN, October 2000.
40 Fowler and Mooney, *The Threatened Gene*.
41 UBINIG, 'Uncultivated Shaks: Food Security for the Poor in Bangladesh', Proceedings of the South Asian Workshop on Uncultivated Foods and Plants, Bishnupur, Tangail, Bangladesh, 2–4 October 1999.
42 Fowler and Mooney, *The Threatened Gene*.
43 David Korten, *When Corporations Rule the World*, London: Earthscan, 1995, p. 165.
44 'Debt Relief under the Heavily Indebted Poor Countries (HIPC) Initiative, a Factsheet', August 2002. www.imf.org/external/np/exr/facts/hipc.htm
45 'Facing the Farm Crisis: Farming at Peril', special supplement to *Ecologist*, 22 May 2002.
   http://www.theecologist.org/archive_article.html? article=181&category=52
46 'GM Crops: Food Production and World Hunger', Unison Policy and Public Affairs Report, June 2000. (Unison is one of the largest unions in the UK.)
47 UNCTAD, *World Investment Report 1998*, New York and Geneva: UN Conference on Trade and Development, 1998.
48 A. V. Krebs, *The Corporate Reapers: the Book of Agribusiness*, Essential Books, 1992.
49 American Corn Growers Association Press Release, August 2000.
50 'DuPont and Monsanto Reach Agreement That Brings New Technologies To Growers Worldwide', press release, Wilmington, Delaware and St Louis, Missouri, 2 April 2002. www.dupont.com/corp/news/releases/2002/nr04_02_02.htm

2

Corporations:
from Royal Charters to Biotech Gold Rush

A brief history of the corporation

> *By becoming a corporation, a business is given a distinct legal identity separate from the people that run it. The effect of this arrangement is to shield those who actually run the business from responsibility for their actions.*
>
> Dan Bennett, Helena Paul and Bill Bachle, *Who's in Charge?*[1]

The rise of the modern corporation, with its increasing freedom to operate and its lack of obligations, except to make profits, has helped to shape modern technology in general, and the development of genetic engineering in particular. Corporations were first created in Europe for charitable activities such as establishing hospitals during the medieval period of European history (eleventh–fifteenth centuries). They were meant to advance the public good and were non-profitmaking. However, the commercial corporation has become a very different entity.

During the medieval period in Europe, businesses typically operated as groups of people in partnership who shared the risks of an enterprise, which did not have a separate legal identity. During this period the restrictions on usury, or lending at interest, gradually broke down and the use of money was replacing payment in kind or barter of goods. Thus the conditions for the accumulation of capital were created. At the same time, the voyages of 'discovery' meant that new trade routes were being opened up, offering possibilities for the investment of capital for commercial enterprise. Towards the end of the sixteenth century, certain trade associations were granted royal charters of incorporation by the British Crown to act as not-for-profit corporations with a monopoly over a certain area of business.

The British East India Company was granted its royal charter by Queen Elizabeth I on 31 December 1600. Its members gradually put all their assets together until they became a single partnership, which owned the goods and assets (stock) jointly. This partnership then sold its stock to the East India Company itself and received in return a share in the Company. The Company traded their stock in its own name and the profits were distributed amongst the members, so creating the first for-profit corporation. This action was illegal but was not challenged at the time. The East India Company made immense profits and its 'vast expansion in India meant that it not only had a monopoly on trade but was also in charge of the army, the roads, food supply, in fact all the domestic and foreign powers of a government'.[2]

During the early eighteenth century, many new corporations were created which sought public investment to profit from the opening up of the British colonies around the world. One of these companies, the South Sea Company, attracted vast amounts of investment until confidence collapsed, and the stock market, which had been overinflated by this 'South Sea Bubble', crashed. The UK government then passed the 1720 'Bubble Act' ostensibly designed to prevent the speculative buying and selling of shares and curb fraudulent corporate activity. However, the government continued to borrow at interest from the East India and the South Sea companies for wars and other adventures, further fuelling the process of empire building and assisting the expansion of the national debt.

Benefiting the colonial powers

By the East India Act of 1784 the [British] government assumed more direct responsibility for British activities in India, setting up a board of control for India. The company continued to control commercial policy and lesser administration, but the British government became increasingly the effective ruler of India. Parliamentary acts of 1813 and 1833 ended the company's trade monopoly. Finally, after the Indian Mutiny of 1857–58 the government assumed direct control, and the East India Company was dissolved.[3]

Colonial powers in general benefited from the activities of their trading companies and corporations by adding to their empire many of the territories formerly controlled by these companies. Examples for Britain are the East India Company, the Hudson Bay Company and the Africa Company.

During the nineteenth century, restrictions on corporate activities and rights were gradually lifted by the courts and by government, and corporations began to take on their current shape. They consolidated their legal status as individual persons, gradually assuming most of an actual human being's rights. However, unlike people, these corporate persons are potentially immortal, can merge with another corporate person, divide themselves into several persons, cannot be imprisoned, and have no feelings. During this same period, the liability of shareholders was gradually limited and they became the most privileged of all stakeholders. The Bubble Act was repealed in 1825. Previously limited by the charter under which they were created, the powers of corporations were gradually extended with the collusion of the courts, until the board of directors acquired total freedom to decide and to change the activities and objectives of the corporation without any public consultation. The creation of subsidiary companies also shields corporations from the consequences of their actions. This is achieved by ensuring that the subsidiaries carry out the activities of greatest risk but have no assets, while the parent corporation is merely a shareholder in the subsidiary and thus is not liable for its acts. In the event of any problem, the subsidiary simply folds and the parent is left unscathed because of 'the corporate veil' between parent and subsidiary. 'The consequences of granting freedoms to fictitious persons who existed only to make profits were never discussed.'[4] Finally, the Companies Act of 1989 abolished the right of 'anyone who isn't the corporation to challenge the right of the corporation to take various courses of action'.[5]

Although the American Revolution began as a rebellion against the British monarch and his corporations, with a number of corporate charters being revoked, a similar path was followed in the US, with judges steadily increasing corporate powers through landmark decisions in the courts.[6]

From colonial empire to corporate recolonisation

Since the Second World War, corporations have used events in the international political arena to further globalise their reach. These include the Cold War, and the dismantling of the colonial empires established by the British, French, Dutch, Portuguese, Spanish, Germans and other nations in the previous few centuries. They have also used the Bretton Woods institutions – the World Bank, the International Monetary Fund (IMF) and the General Agreement on Tariffs and Trade (GATT) – and the speculative financial markets. The World Trade Organisation (WTO), created out of the GATT in 1994, is a perfect vehicle for extending corporate rights. Unlike other international instruments, it has legislative and judicial powers that can be enforced against states through its complaints mechanism. Governments can use this procedure to force other governments to change laws and lower environmental and social standards in the interests of 'free trade'. Yet it does nothing to limit the ability of the transnationals to 'use their economic power to drive competitors out of the market by unfair means; absorb competitors through mergers and acquisitions; or form strategic alliances with competitors to share technology, production facilities, and markets'.[7]

Besides the WTO itself, free trade agreements are strongly promoted by the corporations. The North American Free Trade Agreement (NAFTA) was the first regional treaty, linking Mexico, Canada and the US. Bitterly opposed by indigenous and small-farmer communities in Mexico, it is seen by the corporate fraternity as a model to be replicated wherever possible, even though the impacts of NAFTA on jobs and the environment have already proved detrimental to ordinary people.

Recently, representatives from 34 countries have been working to expand NAFTA to Central America, South America and the Caribbean, in order to create the Free Trade Area of the Americas (FTAA).[8] Some have called this a smaller version of the Multilateral Agreement on Investment (MAI), which was defeated but nevertheless enunciated a principle too important to corporations to be dropped: the freedom to invest. There are other possible free trade configurations being discussed for the Americas. The African Growth and Opportunity Act, passed in 2000 in the US, provides the basis for constructing free trade agreements within Africa, and the US is targeting the Southern African Customs Union of five countries as a first step (see Chapter 8). Agreements were signed in November 2002 regarding future free trade between the countries of the Association of South-East Asian Nations (ASEAN), China and Japan.[9] Following war in Iraq in 2003, President Bush announced proposals to create a free trade zone in the Middle East by 2013. There are also a number of bilateral free trade agreements, the majority of them between the US and other countries. These are but some of the initiatives being discussed or put into effect.

Getting intellectual property into the trade arena

As we shall see later, the US administration decided to move the intellectual property debate out of the World Intellectual Property Organisation and into the trade arena, specifically the Uruguay Round of trade negotiations, which ended in 1994. The impact of this was enormous, especially since it made patent protection of micro-organisms mandatory, without defining them, so providing the first international framework for patents on living organisms.

Factors in the growth of the biotechnology industry

What you are seeing is not just a consolidation of seed companies, it's really a consolidation of the entire food chain.

Robert Fraley, Executive Vice-President, Monsanto, 1996[10]

Just as the green revolution had its enabling context, so also does the gene revolution. The freeing up of the financial markets has played a vital role.

The tide of investment has ebbed and flowed massively in response to the promises of biotechnology and the tension between the need for quick returns as against the long period of time required to bring products to market. The extension of patents to living organisms and their parts was a crucial part of the gene revolution, assiduously lobbied for by the corporations in every available arena. Rapidly developing capacity in genomics led to a race between public and private domains to sequence the human genome and those of other organisms, including oilseed rape (canola) and rice.

The corporations involved have a number of different requirements, including the following:

- compliant financial markets, open to rapid movements of capital and speculative investment;

- access to cheap raw materials;

- methods of protecting intellectual capital and new products from competition, through intellectual property rights, especially patents;

- access to research through universities and independent research companies;

- infrastructure, such as roads, ports, airports, etc.;

- favourable regulations that do not impede the commercialisation of their products.

While they have been working on all these, corporations have continued to develop new technologies with great potential for opening up yet more new territories for corporate colonisation. When the interface with other emerging technologies is added, these territories expand as the elements involved become smaller and move into molecular and atomic levels of investigation. Nanotechnology involves the manipulation of matter at the quantum level – a nanometer is one billionth of a metre. The issues involved are beyond the scope of this book. However, there are two points to be made briefly here: the first is that as biotechnology meets with nanotechnology, informatics and the cognitive sciences, and combines with them, its own development will be profoundly influenced. The second is that development itself will increasingly be driven by these synergies. Development always has been driven by technology, although it is sometimes forgotten that this is the case. The accelerating emergence of new technologies means that human society is less and less able to internalise the implications and respond appropriately. The marketplace can respond without the impediment of ethics or precaution to dreams of vast profits and progress, and no-one wants to be left behind. In the end the key driving force for such development may simply be the technological change itself.

The financial markets – biotech bubbles

The financial markets were liberated from most constraints during the 1980s and 1990s. Capital, freed from all relation to locality, tends to flow to the area of least regulation, and moves at the speed of light. All the major corporations, bar Cargill, are publicly listed, which means they are financed by shareholders as well as bank loans. Winning investor confidence is fundamental to corporate strategy because their market value is determined not only by their assets, but also by the value of their shares.

At the moment, the biotech industry is largely based on a futures market. Investment is absorbed in R&D (research and development), public relations and advertising, and spectacular results are promised in the future. Currently there are more promises than products. This has caused enormous volatility in the market, with share prices soaring and crashing on the basis of rumours. There is also a strong incentive to 'talk up' the potential of products in development, so as to increase the share price. The story of British Biotech and Dr Andrew Millar is a case in point (see p. 27: 'British Biotech misleads investors').

Dr Alan Williams, a British Member of Parliament, said on behalf of the House of Commons Science and Technology Committee in August 1998:

> In an environment, such as the biotechnology industry, where subjective judgements and sentiment are so important in determining share price and company value, and where investors are to a large degree dependent upon the company to inform those judgements, accurate provision of information by the company is essential.[11]

Beyond all borders

Between the late 1970s and early 1997, 'investors have pumped approximately £40,000 million (US$60 billion) into biotechnology enterprises [not just genetic engineering] according to figures from international accounting firm, Ernst & Young'.[12] In 1996, then a record year for biotech investment, only 50 or so of these companies actually made a profit, and few generated significant revenues.[13] By 1997, there were 1,800 biotech research companies registered worldwide. In 2000, biotechnology as a whole raised $38 billion according to the BioIndustry Organisation (BIO, see Chapter 3) – a figure that dropped again to an estimated $11 billion in 2001.[14]

British Biotech misleads investors

British Biotech was founded in 1986 and floated in 1992, becoming the first UK biotech company to be fully listed on the stock market. In May 1996 its shares exceeded 300 pence and the company was valued at £2 billion when two drugs in development – the cancer drug Marimastat and the pancreatitis drug Zacutex – were presented as potential multi-billion-dollar blockbuster drugs. To keep the investors interested, the company substantially overstated the performance of the drugs in its trials. In Spring 1998 this was disclosed to investors by British Biotech's head of clinical research, Dr Andrew Millar, which led to his dismissal. It came further to light that the US Securities and Exchange Commission was investigating British Biotech over allegations that it had issued misleading press releases in 1995 and 1996 about its new cancer drug.

> On 10 June 1999, the American Securities and Exchange Commission (SEC) found that it was in the public interest to impose a Cease and Desist Order on British Biotech and its ex-CEO Dr McCullagh, having found them guilty of violations of Section 13(a) of the Exchange Act and Rules 12b-20, 13a-1 and 13a-16 thereunder on no less than *seven* occasions by making false representations in Press Releases.[15]

With these events in the open, investors rapidly lost faith, shares plummeted and by July 1998 the company was worth less than £330 million.

In June 1999 the London Stock Exchange 'publicly censured British Biotech for a "most serious" case of misleading investors…. Lacking the power to fine British Biotech, an exchange spokesman said it was taking the strongest action it could short of delisting the shares.'[16]

And in the same month British Biotech announced that the dispute was settled with its former director of clinical research. It was stated in a press release that 'British Biotech have withdrawn their claims and allegations of improper behaviour and Dr Millar has agreed not to continue with his proceedings against British Biotech.'[17]

In 2000, with optimism at its height, one commentator wrote:

This year, for the first time, the biotechnology industry became truly borderless. The trend has been building for several years, but it's reached major proportions by now. And it's far more than going global implies, for companies are not just setting up foreign subsidiaries to manage their clinical trials or market their products. They're also creating entirely new companies that are a synthesis of skills and expertise from many different areas of the world. Thanks in large part to the Internet and other high-tech means of communication and data exchange, these borderless firms have come close to transcending both time and distance.[18]

This faith in the power of new technologies and the buoyancy of the market in general meant that biotech shares rose above the level of the rest:

In 2000, high-risk biotechnology stocks outperformed the overall market, fuelled by the promise of the mapping of the human genome. Now that the milestone has been reached, the sector has lost some of its spark since it became all too clear that it would be years before health care felt the impact of the research.[19]

According to the Ernst and Young report 'Beyond Borders 2002', the global biotech industry in 2001 was

> comprised of 4,284 companies (622 public; 3,662 private) in 25 nations. The 622 public companies generated revenues of $35 billion, spent $16 billion in R&D and employed more than 188,000 people.... 72 per cent of the public company revenues were generated by companies in the US....[20]

The UK has developed a strong biotech research base – outperforming other European countries – due to a greater availability of risk capital in the City of London than in the rest of Europe. As John Hodgson explains,

> In 1992, with encouragement from British Biotech and other parts of the UK industry, the London Stock Exchange threw UK biotechnology a lifeline. It altered its listing rules in a way that allowed research-driven small companies to raise money through a public offering even though they had no history of revenues or profits.[21]

The largest shareholders in big corporations are almost always other companies. These might be other blue-chip corporations or financial institutions such as insurance companies, unit trusts or pension funds. Others are simply 'asset managers', whose job is to make as much profit as possible for the real owners of the money (frequently occupational pension schemes or local authorities) by investing it wherever it can generate the highest returns. This means that investment is increasingly removed from local know-ledge and local control. It is not reinvested where it was generated, but flies through speculative virtual markets with no responsibilities attached. There are increasing calls for the localisation of production and investment and for ways to make it harder to externalise or transfer production and consump-tion costs, dumping them on others who did not generate them. There have also been calls for a tax on purely speculative activities in financial markets (one such proposal is known as the Tobin Tax) and for controls on trans-national trade and investment, as well as for regulation to prevent global TNC monopolies.[22] None of these have yet been enacted.

The extension of patents to genes, cells and organisms

> *The most important publications for our researchers are not chemistry journals, but patent office journals around the world.*
>
> from the Hoechst website[23]

Today, the strength of a nation is measured not by the weapons it wields, but by the patents it produces.

Canadian Finance Minister Paul Martin, Budget speech, 2000

Patent law is typically explained as 'a compromise between preserving the incentive to create knowledge and the desirability of disseminating knowledge at little or no cost'.[24] The industrial revolution demonstrated the value of technology or innovation to national competitiveness, and, while not wanting to jeopardise access to new knowledge, states and industrial capital were interested in developing ways to profit from and control technological developments. Patents were a logical choice. They give inventors exclusive rights to their inventions for a limited period of time (usually 20 years) and, in exchange, patent holders must disclose their inventions to the public. In this way, innovation expands, knowledge is diffused and, so the argument goes, the public good is maximised.

Since the late nineteenth century, patents have been an integral part of industrial capitalist economies. But there is no inherent connection between Western industrial development and patent protection. Indeed, there is a basic contradiction between monopoly rights and the free market and, at a practical level, there is little evidence that patents increase investment in R&D.[25] Not that patents are a neutral force. Patents play a major role in determining the context through which innovation occurs and the forms that innovation takes. Patents are based on a narrow, romantic interpretation of innovation, as carried out by author-entrepreneurs – people like Thomas Edison, working in isolation to develop original ideas for profit.[26] In reality, innovation is most often a collective, incremental process, where people build on the knowledge and work of others for a wide range of motivations. This is particularly true of crop development. Any 'new' plant variety is merely a variant of its parents, which were typically developed through careful selection by generations of farmers. Patents are inappropriate in this context, and efforts to bring crop development under patent law have much more to do with the interests of certain actors than with increasing overall innovation.

The corporate push for patents on plants

For practical reasons, plants and animals were not considered for inclusion when the international patent regime was consolidated at the end of the nineteenth century. Even as capital investment in the seed industry increased in the first half of the twentieth century, patent lawyers and officials refused to open most Patent Acts up to living organisms, fearing that it might dilute the entire patent system.[27] The seed industry had other, biological options.

In the 1920s and 1930s the American seed industry began a programme to develop hybrid maize. While the agronomic advantages of hybrids are debatable, the advantage to the seed industry is clear: to produce hybrid seeds (F1) two specific and distinct parental lines are needed. Thus hybrids can only be reproduced by the breeder; replanting saved seeds (F2) is of little use as they will not grow into a crop resembling the previous hybrid plants but rather perform in an irregular and unpredictable way.[28] Hybrids thus force farmers to buy seed every year and prevent other breeders from using the varieties in their own breeding programmes. This built-in 'patent' protection attracted enormous interest from the seed industry, which had the full-fledged support of the Secretary of the US Department of Agriculture, who also happened to be the president of Pioneer, one of the leading maize (corn) seed companies in the US. Hybrids brought big rewards for business, generating revenues of $60–$70 million by 1944, but the gains for the overall public good were less clear: yields for wheat, a crop with no biological patent protection and with little investment from the private sector, increased twice as much as yields for maize in the US between 1920 and 1945.[29]

As it was too expensive and difficult to develop hybrids for most major agricultural crops, the seed industry continued to pursue legal intellectual property protection for plant varieties. Frustrated in its attempts to enter the patent system, it put forward a separate system of legal protection. In 1961, several European countries agreed to a minimum set of standards for the protection of plant varieties that they would implement in their own countries. This convention, known as the international Union for the Protection of New Varieties of Plants (UPOV), led to the establishment of separate legal systems for the property rights of plant breeders.

The criteria for plant breeders' rights (PBRs) are less demanding than those for patents, but the scope of protection is also narrower. 'Patents protect the inventor against all unauthorised commercial use of the invention; a PBR certificate entitles the breeder only to prevent unauthorised commercial propagation of plant varieties.'[30] Similar legislation was introduced in the US in 1970 and 51 countries are now party to UPOV.

The seed industry has never abandoned its objective of full-scale patent rights, and UPOV itself has moved closer and closer to such rights. Under the latest version of UPOV, drawn up in 1991, farmers are prohibited from saving seeds except under highly restricted conditions. And, in the US, new plant varieties can now be patented. Moreover, even in countries where patents are not issued for plant varieties, the seed industry has taken out patents on genes that establish patent-like rights over genetically engineered varieties.

THE PATENT TRAP

Under the Trade-related Intellectual Property Rights (TRIPS) agreement of the WTO, member countries must provide for patent rights on micro-organisms. The term 'micro-organism' is not defined and many patent offices have determined this provision to include patents on genes and DNA sequences. In Canada, for example, Monsanto owns the patent rights to the gene construct genetically engineered into canola (oilseed rape) to give it resistance to the herbicide glyphosate. Monsanto claims that this gives it patent rights over any plant variety containing this patented gene construct, even if the genes arrive in a farmer's canola fields through cross-pollination. In March 2001, the Federal Court of Canada ruled that Saskatchewan farmer Percy Schmeiser had violated Monsanto's patent by growing canola containing the patented genes, even if it was true that the gene had arrived in his crop through cross-pollination, as he alleged, making him in effect guilty of violation through being contaminated.[31] Such contamination is now becoming widespread. Lyle Friesen, a researcher at the University of Manitoba who studied seed lot samples of canola, claims that 'you would have a RoundUp-resistant plant every couple of square yards' in canola crops not planted with RoundUp Ready canola.[32] US farmers have the same problem and face similar legal sanctions, as would any farmer in a country that implements US-style patent law.

Such patents have generated a climate of fear among farmers. Plant breeders' rights, patents, and the notorious growers' contracts are forcing farmers to abandon their age-old practices of seed saving, sharing and selling. No farmer wants to risk a major lawsuit by attracting the attention of the private detectives that now police the countryside for the seed companies. For many farmers, the only way out is to grow the patented genetically engineered crops and abide by the contracts.

Patents have obvious repercussions for farmer seed selection and breeding practices, which still constitute the most important sources of plant varieties in the world, especially in the South. But the push for patents on plants and their DNA is also causing havoc among public breeders. Three-quarters of the patents on agricultural biotechnology in the world are controlled by six companies. Often these patents are broad patents that have a crippling effect on any research in closely related areas. In 1994 the company Agracetus was awarded a European patent (EP 301749) (American patent in 1991 – US 5015580) which covered all GM soybeans using a specific method of gene transfer. Rival companies, including Monsanto, were outraged, saying that it would result in just one company having an effective monopoly over all transgenic soybeans. Monsanto's solution was to buy the company and drop the complaint. Monsanto also holds a patent in both Europe and the US on all genetically engineered cotton (EP 270355 and US 5,159,135). PGS – a biotech company now owned by Bayer CropScience – has been granted a broad patent in the US for genetically engineered plants containing an insecticidal Bt toxin (US-5,460,963 for Bt4 and Bt18, for example, or US-5,633,446 for any Bt toxin modified in a specific way).

Researchers seeking to develop crops through biotechnology encounter labyrinths of interconnected patents blocking their way. The public researchers who developed Golden Rice claimed that the 70-odd patents involved in the GM rice forced them to sell the rights for it to Syngenta. Even research on non-transgenic crops can be derailed by intellectual property rights. In 1999 Steven Price, a plant breeder with the University of Wisconsin, sent out a survey to 187 public breeders in the US asking them about difficulties they might be having in obtaining genetic stocks from private companies. Forty-eight percent of those who responded said that they had had difficulties obtaining genetic stock from companies; 45 per cent said it interfered with their research; and 28 per cent said that it interfered with their ability to release new varieties.[33] Public researchers are beginning to realise that such restrictions are about to get much worse.

Most breeding programmes, public or private, now routinely use molecular marker techniques to speed up the breeding process. These markers allow breeders to identify whether the traits that they seek have been incorporated into their crosses, thereby speeding up the breeding process. However, many of the most important markers that are discovered are patented and the traits that they identify are also being patented. On 30 September 1999 Monsanto filed a patent in 81 countries on soybeans with enhanced yield (WO-0018963). That patent has already been issued in Australia (AU6277599). It covers any cultivated soybean containing certain genes or segments of DNA from 'wild' or 'exotic' soybeans identified through molecular marker techniques. The group of genes, which is only vaguely defined, is said to be responsible for enhanced yield. Not only does the patent claim an important trait in soybean breeding, but it also gives Monsanto monopoly rights on *Glycine soja* (wild soybean), particularly PI407305 from southern China and all its progeny. Further, the patent extends to any soybean carrying the yield genes.

The push for patents on plants and their parts is extending corporate control over agricultural R&D. It is also linked to the decline of cooperative and collaborative work between different research groups and a breakdown in open communication in the scientific community. Jonathan King, Professor of Biology at the MIT, USA, in oral evidence to the Royal Commission in New Zealand in 2001, stated:

> I'd like to clarify two further points. Patent lawyers often speak about how patents require the revealing of the information. In the area of modern biological research this profoundly misrepresents the actual use of patents. In the normal

course of modern biological research, scientists are striving to publish and reveal their results; this is their stock and trade in currency. The intervention of the patent system reverses that.

Patent law requires that the subject of the patent, if it's been previously revealed, that is it becomes prior art, then the patent would be disallowed. Thus oral reports, abstracts, grant proposals, public papers all constitute prior art. As a result individuals or groups planning to file for a patent have to avoid public disclosure of their work prior to the filing of a patent claim. Patent attorneys regularly advise researchers to restrict their presentations to colleagues, don't show your work, don't show your notebook, don't give that talk, so as not to jeopardise the planned patent submissions.

This has reversed the half-century culture of free and open communication in the scientific communities.[34]

Unfortunately, few public researchers are raising objections, deciding instead to jump aboard the corporate bandwagon, especially since funding may depend on whether a 'result' might be patentable. There are already instances of researchers developing complicated techniques in genetic engineering to give plants certain traits, when such plants could be produced through conventional means.[35] Areas of research that cannot be controlled through patents are neglected by the private sector and many public institutions that are now pursuing partnerships with private companies. For example, in October 2002 the Consultative Group for International Agricultural Research (CGIAR), perhaps the most influential non-commercial research organisation operating in the South, announced that the Syngenta Foundation was now an official member, joining 46 member countries and three other member foundations.

Essential conditions for countries to profit from patents

Commentators agree that certain conditions are essential for operating a successful patent system. These include facilities for high technology research, active investors, an efficient patent office, trained patent examiners and lawyers, and an effective judicial system. Many Southern countries can satisfy none of these conditions. Operating in the patent world can be extremely expensive. Some have unkindly said that the legal complexities are even more formidable than the scientific complexities. Many countries of the South are faced with trying to bridge a wide gap in time and capacity before they have established the conditions that would enable them to benefit from patents. Meanwhile they will experience a huge outflow of resources in the form of royalty payments and the patenting of their natural and intellectual resources and knowledge by developed countries and their corporations.[36]

Trade-related Intellectual Property Rights (TRIPs) agreement

The pharmaceutical lobby has close connections with the US government. In 1981 US President Reagan appointed Ed Pratt, the chief executive of pharmaceutical giant Pfizer Inc., to head the United States' top private sector trade advisory panel.[37] Gerald Mossinghoff was Reagan's Assistant Secretary of Commerce and Commissioner of Patents and Trademarks until 1985 when he became President of the Pharmaceutical Manufacturers Association, the world's most important pharmaceutical lobby.[38] According to Mossinghoff

> There was a lot of frustration during negotiations about intellectual property matters. As the US ambassador to the diplomatic conference of the World Intellectual Property Office, I personally felt this frustration because I was representing the United States of America – the wealthiest, most powerful, biggest free market in the world – and I had just one vote. As a result, the Reagan administration decided to move these intellectual property negotiations out of WIPO [the World Intellectual Property Organisation] and into the trade world.[39]

Results came swiftly, as Tony Clarke explains:

> It is well known that the Intellectual Property Rights Committee, composed of 13 leading US corporations (for example, Bristol Myers Squibb, DuPont, Pfizer, Monsanto, and General Motors) effectively wrote, word for word, the TRIPS agreement that was adopted at the Uruguay Round of the GATT negotiations and subsequently became part of the WTO body of rules.[40]

Compulsory for all WTO member countries, TRIPS was a big victory for the biotech industry. It consolidated corporate power over information and extended intellectual property rights (IPRs/patents) to cover genetic material, including seeds, plants, animals and the genes and cells of all species, including humans. In agricultural biotechnology, the top six corporations control 74 per cent of all agricultural biotechnology patents, and five corporations control 70 per cent of all patents on genes for wheat and 47 per cent of all patents on genes for sorghum.[41] Patent protection and the move to genetic engineering give the biotech corporations unprecedented control over research and development, which has traditionally been the domain of farmers and public scientists. Together patents and genetic engineering provide the instruments for transnational corporations to gain control over agriculture and the food chain.

A RESPONSE FROM AFRICA – THE AFRICA POSITION ON TRIPS

In 1999, the part of the TRIPs agreement that explicitly extended patents to cover living organisms – Article 27.3(b), Protection Of Plant Varieties – was meant to be reviewed, as mandated during the original negotiations. There were arguments over the scope of such a review process and some countries were afraid of emerging with a worse situation than before. A group of African countries produced a strong statement setting out their fundamental difficulties with the article. After calling for developing countries to be given more time to consider the implications of implementing TRIPs, they made a number of recommendations.[42]

The African group insisted that countries should be allowed to meet their obligations under other international treaties, especially the Convention on Biological Diversity (see Chapter 6), which gives a country the right to prior informed consent about access to and use of its genetic resources (including benefit sharing), and the International Undertaking, now the Treaty on Plant Genetic Resources (see Chapter 5). They called for the wording of TRIPs to be changed to recognise explicitly the right of countries to 'satisfy their need to protect the knowledge and innovations in farming, agriculture and health and medical care of indigenous people and local communities'. They also called for food sovereignty, plus the right of farmers to save and exchange their seed and sell their harvest, to be enshrined in a revised TRIPs agreement. They pointed out serious inconsistencies in the agreement arising from the fact that, while plants and animals could be excluded from patenting, micro-organisms could not. And they demanded that

> The review process should clarify that plants and animals as well as micro-organisms and all other living organisms and their parts cannot be patented, and that natural processes that produce plants, animals and other living organisms should also not be patentable.

The Africa statement still represents the core position of the South in the face of the onslaught from the North for IPR/patent protection to be extended to living organisms. Neither Article 27.3b nor the agreement as a whole have been revised. However, the US has led the push for bilateral agreements that go beyond TRIPs and the fight may be shifting away from the trade arena to WIPO.

Pushing for a world patent system

The TRIPs agreement set a basic framework for intellectual property protection. However, protection worldwide remains a mosaic, with different rules and frameworks in each country and wide differences between the levels of protection in North and South. There is also an increasing backlog of patent applications awaiting examination, increasing the length of time it takes to process a patent. Industry would prefer a simplified system, set at the highest level of property rights protection (the US level) that would cover all countries, speed up the granting of patent rights and remove the need to make separate applications in different jurisdictions. The dream scenario for the biotech industry would be a uniform set of procedures across the globe, with a single patent application giving global cover. WIPO is mandated to promote intellectual property protection. As we saw above, the Reagan administration moved negotiations away from WIPO to the trade arena, but it could become the focus once more, this time for attempts at 'harmonisation' of patent law.

The Patent Cooperation Treaty (PCT) came into force in 1970 and is currently being reformed. Besides being an important source of revenue for WIPO, it provides a common international facility for the preliminary examination of an application, to establish whether or not it is valid, before proceeding to make national applications. Reform of the PCT could involve pressure for the grant of world patents.

In 2000, WIPO members adopted the Patent Law Treaty, which has yet to come into force. It is designed to harmonise procedures for patent applications. Countries then moved on to consider a Substantive Patent Law Treaty (SPLT), which would further harmonise and tighten patent law. The US is prepared to give up its principle of 'first to invent' and adopt the more general 'first to file' principle if the SPLT follows US patent law in other important ways, such as allowing the patenting of 'business methods'. The US and industry also want to ensure that, under the SPLT, countries would not be allowed to exempt plants and animals from patenting, while Europe and the countries of South oppose this. Some countries (Brazil, Peru) have also indicated their refusal to cooperate with SPLT unless prior informed consent and disclosure of the country of origin of the material to be patented are made part of the regime. This has been rejected by the North and by industry.

If SPLT were adopted, it could perhaps supersede TRIPs itself. Certainly, a harmonised global patent system would remove the ability of countries to use patent regimes as a tool for development. It would totally undercut Southern country attempts to build capacity in this field, reducing many of them to mere observers rather than players in the increasingly important intellectual property (IP) arena.[43]

'Independent' research companies

In the late 1970s only a few biotech companies existed in the USA. By 1997 there were around 1,800 worldwide. The excitement about biotechnology from the mid-1990s onwards led to a proliferation of companies. These new ventures could not operate in isolation, as they needed to attract both public and private investment for expensive research. This was one reason why many independent research companies were bought up by the corporations:

Biotechnology research was initially conducted by small specialised industry 'boutiques', hatched out of the basement labs of moonlighting university scientists with supplementary cash from the big corporations who were unwilling to invest their own research programmes … in what was undoubtedly a high-risk endeavour. As the science has developed and the risk receded, however, the big players have moved in, picked up their options, and now dominate the high-tech field.[44]

Genentech, founded in 1976 by Stanford University geneticist Herbert Boyer and the entrepreneur Robert Swanson, was the first biotech company to go public. It raised $39 million in its initial public offering in 1980. More significantly, perhaps, on its first day of trading Genentech's share price climbed from $35 a share to a high of $89. This raised not only money for one company, but investor and public awareness of biotechnology in general. After successfully bringing two new drugs to market, Genentech shocked the biotech world in 1990 by allowing Swiss multinational, Hoffman–La Roche to acquire a controlling stake. Whilst it was spending vast sums on R&D, its products were not raising enough revenue and it had no new products coming through. The Roche buy-out left many people asking: 'If Genentech can't make it on its own, who can?'[45] The same fate befell successful independent agribiotech research companies such as Calgene and Mycogen, now owned by Monsanto and Dow respectively.

In general, it suited the big corporations for initial research to be carried out in universities, research institutes and independent companies. If they liked what they saw, they could always take over, once the groundwork had been done. This way they limited their own risk and could reap the benefits. With universities becoming more dependent on corporate funding, as research became more expensive, they could more easily be persuaded to respond to corporate priorities. Increasingly, they have been willing to under-write contracts that either allow the corporations ownership of resulting IPRs/patents, or make them sole licence holders. In addition, universities themselves are becoming active pursuers of patents in the hope of increasing their incomes.

Many of the small private biotech firms found it difficult to survive.[46] Often the only way to do so was by licensing their patented technologies to bigger corporations. The university spin-off companies had more stability, as they often benefited from direct public subsidies and access to the resources and students of the universities. One way to remain independent was to focus on specific areas of genetic research, such as bioprospecting, writing software or carrying out genomics research, or on a particular technology such as vaccine-producing crops. According to Roger Wyse, a venture capitalist at Burrill and Co., agricultural biotechnology firms have had to deal with the same problems over patent rights and product development as their counterparts in pharmaceuticals, but with far less investor interest. In 2000, according to Burrill and Co, the number of medical biotech firms rose by 58 per cent, compared with a fall of 11 per cent for agbiotech firms.[47]

A new gold rush: the run on genes and genomes

Genomics is the study of genes and their functions within an organism, and includes the sequencing of whole genomes (the complete genetic information of one species). Such knowledge is valued for its potential to enhance conventional practices of crop and livestock breeding. However, if the function of a gene has a potential application, a company will file a patent. Ownership and profit from identifying specific genes has over the years been determined at least partly by access to gene sequencing equipment, largely owned by corporations and specialist research companies.

Five pesticide companies – DuPont, Syngenta, Aventis (now Bayer CropScience), Monsanto and Dow – controlled 71 per cent of all patents on agricultural biotechnology by 2000.[48] Through patenting genes, these corporations are privatising valuable information and plant varieties that have been developed through generations of farmer selection. This they justify on the grounds of recouping R&D costs when products developed from these patents finally come to market. However, it also helps them control the direction of plant breeding, develop new products that suit their commercial aims and prevent others from using the genes.

The race for the rice genome

Whilst most of the public interest around genomics research has focused on mapping the human genome, there has been a race for the genes and the genomes of major crops such as rice.

Ed Kaleikau, director of the plants division at the US Department of Agriculture, stated in 2002:

> Rice is a model for all cereal plants … [Its sequencing] will lead to the identification of genes important not only in rice but in other cereals. Eventually it will lead to a better understanding of rice and all cereal crops including wheat, barley, and corn – for ag[riculturally]-important plants, this could be compared to the [sequencing of the] human genome….[49]

Concerning this sequencing of the rice genome the National Center for Biotechnology Information (NCBI) stated on its website in 2002:

> There is a publicly funded effort and there is a commercially funded effort. The first commercial effort, by Monsanto, resulted in a database[50] of genomic sequence

and SSR [simple sequence repeat] objects. The genomic sequence has been shared with the International Rice Genome Sequencing Project members. The second commercial effort, a collaboration between Myriad Genetics[51] and Syngenta,[52] has allegedly completed the genomic sequence. This effort has entered no sequence into the public domain.[53]

When Syngenta AG and Myriad Genetics Inc. announced the mapping of the rice genome in February 2001, the FAO declared that 'this was a breakthrough to increasing the productivity and nutritional value of rice, a staple for more than half the world's people'.[54] This statement reflects once again a narrowly focused faith in genes to improve food security and diets. Furthermore, it avoids drawing attention to the fact that the completed genome map is being held in the private and corporate domain and that IPRs will allow Syngenta to benefit from any applications derived from the sequencing information.

Myriad, Syngenta and the rice genome

In 2002, Myriad stated on its website:

Myriad and Syngenta make the rice genome publicly available through collaboration agreements. Application information is available on the Syngenta website, www.nadii.com. Collaboration proposals are evaluated bimonthly. Criteria for evaluation include scientific significance and potential for social benefit.

Myriad and TMRI [Torrey Mesa Research Institute – a subsidiary of Syngenta] will seek patent protection for inventions relating to specific gene uses that result from this project. In some cases, these inventions will include the composition of a gene.

The sequence generated by this project will be made available to researchers via a genome technology access agreement.[55]

The publicly funded International Rice Sequencing Group (IRGSP) announced in December 2001 that it intended to complete the high-quality draft of the rice genome by December 2002.[56] On 18 December 2002 a press release announced the completion of this draft for the *japonica* sub-species of rice that is cultivated in Japan, South Korea and the United States. The final, 'finished' genome sequence is now expected to be completed by 2005.

The focus so far has been on the *japonica* strain of rice (*Oryza sativa japonica*). Chinese researchers announced in early 2002 that they had sequenced the *indica* rice strain, the one most commonly used in China, India and other countries. It is said that the information, once finalised, will be made completely available with no strings attached.[57]

The Monsanto rice genome sequence site ceased operations on 30 December 2002. Monsanto stated that owing to accelerated progress of the public sequencing project, 'the unique role that the Monsanto rice genome site played in support of public research is no longer needed'.[58] Monsanto claims further that 'more than 90 per cent of the sequences contained in the Monsanto draft rice genome sequence data can now also be found in public databases'.

Other genomes

The first genome of a higher organism (eukaryote) to be sequenced was that of the yeast *Saccharomyces cerevisiae* (1997), followed by the nematode worm *Caenorhabditis elegans* (December 1998), the fruitfly *Drosophila melanogaster* (2000) and the Thale cress *Arabidopsis thaliana* (December 2000). The sequencing of the human genome was announced in 2001 and that of the mouse genome in November 2002. There are still very few complete genome sequences available. Translation of the sequence data into profitable applications is still seen to be a long way off.

Knowing the sequence of a gene is one thing, but knowing how this gene functions and interacts as an integral part of an organism is quite another. It is the product of a gene, a protein, that is usually of interest, yet little is known of how most proteins interact. Thus a new branch of science is developing, termed *proteomics*, which involves studying protein–protein interactions. Its stated goal is the identification and characterisation of complete sets of proteins. The study of *proteomes*, an organism's total set of proteins, is now overtaking the race to acquire and sequence genomes, an organism's total set of genetic information.

As organisers for a proteomics conference stated: 'There is growing recognition that one of the key ways in which companies are going to obtain maximum return on their investment in genomics is to include strong capabilities in the field of proteomics.'[59]

The human genome

In 2000 the exuberance that surrounded the race to complete the human genome led to a rapid rise in biotech stocks. This was mainly fuelled by the belief of investors that exciting new drugs, crops and other products were only a few years away. In a year in which the NASDAQ index posted its worst performance ever, with Internet and hi-tech stocks plummeting, the biotech index rose 15 per cent. In 2001, however, the biotech index began the year by losing 25 per cent of its value, prompting fears of a bursting bubble in the sector. Investors feared that genomics would not speed up the discovery and development of drugs or bring products to the market as quickly as expected. Genentech's chief executive Arthur Levinson warned investors that the sequencing would not translate into shorter development time for new drugs.[60] No matter how promising, potential drugs still must be tested in laboratories and human clinical trials; regulatory procedures continue to be burdensome. This market anxiety was reflected in the response to announcements by Celera Genomics in 2000 and 2001. In February 2000 Celera announced that it was entering the final phase of its genome sequencing. In response the market soared by 30 per cent. However, when in February 2001 Celera announced that it had published the map of the human genome, the market rose by only 17 per cent.

The publication of the human genome was not the great triumph that the life science industry had expected. Instead – as pointed out in a recent article by Barry Commoner, a senior scientist at the Center for the Biology of Natural Systems at Queens College, New York – the publication of the complete human genome put to rest the 'central dogma' of molecular biology and the biotech enterprise: the assumption 'that an organism's genome (its total complement of DNA genes) should fully account for its characteristic assemblage of inherited traits'.[61] To the astonishment of the genomics industry and scientists, there were far fewer genes than would be necessary to account for the entirety of human proteins and traits.[62] Out of at least 100,000 genes predicted the actual gene count was only about 30,000. The assumed correlation between genes and traits appears to be spurious, bringing the foundations of genetic engineering and the biotech industry into doubt.

Notes

1 Dan Bennett, Helena Paul and Bill Bachle, *Who's in Charge?*, pamphlet from the Programme on Corporations, Law and Democracy, 1997. See also Corporate Watch website. www.corporatewatch.org
2 *Ibid.*
3 See 'East India Company, British', http://www.encyclopedia.com/articlesnew/03917.html
4 Bennett, Paul and Bachle, *Who's in Charge?*
5 *Ibid.*
6 Richard L. Grossman and Frank T. Adams, *Taking Care of Business*, pamphlet, Massachusetts: Charter, Ink, 1993. www.poclad.org
7 Bennett, Paul and Bachle, *Who's in Charge?*
8 www.globalexchange.org
9 'Moves on Free Trade Agreements Gain Momentum in East Asia', 14 November 2002. www.fpcj.jp/e/shiryo/jb/0241.html
10 R. Fraley (then co-president of Monsanto's agricultural sector), *Farm Journal*,

October 1996, p. 19.

11 Dr Alan Williams for the UK House of Commons Science and Technology Committee, Press Notice No. 34 of Session 1997–8 (17 August 1998) regarding its report on British Biotech.

12 Diane Gershon and John Hodgson, 'The Assembly Line Evolves: How Biotechnology Companies Have Grown Up', *Nature* Biotechnology Supplement, June 1997.

13 *Ibid.*

14 'About BIO: Partner to a Dynamic Industry Coming of Age', December 2002. http://www.bio.org/aboutbio/history.asp

15 Information on British Biotech and its cancer drugs Batimastat, Marimastat and Zacutex. http://www.classlaw.co.uk/biotech/archive/20-3-2002.html

16 ★★R: Issue No. 245; 1–7 July 1999; Investors' Corner, The Market. From cache of http://www.business-line.com/business-weekly/archives/245/investor.html.

17 'British Biotech and Dr Millar Settle Their Disputes', press release by British Biotech plc, 8 June 1999.
  http://www.britbio.co.uk/news/settle.txt

18 Jennifer van Brunt, 'Borderless Biotech', *Signals* (online magazine), 13 December 2000. http://www.signalsmag.com/signalsmag.nsf/0/3BB72467A85394E1882569B2005 ED830

19 Kirsten Philipkoski, 'Biotech in the Market for a Cure', 16 March 2001. http://www.wired.com/news/technology/0,1282,42473,00.html

20 Ernst & Young, LLP, *Global Biotechnology Industry Report: Beyond Borders*, 2002, one of a series produced annually since 1993. http://www.ey.com/beyondborders

21 Gershon and Hodgson, 'The Assembly Line Evolves'.

22 David Korten, *When Corporations Rule the World*, London: Earthscan, 1995, p. 323.

23 http://www.hoechst.com/press_e/13096e3.htm

24 World Bank, *Knowledge for Development – World Development Report 1998/99*, Oxford and New York: Oxford University Press, 1998, p. 33. http://www.worldbank.org

25 Geoff Tansey, *Trade, Intellectual Property, Food and Biodiversity: Key Issues and Options for the 1999 Review of Article 27.3 (b) of the TRIPS Agreement: a Discussion Paper*, London: Quaker Peace and Service, February 1999.

26 James Boyle, *Shamans, Software and Spleens: Law and Construction of the Information Society*, Cambridge, MA: Harvard University Press, 1996.

27 Robin Pistorius and Jeroen van Wijk, *The Exploitation of Plant Genetic Information: Political Strategies in Crop Development*, Cambridge: CABI Publishing, 1999, p. 79.

28 J. P. Berlan and R. C. Lewontin, 'The Political Economy of Hybrid Corn', *Monthly Review,* 38 (1986): 35–47.

29 Jean-Pierre Berlan, 'La génétique agricole: Des origines aux chimères génétiques', in Jean-Pierre Berlan (ed.), *La guerre au vivant: OGM et mystifications scientifiques*, Marseilles: Agone Éditeur, 2001.

30 Pistorius and van Wijk, *The Exploitation of Plant Genetic Information*, p. 83.

31 Federal Court decision can be seen at http://www.percyschmeiser.com/T1593-98-%20Decision.pdf

32 Les Kietke, 'Research Shows: Herbicide Tolerance Everywhere', *Manitoba Co-operator*, 1 August 2002.

33 *Nature Biotechnology*, 17 (October 1999): 936.

34 Jonathan King, Professor of Biology at Massachusetts Institute of Technology, Boston, 'Patents on Life', oral submission to the New Zealand Royal Commission on Genetic Engineering, appearing by video link to Auckland, 16 February 2001.

35 Devlin Kuyek, 'Blast and Biotech: Implications of Corporate Strategies on Rice Research in Asia', GRAIN, Barcelona, August 2002, http://216.15.202.3/ publications/blast-en.cfm and 'BB Rice: IRRI's First Transgenic Field Test', GRAIN, Barcelona, May 2000, http://216.15.202.3/publications/bbrice-en.cfm

36 Keith Maskus, World Bank, speaking at the Conference of the Commission on Intellectual Property Rights: How Intellectual Property Rights Could Work Better for Developing Countries and Poor People, 21–22 February 2002.

37 Joel Lexchin, 'Canada, Free Trade Agreements and Drugs Costs', October 2001. http://apha.confex.com/apha/responses/129am/242.DOC

38 Centre for Responsive Politics, 'Revolving Door between the US Government and Industry', January 2001. http://www.cptech.org/ip/health/politics/revolvingdoor.html

39 Gerald J. Mossinghoff, 'World Patent System Circa 20XX, AD', Yale Symposium on Law and Technology, Spring 1999. http://lawtech.law.yale.edu/symposium/98/speech_mossinghoff.htm

40 Tony Clarke, Director, Polaris Institute, 'Global Economic Governance: the WTO's Ongoing Crisis of Legitimacy', 2002. http://www.polarisinstitute.org/polaris_project/corp_security_state/publications_articles/canada_watch_sept_2002.html

41 ETC Group, *Globalization Inc.*, Communique No. 71, July/August 2001; John Madeley, *Crops and Robbers*, ActionAid, October 2001.

42 Communication from Kenya on behalf of the African Group, Preparations for the 1999 ministerial conference on the TRIPS agreement. WT/GC/W/302.

43 'WIPO moves towards "World" patent system', GRAIN, July 2002. http://www.grain.org/publications/wipo-patents.2002-en.cfm

44 Pat Mooney, 'The Parts of Life: Agricultural Biodiversity, Indigenous Knowledge and the Role of the Third System', *Development Dialogue*, Special Issue, 1996, p. 143.

45 Gershon and Hodgson, 'The Assembly Line Evolves'.

46 'Dry Season', *Economist* (2 November 2000).

47 *Ibid.*

48 ETC Group, *Globalization Inc.*

49 Ken Howard, 'Rice Genome Sequence Revealed', GenomeWeb, 16 January 2002. http://www.vlifescience.com.au/Article/Display/1,2906,599,00.html

50 www.rice-research.org/

51 http://www.myriad.com/pr/20010126.html

52 http://www.syngenta.com/en/media/article.asp?article_id=126

53 Website of the National Center for Biotechnology Information (US), October 2002 http://www.ncbi.nlm.nih.gov/mapview/map_search.cgi?chr=rice.inf

54 Reuters News, 'Rice Genome Mapping Helps War on Hunger – FAO', 1 February 2001

55 Myriad website (March 2002) on rice genome, http://www.myriad.com/research/rgfaq.html#rg4

56 National Institute of Agrobiological Sciences (NIAS), press release, 21 December

2001. http://www.nias.affrc.go.jp/pressrelease/2001/20011221e.html

57 Howard, 'Rice Genome Sequence'.

58 www.rice-research.org/

59 Introductory paragraph from the Cambridge Healthtech Institute's Fifth Annual Conference, Proteomics Program, 21–22 June 2001, Fairmont Hotel, San Francisco, California. http://www.beyondgenome.com/pro.htm

60 Victoria Griffith, 'Biotechnology Sector Gets a Sinking Feeling', *Financial Times*, 9 January 2001.

61 Barry Commoner, 'Unraveling the DNA Myth: the Spurious Foundation of Genetic Engineering', *Harper's Magazine*, 304, 1821 (February 2002): 39–47.

62 *Ibid.*

3

Image Control:
Manipulation and Public Relations

The PR industry is so huge because of corporations. Most every issue in the news today – global warming, globalisation, genetically modified foods, tobacco legislation – affects corporations who stand to gain or lose heaps of money, depending on public reaction. Therefore, the 'management' of public reaction is crucial....

With so much cash riding on public opinion, industry has always viewed public relations as a valuable, even necessary investment. Why else would corporations throw billions of dollars a year at the PR industry?

Michael Manekin[1]

The use of public relations (PR) has become so familiar that we take it as much for granted as the existence of the corporations which employ it. The term 'public relations' was invented by Edward Bernays in the early twentieth century. A nephew of Sigmund Freud, he was born in 1891 and came to the US as an immigrant. After working with the US Committee on Public Information (CPI) – 'the vast American propaganda apparatus mobilized in 1917 to package, advertise and sell the [First World] war as one that would "Make the World Safe for Democracy"', he came to the aid of the corporations after the war as part of the effort to help 'shift America from a needs to a desires culture'.[2]

Bernays published *Crystallizing Public Opinion* in 1923 and *Propaganda* in 1928. In 1947 he wrote *The Engineering of Consent*, a title which describes in a single phrase what public relations aims to achieve. His early campaigns included the promotion of cigarette smoking among women and softening up public opinion for further US government intervention in Latin America by projecting Guatemala's struggles against the United Fruit Company in the 1950s as dominated by Communists.

Public relations is meant to be an invisible means of securing the consent of the 'masses' in a modern democracy, where, although people are not actually consulted over most of the major issues, their mass opposition can make it impossible to implement what government or business wants, whether it is war or new technologies. As Stuart Ewen says,

> Bernays was also a far-sighted architect of modern propaganda techniques who, dramatically, from the early 1920s onward, helped to consolidate a fateful marriage between theories of mass psychology and schemes of corporate and political persuasion.[3]

Growth and consolidation of the public relations industry

Does it matter that four of the world's largest public relations firms are now owned by the same corporation? WPP is a potential powerhouse, a huge propaganda machine, with the reach and coordinated skills in people manipulation that might allow it to rule the hearts and minds of the entire global population.

Sharon Beder and Richard Gosden, 2001[4]

Corporate public relations has become a growth industry in its own right. Like those they serve, the PR companies are swallowing each other up so fast, it is hard to keep up. For example, Wire and Plastic Products (WPP), a UK company which started out making wire shopping baskets and filing trays, has now become one of the three major global PR firms (the others are Omnicom and Interpublic), owning 80 companies. In 1987, it acquired J. Walter Thompson Group, which included Hill and Knowlton. In 2000 it acquired Young and Rubicam, which included Burson–Marsteller (see below). Now known simply as WPP, it enjoyed sales of $4,456.7 million and a net income of $365.9 million in 2000, and followed this with sales of $5,856 million and a net income of $395 million in 2001 – growth leaps of 31.4 and 7.9 per cent respectively.[5]

Whatever corporations are involved in, they all increasingly use PR companies that combine glossy presentation with careful attention to language, often appropriated from the civil society organisations and NGOs that oppose corporate activities. Words like 'dialogue', 'transparency', 'sharing', 'respect' and 'democracy' are all freely used. Corporations rely heavily on public relations companies to advise them on strategies to get their message across to governments, public institutions and the public in general. The tactics used by the biotech corporations include:

- engaging key scientists or respected figures who appear independent (former President Carter, for example) to speak in favour of biotechnology;

- commissioning new research to promote the benefits of biotechnology as a whole or to denigrate alternatives such as organic food;

- lobbying governments and international institutions both directly and through trade associations;

- launching personal attacks to discredit the opposition, including scientists, NGO representatives and environmentalists;

- attracting known environmentalists to work for them;

- creating civil society organisations – such as the [US] Citizens Network for Foreign Affairs (CNFA) – to promote their point of view (see Chapter 5);

- avoiding the controversial areas of the debate and trying to forestall awkward questions (as when Burson–Marsteller leaked advice to the industry in 1997 – see below);

- using PR as education;

- seeking to transform the image of industry through major new campaigns such as converting themselves into 'life science' companies (see Chapter 4);

- using grassroots tactics (see below);

- setting up 'dialogues' with NGOs, the public, government and others.

Cleaning the corporate image

The brochures, websites and company pronouncements of the big biotech corporations give the impression that they are sincerely concerned for the planet and the welfare of all.

Dow Agrosciences, for example, used a Native American proverb for its website in 2000, stating: 'We do not inherit the land from our ancestors; we borrow it from our children.'

The *DuPont* vision statement begins, 'We, the people of DuPont, dedicate ourselves daily to the work of improving life on our planet', and ends: 'Our principles are sacred. We will respect nature and living things, work safely, be gracious to one another and our partners, and each day we will leave for home with consciences clear and spirits soaring.'[6]

Neatly, its CEO assures its investors that they can save the planet, its people *and* make lots of money:

> However, there are still enormous challenges. Extrapolation of current trends paints a picture of an unsustainable world: an increasing gap between the rich and the poor; billions of people who do not have access to clean water, proper sanitation, adequate food, shelter, and health care; and the steady decline in key global ecosystems.

As a company that is owned by thousands of investors, our challenge is to address these issues in a way that makes business sense. We define this direction as sustainable growth – the creation of shareholder and societal value while decreasing our environmental footprint along the value chains in which we operate.[7]

In its vision, *Syngenta Biotechnology* modestly proclaims a 'New Agricultural Renaissance' and says:

WE are the generation of individuals committed to applied biology with potent new technologies and knowledge;

WE have the ability to see opportunities to create a high-value agriculture with expanded benefits for people and the planet.[8]

Skeletons in the cupboard: challenges for the PR machine

Not surprisingly, the websites of the major agrochemical corporations are silent as regards their less laudable activities. Yet it is instructive to look at the past and gain some perspective on the history of some of the leading biotech corporations. For instance, Monsanto's history includes the production of DDT (an indiscriminate insecticide, also produced by other companies such as Ciba–Geigy and banned in 1976 in the North, but still manufactured in the North and available in many Southern countries) and the development of other extremely hazardous and toxic pesticides, defoliants and chemicals such as PCBs and Agent Orange (see page 49), which have caused untold human suffering and environmental damage in the North as well as in the South. Some of the many other examples are reviewed below.

RISEN FROM THE THIRD REICH

IG Farben's profits were built on forced slave labour under the Nazis during the 1940s. Members of IG Farben included Hoechst, BASF, Bayer and Agfa. 'By 1944, more than 83,000 forced labourers and death camp inmates were put to work in the IG Farben camp at Auschwitz, where more than 120,000 people perished.'[9] IG Farben subsidiary Degesch also manufactured the chemical Zyklon B, used for genocide in the gas chambers at extermination camps. Surviving slave workers have been suing German companies for compensation, with no satisfactory outcome so far.[10, 11]

Telford Taylor, US Chief Prosecutor at the 1947 Nuremberg War Tribunal against the managers of Bayer, BASF and Hoechst (IG Farben) stated:

These companies, not the lunatic Nazi fanatics, are the main war criminals. If the guilt of these criminals is not brought to daylight and if they are not punished, they will pose a much greater threat to the future peace of the world than Hitler if he were still alive.[12]

This history shows that the dangers of allowing corporations to become too powerful goes far beyond mere matters of competition and the domination of markets.

THE HEIRS OF UNION CARBIDE

In December 1984 the Union Carbide Corporation's pesticide plant in Bhopal, India was the site of the world's worst industrial accident. Thousands of people died, and an estimated 140,000 survivors still suffer from a range of diseases linked to exposure to the gas methyl isocyanate that leaked from the site, spreading over a 25-square-mile area. Survivors are still fighting for fair compensation.

In 1986 Rhone-Poulenc (now Aventis), under the chairmanship of Jean-René Fourtou, picked up the agrochemical division of Union Carbide for $575 million. Union Carbide was anxious to sell in order to protect itself from a worldwide boycott following the Bhopal disaster. Over the next 5–10 years Union Carbide shed more of its divisions and finally announced in 1999 that it was to merge with Dow Chemical Company. In February 2001 Union Carbide became a wholly owned subsidiary of Dow, whilst its former agrochemical plants changed hands from Aventis to Bayer in 2002.

> The Chemical Manufacturers Association [USA] created its much-touted Responsible Care Program in the aftermath of the 'public relations problem' caused by Union Carbide's gas disaster in Bhopal. Ironically, a representative from Union Carbide was among the first to chair Responsible Care.[13]

DOW CHEMICAL

This US company gained notoriety in the 1960s for the manufacture of napalm, a jellied gasoline which stuck to its victims and caused frightful burns. It was also one of the makers of the herbicide known as Agent Orange, used as a defoliant during the war in Vietnam. The watchdog INFACT reported in 1999:

> Dow's own history includes covering up information about dioxin contamination in Agent Orange … as well as problems related to its consumer products including silicone breast implants, and the pesticide DBCP which Dow continued to sell abroad even after it was banned in the US because it causes sterility. Dow has made efforts to clean up its image with advertising campaigns like its recent 'What Good Thinking Can Do'.[14]

THE VITAMIN CARTEL

In 1999, companies including Rhone-Poulenc (now Aventis), Roche and BASF were all exposed over a major price-fixing controversy in the vitamin business; they had formed a cartel that controlled the world market for nine years. Vitamins are widely used by the food processing and animal feed industries, and their inflated prices are estimated to have affected US commerce by $5–6 billion and global commerce by over $20 billion.

> The conspiracy appears to have begun in 1989 when executives at Roche AG and BASF began holding talks about price fixing. They decided to carve up the vitamin market and to recruit other major vitamin makers to come in on the arrangement, like Rhone-Poulenc of France and Takeda Chemical Industries from Japan. Later, yet further vitamin producers joined the cartel. Nearly all world vitamin producers now face massive fines.[15]

Roche had to pay a record fine of US$500 million and one of its directors went to jail in the US; BASF paid US$225 million; Rhone-Poulenc escaped conviction and hundreds of millions of dollars in fines by testifying against the other two. Record fines were also set by the European Union in September 2001 for eight distinct price-fixing cartels in vitamin products (Roche paid 462 million euros; BASF E296 million; and Rhone-Poulenc only E5 million).

SANDOZ AND CIBA–GEIGY – THE PAST OF NOVARTIS

Both Novartis's merger partners Sandoz and Ciba–Geigy are remembered for past scandals. So are Ciba and Geigy. Although dwarfed by the mega-mergers of the 1990s, the merger of Ciba and Geigy in 1970 was extra-ordinary for its time. With the merger, Ciba–Geigy became the world's third-largest pharmaceutical manufacturer, the second-largest producer of pesticides, and the largest producer of chemical dyes.

- **SMON tragedy in Japan:** The merger also came at the time of one of the company's worst scandals, the SMON tragedy in Japan, brought about by Ciba's drug clioquinol. Holly Knaus called it 'one of history's most horrifying cases of corporate negligence'.[16] Ciba's clioquinol had entered the Japanese market in 1953 for all forms of dysentery and all types of abdominal pain. Whilst increasing numbers fell ill with severe optic disorders and paralysis in the feet and legs, the syndrome was only identified as a 'disease' called SMON (subacute-myelo-optico-neuropathy) in 1965. Not until 1970, with 10,000 Japanese affected by devastating symptoms, could Japanese researchers link their suffering to the use of the popular clioquinol. Ciba was the largest producer worldwide of clioquinol and oxyquinoline-derived drugs. Though the company immediately dismissed the links to oxyquinoline, it was shown later that Ciba had known about problems since 1953 and had been in possession of proof since at least 1962.[17] Over 5,000 lawsuits were filed in Japan against Ciba–Geigy, resulting in a pay-out of over $490 million to Japanese SMON victims by 1981. It was not until 1985 that

Ciba–Geigy finally took the drug off the global market. In an apology to the victims of its drug the company stated:

We who manufactured and sold clioquinol drugs deeply sympathise with the plaintiffs and their families in their continuing unbelievable agony; there are no words to adequately express our sorrow. In view of the fact that medical products manufactured and sold by us have been responsible for the tragedy, we extend our apologies, frankly and without reservation, to the plaintiffs and their families.[18]

The SMON incident put Ciba–Geigy in the spotlight and led to the discovery of other cases of negligence concerning the sale of its drugs.

• **Poisoning the Rhine:** Sandoz was responsible for a notorious chemical disaster that occurred in November 1986 as a result of a fire at its production and warehouse facility in Switzerland. Eight tons of mercury and approximately 30 tons of extremely hazardous organophosphate pesticides spilled into the Rhine River and killed fish, wildlife and plants for hundreds of miles. According to Greenpeace researchers Jed Greer and Kenny Bruno, following the spill, Sandoz 'cleaned up' its operations by moving 60 per cent of its organophosphate production to Resende, Brazil. In 1989, shortly after another ton of Sandoz disulfoton nearly spilled into the Rhine, Sandoz moved the rest of its organophosphate production to Brazil.[19]

• It also emerged in November 1986 that Ciba–Geigy, then neighbour to Sandoz, had played its part in the toxic pollution of the Rhine. A day before the Sandoz fire an accidental leak at Ciba–Geigy sent 88 gallons of the weedkiller Atrazin into the river. A spokesman for Ciba–Geigy said the leak happened when staff accidently released chemicals into the river before they had been treated.

• **Biotech companies versus nature – the case of multiple resistance:** GM contamination and herbicide resistant canola (oilseed rape) volunteers (plants that germinate from seeds of previous crops in succeeding years) have become a serious problem in Canada. Resistance to more than one herbicide is caused by successive cross-pollination of canola plants engineered to be resistant to different herbicides. At present 3 classes of herbicide tolerant oilseed rape are grown in Canada, each tolerant to a different herbicide (glyphosate, glufosinate and imidazolinone (non GM)).

In 1999 and 2000 various reports showed that crosses amongst these oilseed rape cultivars have resulted in the unintended creation of plants with multiple resistance to either two or three classes of herbicides. Such 'accidental gene stacking' is a serious development that could easily have been foreseen by the companies. Canadian farmers are now saying that any advantages that GM technology might have conferred are already being outweighed by the problems caused, and it is getting worse.[20]

English Nature, which is the UK Government's chief conservation agency, has expressed concern over such resistant crops, saying that, if GM crops are introduced in the UK, farmers might turn to old herbicides which are highly toxic, such as Paraquat and 2,4-D, in order to rid themselves of such volunteer crops or superweeds.[21]

Sidestepping the consequences

These stories highlight recurring patterns in corporate activity. However, corporations and their PR companies rely on our short memories and their sales tactics to ride any public challenge about their pasts. They are free to constantly reinvent their images. Moreover, mergers, divestments and changes of name make companies difficult to track. They can also change their objects freely without returning to the public to ask for permission. They can set up subsidiaries without assets to take the blame for disasters, leaving the parent company untouched. This is often called the 'corporate veil' (see Chapter 2). These tactics make it hard for people to hold corporations to account for their actions.

Corporate mind control

When asked about the links between US domestic and foreign policies and the sophisticated PR machinery, John Stauber stated:

> They're really one and the same, because the push for corporate globalization – the push to lower and destroy regulatory standards in other countries that do care about protecting human health and safety – is based here in the United States. And the biggest PR firms that work for these corporations are very much active in trying to impose the US definition of globalization on the rest of the world, including definitions that say, 'Well, yeah, there's no real need for countries to provide universal health care; there's no need to safety-test genetically engineered food.'
>
> John Stauber, co-author of Trust Us, We're Experts – How Industry Manipulates Science and Gambles With Your Future[22]

Corporate PR campaigns

Corporations use a number of different methods to promote or disguise their public relations campaigns. One is to package them as education. Others include engaging in stakeholder dialogue and using scientists – like the members of Cropgen UK, a lobby group 'funded by but independent from the biotech industry' – as the main mouthpieces for biotech PR. It also helps their cause if they can ensure that news of 'scientific breakthroughs' comes from the mouths of scientists, charities and research institutions rather than from industry itself. Deploying the grassroots can also help the cause – and if none of these things are effective, then apologies may be used.

PR AS EDUCATION

In September 1999 Novartis and others launched a biotech PR campaign aimed at students and teachers. Novartis gave the (then Washington-based)[23] Biotechnology Institute $150,000 for the production and distribution of *Your World: Biotechnology & You*, a student magazine. Amongst the many other 'founding sponsors' of the Institute, all of which put funds into *Your World*, there were well-known names which included: BIO (Biotechnology Industry Organisation – see below), Amgen, Aventis, Biogen, Council for Biotechnology Information (see below), Genzyme, Merck, Monsanto Fund, Novartis Foundation, Pennsylvania Biotechnology Association, Pfizer, Scottish Enterprise and the US departments of Commerce and Energy.[24]

> Our vision is to engage, excite and educate as many people as possible, particularly young people, about biotechnology and its immense potential for solving human health and environmental problems.[25]

According to its president Paul Hanle, the Biotechnology Institute was specifically established to be:

- The authoritative national source of reliable, scientifically sound information about biotechnology for teachers and students;
- A leading independent resource for opinion leaders and the general public.[26]

Consequently, the goal was to achieve a 'measurable increase in appreciation of biotechnology among young people and general audiences'. Each issue claimed to provide an 'in-depth exploration of a particular biotechnology topic by looking at the science and its practical applications'. Subscribers received 30 copies of the glossy magazine, a classroom poster and 16-page Teacher's Guide. According to Jeff Davidson, the Institute's Director of Bioscience Education,

> *Your World* gives teachers access to up-to-date, real-life examples of biotechnology at work, information that simply isn't available from most textbooks currently in use. Equally important, we present the material in a fun-to-read, magazine-style format, which students find more interesting than most traditional classroom material.[27]

Whilst over 5,000 schools with 7th–12th grade students in the US were being supplied with copies of the biannual magazine, the intention was to achieve global distribution. Scotland became one of the 'worldwide' targets, with its schools receiving tens of thousands of copies. On 15 April 2001 the Scottish *Sunday Herald* reported:

> Up to 20,000 copies of seven editions of *Your World* are this month being sent to 600 schools and colleges throughout Scotland as a 'teacher's resource for biotechnology education'. In promoting the magazine, neither Scottish Enterprise nor HM Inspectorate of Education mentioned the fact that it has been sponsored by multinational GM companies.

Jeff Davidson of the Biotechnology Institute was quick to point out that *Your World*, 'though sponsored by GM companies, was actually produced by academics and science writers'. One of these was Professor Prakash (see pp. 70–2) who was scientific adviser and editor to the *Your World* issue (Volume 10, Issue No. 1 – 'The Gene Revolution in Food') addressing genetically modified food crops.

OTHER PAST EXAMPLES OF 'EDUCATIONAL' PR CAMPAIGNS

- Monsanto funded the 'Beautiful Science' exhibit at Walt Disney World, in February 1999.

- Novartis Seeds donated $25,000 towards the establishment of a Biotechnology Education Center at Iowa State University in February 1999.[28]

- In September 1999 Novartis contributed $300,000 towards an exhibit at the Museum of Science and Industry in Chicago entitled 'Farm to Plate'. Approximately two million people toured the exhibit annually, including 400,000 children on school tours. Ed Shonsey, President of Novartis Seeds, stated, 'In order to realise the potential [of biotechnology], we must help American consumers understand the immense possibilities biotechnology places within our grasp.'[29]

Stakeholder dialogue

A number of companies have invited key stakeholders such as NGOs to participate in dialogue with them, often stating that this will help them (the companies) to understand the issues better. Such dialogue may not only circumvent open democratic processes, public debate and participation, but may also split campaign alliances and isolate the 'radicals' who can then be portrayed as hardliners, uninterested in resolving the issues. It is also a useful method of finding out what current concerns are and what language is being used by the opposition, in order to massage the concerns and appropriate the language.

Masquerading as grassroots

Industry has long used what John Stauber of PR Watch calls 'phony corporate grassroots organizing':

> Unfortunately, most of what passes for citizen activism these days is actually paid for by corporate interests like the tobacco industry using Burson–Marsteller to create the National Smokers Alliance. They spent easily over 100 million dollars creating a 3 million member strong organization – all in a computer database – all able to be contacted by mail, by phone, even local organizers. And when the tobacco industry needed to dump phone calls and letters into Congress or into the local [legislature] or into cities to oppose restrictions on smoking, there was the National Smokers Alliance.[30]

As the US public became aware that GMOs were in their foods, the biotechnology industry in the US was encouraging people, such as groups of church members, union workers and the elderly, to speak in favour of GM food at public hearings held by the Food and Drug Administration (FDA). According to the *New York Times*,[31] in one demonstration, Monsanto paid for 100 members of a Baptist church to attend a rally in Washington, waving signs that said 'Biotech saves children's lives' and 'Biotech equals jobs'. They reportedly also paid for their lunch. A spokesperson for Monsanto said that the company had authorised the PR company Burson–Marsteller to reach out to people supporting biotechnology.

Before another FDA hearing in Chicago in November 1999, Burson–Marsteller hired Jerry Morrison, a long-time labour organiser. Morrison said that he had spoken to eight groups, asking them to speak at the Chicago hearing. Morrison readily admitted that Burson–Marsteller hired him to meet with farmers, unions, consumer and 'faith-based' groups to counter what he describes as 'environmentalist public hysteria' about biotech foods.[32] (See also Direct Impact Company, p. 57.)

THE FAKE PARADE

At the World Summit for Sustainable Development in Johannesburg, in August 2002, a march by poor farmers drew worldwide press attention. These farmers challenged opponents of genetic engineering and accused them of perpetuating poverty. However, careful examination revealed that all was not as it seemed. Behind the marchers and their 'bullshit' awards for the likes of Vandana Shiva was a web of interconnected groups and individuals. The Sustainable Development Network, which organised the march, is based in London and directed by Julian Morris, who is also linked with the Institute of Economic Affairs (UK). Its network includes the AgBioworld Foundation, linked to Agbioworld (see Professor Prakash, pp. 70–2), and the European Science and Environment Forum (see pp. 64–6),

Consumer Alert, the Free Market Foundation (Johannesburg), the Free Trade Institute (Lima, Peru), and a number of other organisations based in the South.[33] Most of these echo similar aims: strict limits to government, and individual and economic freedom. After the Summit, Val Giddings, Vice-President for Food and Agriculture of the Biotechnology Industry Organisation (BIO), wrote for the November issue of *Nature Biotechnology* (2002) about how the farmers were speaking for themselves at last, against those who profess to be their advocates.[34]

Apologies and pledges

Finding that the public would not simply accept the technology gratefully appears to have been a considerable shock to the biotech corporations, especially Monsanto. In October 1999 Monsanto's chief executive Robert Shapiro acknowledged that his company's aggressive biotech campaign probably 'irritated and antagonised' more people than it persuaded and was perceived as 'condescension or indeed arrogance'.[35]

This was followed by the Monsanto pledge, first issued in 1990 and renewed to cover biotechnology in November 2000. It reaffirms that it will not pursue Terminator technologies. It commits itself to dialogue and transparency, and promises to respect other people's concerns by not using genes from animals or humans in food or feed. It also promises to share Monsanto research with universities, supports a requirement for firms to notify US regulators about plans to market a biotech product, seek global standards on biotech seed, grain and food products, and sell only grain products approved as human food and livestock feed. And it will only launch products if they have regulatory approval in the US, Europe and Japan.

Similar sentiments come from William F. Kirk, president of DuPont's agricultural division:

> I think we totally underestimated the effect at the consumer level. Product acceptance went so fast with the farmers that maybe the consumer side didn't get worked on well enough for long enough. There is more work to be done around communicating and talking about benefits and being able to understand and listen for concerns.[36]

Burson-Marsteller: 'crisis management' company

> *I remember one conversation with a PR lobbyist for Monsanto, and I basically asked him how he did it. And he said, 'Well look, it's a great job, it pays me lots of money, I love my wife and my kids, and when I go home I just turn on the TV and pour a stiff drink and leave it all behind me.' At work here is the Nuremberg principle: 'If I don't do this,*

then somebody else will.' This view is the worst sort of cynicism because it allows one to rationalise any sort of behaviour, to the point of what was done in Nazi Germany.

John Stauber[37]

Burson–Marsteller – owned by WPP (see p. 46) – is a good example of the kind of company that the biotech corporations use to improve their image. It is an international PR company that specialises in 'altering public perception' and 'crisis management' for corporations, governments and military dictators in need. The last category has included the governments of General Jorge Rafael Videla in Argentina, Suharto in Indonesia and Abacha in Nigeria.[38] Burson-Marsteller is an expert in working on and changing public perception. Its public relations portfolio includes some of the worst ecological disasters such as the *Exxon Valdez* oil spill, the BSE crisis and the Union Carbide chemical leak in Bhopal, India.

Burson–Marsteller also put in a tender to advise EuropaBio, the pan-European biotechnology industry trade association. A report leaked in 1997 illustrates some of its advice.[39] For example, the biotechnology industry is advised to 'stay off the killing fields' – that is, not to engage in debate on environmental issues and health. They should be aware that adversarial voices will try and lure them into those areas as 'they enjoy high public credibility and because they know that direct industry rebuttals usually feed the story instead of killing it'. EuropaBio is instructed to turn itself into the journalist's best and most reliable continuing source of biotechnology/bioindustries inspiration and information – the first-stop help-desk, not for industry propaganda, but for practical, editor-pleasing, deadline-beating connections to interesting stories and personalities, even adversarial ones, relevant to their readerships.

DIRECT IMPACT COMPANY

Direct Impact became a subsidiary of Burson–Marsteller in 1999. According to the *Washington Post*:

> Burson–Marsteller, the public relations firm that perfected the art of astroturf lobbying, has taken over Direct Impact, another PR firm known for its somewhat disingenuous 'grassroots' efforts. Direct Impact has considered themselves the non-traditional 'third leg' of the 'lobbying stool.' The other two legs are 'traditional public relations and traditional lobbying.' Because Direct Impact do not lobby Congress directly, they are not required to file disclosure reports, making it impossible to find out how much money they spend on their 'grassroots' campaigns.[40]

Direct Impact specialised in 'grassroots PR', creating grassroots support for corporate interests. In the early 1990s, a dairy organisation hired Direct Impact to recruit New York residents to speak in favour of Monsanto's artificial GM growth hormone (rBST or rGBH) for milk cows, which caused one of the first battles over products created by genetic engineering. Direct Impact's list of customers in need of grassroots PR includes

> the American Petroleum Institute, a member of the Executive Committee of the Air Quality Standards Coalition (the lead organisation fighting the EPA's stringent air pollution standards), and a supporter of several anti-global warming treaty organisations, including the Global Climate Information Project, the Alliance for a Responsible Atmospheric Policy, the Global Climate Coalition and the Coalition for Vehicle Choice.[41]

Burson–Marsteller itself houses the Foundation for Clean Air Progress, another anti-environmental corporate front group.

Industry lobby groups

Bios is the ancient Greek word for 'life' and 'biology' refers to the science of life. Industry has chosen to award this positive meaning to the Biotechnology Industry Organisation (BIO). It was first called into life in the US in 1993 as a merger of the Industrial Biotechnology Association and the Association of Biotechnology Companies. By 2002 it held a membership of 'more than 1,000 companies, academic institutions and public biotech centres in all 50 US states and 33 other nations'. Its board (2001–2) included DuPont, Monsanto, Novartis, Bayer, Dow AgroScience, Syngenta and many of the leading pharmaceutical and genomics companies. BIO sees itself as the voice of all biotech interests, including genetic modification of crops, food and pharmaceuticals.

According to its website it is pursuing a 'three pronged mission':

- 'Advocate the industry's positions to elected officials and regulators [including international negotiations, trade talks, etcetera].

- Inform national and international media about the industry's progress, contributions to quality of life, goals and positions.

- Provide business development services to member companies, such as investor and partnering meetings.'[42]

Other organisations of the same type as BIO have appeared over the last decade in different parts of the world to ensure that biotechnology industry interests are pursued at the highest level of government, at international negotiations and in global trade. The most visible work is the organisation of industry conferences and BIO conventions. These widely publicised and expensive events feature company and salespeople, exhibitions, press conferences, industry workshops, lectures focusing on the benefits and progress of biotech, free banquets and gifts for journalists, and more. In the US, for example, BIO 2001 (San Diego) hosted 13,700 participants from 44 different nations, with 630 press registrations. The annual BIO conferences have been attracting increasing attention from critics. Counter-conferences, several entitled 'Biodevastation', have attracted thousands of concerned citizens to rally and march against what they believe BIO stands for.

Australia established its BIO equivalent, the Australian Biotechnology Association, in 1995; it was renamed AusBiotech in 2001. EuropaBio, founded in 1996 and based in Brussels, has proved to be a cunning and powerful lobbyist at the European Parliament and the European Commission, especially in the debate over the Patent Directive, on which large sums were spent. AfricaBio, established in 2000 in South Africa, is the only BIO organisation that focuses solely on biotech interests in food and farming. It is strategically placed to open the door of this vast continent for the GM seed industry. One of its tasks is to ensure that IPRs for 'biotechnological inventions' (such as genes or GM seeds) are embedded in the laws and regulations of the various African nations.

The following section gives further information on BIO organisations for those interested in industry lobby groups.

BIO

BIO, founded in 1993, has its headquarters in Washington DC, perfectly placed for its lobbying tasks. BIO reports that it has successfully prosecuted its core lobbying agenda points in the 1990s. It has, for example, repeatedly 'beaten back' federal [governmental] price control initiatives on breakthrough drugs. It claims that its core agenda point of 'shaping political and public reaction to the genetically modified foods that were poised to enter supermarkets' was also successfully executed: 'A host of genetically modified agricultural products traversed the regulatory gauntlet, including improved varieties of corn, potatoes, tomatoes and cotton.' BIO also takes credit for the fact that 'a variety of tax incentives were enacted at the state and federal level to encourage biotech investment'.[43]

Besides lobbying, BIO promotes huge PR and media campaigns. In March 2000 it launched a six-month television advertising campaign called 'Biotechnology: a Big Word That Means Hope', based on themes of US entrepreneurship, pioneering technology and the biotech industry's R&D into medicines for heart disease, cancer, diabetes, Alzheimer's and Parkinson's diseases. Interestingly, this PR campaign bundles the pharmaceutical and agricultural applications of the technology together. Further, little distinction is being made between genuine breakthroughs and ideas that have yet to be tested.

EUROPABIO

EuropaBio, the European Association for Bioindustries, was founded in 1996 as the 'voice of the European biotech industry'.[44] With its headquarters in Brussels, its major purpose is to influence legislation relevant to the biotech industry by lobbying the relevant institutions. 'EuropaBio's primary focus is the European Union [the Parliament, the Commission, the Council of Ministers and the presidency] but because of the global character of the business, we also represent our members in transatlantic and worldwide fora.'[45] One of its aims is to create coherent European legislation for bio-industries:

> Through its working groups and task forces, EuropaBio proactively contributes to the preparation of this regulatory framework, by providing constructive comments on proposed legislation or by drafting discussion documents and position papers.[46]

EuropoaBio and its members have been remarkably successful in convincing the European Commission of the desirability of biotechnology industries in Europe and in supporting the respective industries. We have mentioned that one of its major 'battles' was around the Life Patent Directive – the EU Directive on the Protection of Biotechnological Inventions:

> This Directive, which had been fiercely opposed by the European Parliament in 1995, was adopted by the same Parliament in 1998, after what had been one of the biggest and most expensive industry lobby campaigns in Brussels to date.[47]

According to its website, in 2003 EuropaBio had 35 corporate members operating worldwide, 21 national biotechnology associations with 1,200 small and medium-sized enterprises. The first European Biotechnology Convention (Cordia EuropaBio Convention 2003) has been announced for Vienna, 2–4 December 2003. (See also Chapter 7.)

AFRICABIO

AfricaBio was publicly launched in South Africa in January 2000 'to promote the enhancement of food, feed and fibre through the safe and responsible application of biotechnology'.[48] In contrast to other BIO organisations it focuses solely on genetic engineering in food and farming. By December 2002 it claimed a membership of 90 stakeholder organisations.

South Africa is a major entry-point into the African continent for industry. It has the infrastructure and wealth to support biotech research and is a large exporter to the region, with obvious implications for any African country seeking to remain GMO-free.

BIO offers this assessment of AfricaBio's impact on its website:

> While South Africa, Zimbabwe, and Mauritius lead the way with respect to modern biotechnology, Malawi, Zambia, Namibia, and Mozambique are actively

reviewing the technology and preparing a policy and biosafety platform for safe introduction and testing of GMOs.

AfricaBio aggressively pre-empted the launch of a citizen initiative for a five-year freeze (moratorium) on genetic engineering for food and farming in South Africa by issuing a press release denouncing it. Accusations included

> The so-called 'freeze alliance' fails to properly identify itself other than by the acronym SAFeAGE, 'a coalition of organisations who support the 5-yr Freeze Manifesto', in a pamphlet recently distributed to the public. According to Dr [Jocelyn] Webster [Executive Director of AfricaBio], the document is fraught with hackneyed generalisations and claims inconsistent with the latest scientific evidence. (AfricaBio Media Release, 25 July 2000)

AUSBIOTECH LTD

AusBiotech Ltd represents 685 members and describes itself as

> a national body of companies and individuals dedicated to the development and prosperity of the Australian biotechnology industry. It is the main body for the Australian Biotechnology industry, and provides a 'platform' which brings together all the relevant players involved in the Australian biosciences community. Its mission is to facilitate the commercialisation of Australian bioscience in the international marketplace.[49]

Established in 1995 as the Australian Biotechnology Association, it changed its name to AusBiotech Ltd in 2001; it has also changed the definition of 'corporate member' to include university and government research departments as well as hospital departments, which it invites to join alongside R&D corporations.[50] Maybe it is a brave step into the open, the public outing of university and governmental research departments as members of the corporate community. Whatever the intention, having institutions previously regarded as independent as members could make AusBiotech a well-cloaked advocate for profit-motivated genetic engineering solutions.

OTHER BIOTECH INDUSTRY ASSOCIATIONS

Other national or regional biotechnology industry organisations listed on BIO's webside include the All India Biotech Association (AIBA), New Delhi, India (established 5 July 1994; with more than 200 members by 2002; affiliated to BIO–USA); the Japan Bioindustry Association (established 1942; membership of 400 companies and 1,300 individuals); New Zealand Biotechnology Association; BIOTECanada; the BioIndustry Association (BIA) in the UK (established 1989, 130 corporate and 121 associate members by 2002); Israel Biotechnology Organisation; and Foro Argentino de Biotecnología in Argentina (established 1986; 35 members).[53]

The Council for Biotechnology Information (CBI)

This is a coalition of seven leading companies with an interest in biotechno-
logy, plus the industry trade association, BIO. The founding members of the
Council are: Aventis CropScience, BASF, Dow Chemical, DuPont,
Monsanto, Novartis, Zeneca Ag Products and BIO. Associated with the
Council are a range of other organisations and trade and industry groups that
support genetic engineering.

The Council's stated goal is to make it easier for people to get information about biotechnology. Its latest PR campaign in the US and Canada,
costing $50 million over three to five years, includes a website
(www.whybiotech.com), toll-free consumer number, information materials,
and television and print advertising. The CBI is also a founding sponsor of
the Biotechnology Institute.

Canadian secondary schools, colleges and universities got a special
present in 2001. The CBI – in cooperation with Oxford University Press
– sent a free copy of Alan McHughen's book *Pandora's Picnic Basket*
addressed to the librarians of all these institutions. The Canada-based *Ram's
Horn* newsletter reported in December 2001 that this industry practice was
not going unnoticed. The husband of a high school biology teacher had
sent a note in which he stated: 'I intend to pursue this practice [of industry
lobby group propaganda disguised as books for libraries or educational
resource 'kits' free to teachers] with the provincial deputy minister of
education.'[52]

Helping hands

It is very helpful for the corporations and their public relations contractors
to have supportive sources of opinion that appear to be completely
independent. Their value is increased by their status. Think tanks have
been well established in the US and the UK for many years. The media
quite often fail to give the affiliations of information providers, and help to
increase the illusion that they are all neutral or independent. Think tanks
are now appearing in the South. There is also a wide range of scientists and
opinion formers who operate as advocates for biotechnology. Many of
them oppose any regulation which is seen by industry as posing a threat to
the freedom to operate, such as campaigns associated with the Convention
on Climate Change, to reduce CO_2 emissions. Often a little investigation
shows how these apparently independent spokespersons, groups and
networks are linked together in an intricate web of connections. What
follows is just a sample of the individuals and organisations involved.

Often quoted, less often named: US conservative think tanks

Think tanks are usually recognised for their policy research, their particular approach to problem solving and, possibly, their lobby work. The background of particular think tanks, their closeness to industry or government, their sources of funding and their role in influencing the course of events through the media are less well known. Right-wing think tanks can serve the useful purpose of promoting free-market philosophy in the media.

The US national media watch group, the 'Fairness and Accuracy In Reporting' or FAIR collective[53] found that in 1997 conservative or right-leaning think tanks provided more than half the main US media's think tank citations for the third year running.[54] Think tanks of the right provided 53 per cent of citations, centrist think tanks 32 percent, while progressive or left-leaning think tanks received just 16 per cent of all citations. Five of the ten most-cited think tanks are conservative or right-leaning, including three of the top four: the Heritage Foundation, the American Enterprise Institute, and the Cato Institute. The Brookings Institute was the most cited and is defined as centrist. The top four think tanks were each cited more than a thousand times, and provided over 40 per cent of all think tank citations. Expert spokespersons quoted in the media were often not identified as representing think tanks, which also went unnamed in a majority of the citations. Nor was the fact that many of these think tanks receive significant corporate support.

> By failing to politically identify representatives of think tanks, or identify the financial base of think tanks, major media deprive their audiences of an important context for evaluating the opinions offered, implying that think tank 'experts' are neutral sources without any ideological predispositions.[55]

These think tanks also form opinions on genetic engineering in food and farming, influencing the debate and shaping its agenda. For example, the article 'Con Game', published to influence the Oregon State vote on labelling, was written by Jessica Melugin, a researcher at the American Enterprise Institute's Federalism Project, and Roger Bate, Director of the International Policy Network. In the article Melugin and Bate argue that

> the Food and Drug Administration – as well as all major international food and health bodies – have declared GM foods safe. For millennia technology has been employed to fight off pests, whether it's the application of tons of sulfur on organic crops, or inserting a single gene into a crop. The battle is ongoing, and with new technologies – from sulfur to DDT to newer pesticides and now GM techniques – we have increased food safety and helped feed billions of people. GM food doesn't deserve the stigma of mandatory labeling.[56]

In fact, neither the FDA nor 'all major international food and health bodies' have declared GM foods safe. The FDA only acknowledges that the notifying company regards the GM food as safe (see Box, p. 168, 'GM foods: not approval – just acknowledgement').

The Cato Institute is equally in favour of biotech crops and features pro-GM articles on its website. Examples include: 'GM Trade Wars' by Ronald A. Bailey, an adjunct scholar at the Cato Institute, who lays all the blame for current trade as well as food aid problems at the feet of Europe, reducing it all to a case of 'protectionism'.[57]

LINKING BUSH'S CABINET MEMBERS TO POLICY GROUPS AND THINK TANKS

Revolving doors between right-wing think tanks and the US government are many.[58]

- Ann Veneman, Secretary of Agriculture, is a member of the International Policy Council of Agriculture, Food and Trade (a policy group financed by Monsanto, Cargill, Archer Daniels Midland (ADM), Kraft and Nestlé) (see Dennis T. Avery, discussed on p. 73).

- Elaine Chao, Secretary of Labor, was formerly a distinguished fellow at the Heritage Foundation, the Washington-based right-wing policy group.

- Lynn Scarlett, Assistant Secretary for Policy, Management and Budget, is president of the Reason Foundation, a 'wise use' think tank.

- Paul H. O'Neill, Treasury Secretary, is a trustee at the Rand Corporation and the American Enterprise Institute, and the director of the Institute for International Economics.

- Lawrence Lindsey, top economic adviser to the President, is Arthur F. Burns chair at the American Enterprise Institute.

- Diana Furchgott-Roth, staff chief to the Council of Economic Advisers, is a resident fellow at the American Enterprise Institute.

- Nina Rees, adviser to Vice-President Cheney, is a senior analyst at the Heritage Foundation.

The Institute of Economic Affairs (IEA) and the European Science and Environment Forum (ESEF)

[The IEA] has played a most valuable role and has obviously had enormous influence. It also did a great deal of good in spreading the message for deregulation and in favour of capital markets.

Lord Taverne, House of Lords speech, 21 January 1999

The IEA is a UK-based, right-wing, pro-free trade and pro-corporate think tank. It was founded in 1955 by the late Sir Antony Fisher, who made a fortune by establishing Britain's first broiler chicken farm. Its general director is John Blundell. Since 1974 it has been developing similar institutions across the globe, evidently impressing Rupert Murdoch, who spoke of

> the remarkable universe of similar think tanks around the world. All are inspired with the principles of classical liberalism that are fundamental to our civilisation. Each one is now following its own independent course, but all can be traced back to a founding 'big bang', the celebrated Institute of Economic Affairs. (Rupert Murdoch, President and CEO of News Corporation Ltd, October 1994)[59]

In common with a number of other think tanks, it receives industry support, while proudly claiming its independence from government funding and political parties. Many people associated with the organisation are well known for attacking the claims of environmentalists about the threat of climate change, the destruction of rainforests, the benefits of organic food and agriculture and the dangers of economic globalisation.

Each year the IEA publishes some 20 books, plus a quarterly journal on various public policy issues. It holds conferences, seminars, lectures and working lunches to discuss its themes (50–80 events a year). There is also a student outreach programme. The Institute's research agenda includes:

- the risk of adopting the precautionary principle;

- private property rights and markets in environmental assets;

- the extent of scientific consensus on issues such as global warming;

- the growth and desirability of EU environmental regulations.

Members of the IEA have been involved in the production, for instance, of documentaries that have highlighted the 'health risks' of organic food and called environmental campaigners middle-class romantics who are attempting to prevent development in the South.

Such documentaries include the TV programme 'Counterblast',[60] which attempted to discredit organic food.[61] Roger Bate, who presented the programme, founded the Environment Unit at the Institute of Economic Affairs in 1993. Another was the Equinox documentary 'The Modified Truth',[62] which featured Professor Phillip Stott, the journalist Richard North, Julian Morris, the Director of the Environment and Technology Programme of the IEA, and Martin Durkin, who produced the Equinox programme. All these contributors were closely associated with the IEA at the time, but this was not disclosed in the Equinox programme, which questioned the motives of environmentalists for challenging genetic engineering.

Roger Bate was also co-founder and Director of ESEF, which was funded by the tobacco industry. According to the Norfolk Genetic Information Network,

> ESEF's task was to smuggle tobacco advocacy into a larger bundle of 'sound science' issues, including attacking such problematic areas for US corporate interests as the 'ban on growth hormone for livestock; ban on rBGH [genetically-engineered bovine growth hormone] to improve milk production; pesticide restrictions; ban on indoor smoking; restrictions on use of chlorine; ban on certain pharmaceutical products; restrictions on the use of biotechnology'.[63]

Roger Bate and Julian Morris, both involved in the IEA and the ESEF, edited a book called *Fearing Food: Risk, Health and the Environment* with contributions from Dennis Avery of the Hudson Institute (see pp. 73-4). They have also repeated and magnified Avery's claim that people who eat organic food are more likely to be affected by E. coli 0157, even though it appears that no research has actually been carried out that demonstrates this.

Richard D. North, well-known contrarian and anti-environmentalist, has written several papers funded by the IEA on the benefits of genetic engineering.[64] The *Ecologist* magazine claims that North's book *Life On A Modern Planet* was funded by ICI and that Shell paid him to visit Nigeria's Ogoniland to report favourably on the company's actions there.[65]

Another stalwart of the IEA is Roger Scruton, a right-wing academic, writer and columnist, who was recently exposed as receiving funds from Japan Tobacco to place stories favourable to the tobacco industry in the media. He wrote a pamphlet for the IEA in 2001 in which he attacked the World Health Organisation without declaring his links to the tobacco industry. In an e-mail to Japan Tobacco proposing an increase in his fees, he suggested further attacks on the WHO and said 'We propose a more general attack on the absurdity of trivial and unworkable transnational legislation, at a time of global crisis.'[66] He told the UK *Independent* newspaper: 'I'm not particularly keen on defending tobacco, but I am keen on defending freedom.'[67]

Some key proponents and 'independent' scientists

As already mentioned, it is a key PR strategy to identify, support and give opportunities to those scientists in good positions who will publicly speak up in favour of biotechnology. Scientists are supposed to be independent, factual and non-partisan, and are thus seen as the ideal communicators of the pro-biotech message. A good candidate is a scientist with a certain mindset and already established links with industry and/or government, or with hopes of gaining or maintaining funding for industry-tailored and application-driven projects.

Many of the most vocal and visible scientists promoting biotechnology seem to conform to a similar pattern. They frequently reflect a strong pro-corporate bias. They actively promote their views in the public domain, often seeking to discredit anyone who puts forward different views. Looking at the websites associated with outspoken biotech proponents whose articles and contributions are frequently found on the AgBioView e-mail list (see Professor Prakash, pp. 70–2), common threads can easily be found, including opposition to the Kyoto Treaty, CO_2 emission regulation, DDT regulation and organic farming and labelling. This is illustrated in Table 3.1 (p. 68). Such views are amplified through bogus consumer alliances and their websites – such as the National Consumer Coalition (www.foodstuff.org) and International Consumers for a Civil Society (www.icfcs.org). With an additional twist, it emerged during 2002 that some of the vocal GM advocates in the discussions do not actually exist at all, but are figments of virtual reality.[68] The Internet lends itself to the creation of illusions and this has not been lost on biotech proponents.

HENRY I. MILLER, MS, MD

Henry I. Miller is included to illustrate the multiple linkages between think tanks, individuals, government and negotiations. He is one of many who could have been selected.

By training, Henry Miller is a physician. At present he is research fellow in 'public policy toward science and technology' at the Hoover Institution, which is part of Stanford University and well known as a conservative think tank (number 14 in the list of quoted think tanks mentioned on p. 63).[69]

During 1979–94 he worked for the US Food and Drug Administration (FDA). According to the Hoover Institution website,

> he was the medical reviewer for the first genetically engineered drugs evaluated by the FDA and was instrumental in the rapid licensing of human insulin and human growth hormone. He served in several posts, including special assistant to the FDA commissioner, with responsibility for biotechnology issues; from 1989 to 1994, he was the founding director of the FDA's Office of Biotechnology.[70]

In 1994–6 he was Robert Wesson Fellow in Scientific Philosophy and Public Policy at the Hoover Institution.

Together with Norman E. Borlaug (see pp. 72–3), he is a director (since 1996) of the American Council on Science and Health (ACSH)[71] and a regular contributor to its magazine *Health Facts & Fears* (which can be read at HealthFactsandFears.com). He is an adviser to the US delegation to the Codex committee on biotechnology-derived food, an adjunct scholar at the Competitive Enterprise Institute (CEI), a member (since 1994) of the scientific advisory board of the George C. Marshall Institute and a director (since 1996) of Consumer Alert, one of the Sustainable Development

Table 3.1 • Examples of biotech proponents, their websites and anti-environmentalist (✔) views

Proponent, organisation and website	Kyoto Treaty	CO_2 emission regulation	DDT regulation	Organic farming & labels	Concern about rainforest destruction	Tobacco taxes & regulation
Philip Stott ProBiotech www.ecotrop.org www.probiotech.fsnet.co.uk	✔	✔	✔	✔	✔	
Steven J. Milloy Citizens for the Integrity of Science www.junkscience.com & www.nomorescares.com	✔	✔	✔	✔	✔	✔
Alex Avery Center for Global Food Issues www.cgfi.com	✔	✔	✔	✔		
Dennis Avery The Hudson Institute www.hudson.org	✔	✔	✔	✔		
Frances B Smith Consumer Alert www.consumeralert.org	✔	✔	✔	✔		
Gregory Conko Competitive Enterprise Institute (CEI) www.cei.org	✔	✔	✔	✔	✔	✔
John Carlisle National Center for Public Policy Research www.nationalcenter.org	✔	✔	✔	✔	✔	✔

Data above partially based on information provided by Robert Vint.[72]
Philip Stott – Professor Emeritus of Biogeography, University of London, UK. An IEA intimate, though not a formal member. Organiser of the UK Seeds of Opportunity conference in May 2001.
Steven J. Milloy – Former tobacco industry lobbyist as well as a former executive director of TASSC (The Advancement of Sound Science Coalition), a front organisation created by

tobacco giant Philip Morris. Steven J. Milloy is the publisher of Junkscience.com, an adjunct scholar at the Cato Institute and a columnist for FoxNews.com.

Dennis Avery – See pp. 73–4.

Frances B. Smith – Consumer Alert is a 'consumer' group opposing consumer safety and rights. Recipient of big tobacco funding.[73] Henry I. Miller (see pp. 67–9) is on its advisory council and sits – according to his own biography – on its board of directors.

Gregory Conko – CEI receives big tobacco funding.[74] Conko has a BA in Political Science and History. According to his biography on the CEI website, he is – together with C. S. Prakash (see pp. 70–2) – co-founder of the AgBioWorld Foundation, where he also serves as vice-president and is on the board of directors. The CEI website states further:

> Mr Conko served as a Principal Investigator for the California Council on Science and Technology's 2002 report 'Benefits and Risks of Food Biotechnology', commissioned by the California state legislature and Governor Gray Davis....
>
> Gregory Conko is a Policy Analyst and Director of Food Safety Policy with the Competitive Enterprise Institute (CEI) where he specialises in issues of food and pharmaceutical drug safety regulation, and on the general treatment of health risks in public policy. Mr Conko is particularly interested in the debate over the safety of genetically engineered foods and the application of the precautionary principle to domestic and international environmental and safety regulations. He frequently participates in international meetings on food safety and trade as a credentialed non-governmental organisation representative.[75]

Network's member organisations (see pp. 55–6). His biography also details his membership of the editorial boards of *Human Gene Therapy*, *Journal of Commercial Biotechnology*, *Medical Spectator*, and *Biotechnology Law Report*.[76,77]

His website at the Hoover Institution provides details of his work contributions in four areas:

> (1) as a federal official, crafting and implementing science-based regulation and (2) explaining these policies to regulated industry, the scientific community, and the public; as a member of international panels and groups of experts, moving consensus toward the scientific view of risk assessment and management; (3) making science and technology and their regulation more widely understood, via articles in newspapers and magazines; and (4) performing research on and analyses of various issues related to science and technology, including the description of models for regulatory reform.[78]

Many of his articles can be found on the AgBioView website of Professor Prakash (pp. 70–2). He often co-authors papers with members of other think tanks (with Gregory Conko, for example). As with other pro-GM think tanks and think-tank members, a main focus is on the EU and its supposed protectionism, he attacks the precautionary principle, the Cartagena Biosafety Protocol, labelling and stringent regulations. In an article ('European Move Will Stifle GMOs') published in July 2002 and posted on AgBioView, Henry I. Miller and Gregory Conko write:

Repeated analyses over two decades have documented Europe's lack of competitiveness in biotechnology, but last week, by formally ratifying the United Nations-sponsored Cartagena Protocol on Biosafety, the EU yet again has embraced an oversight regime that wrongly and excessively regulates the international movement and testing of safe, precisely crafted products, while exempting more problematic ones. ... Although numerous critiques of the so-called precautionary principle, which is not a principle at all but a kind of blanket justification for arbitrarily opposing disfavoured technologies and products, have been promulgated, its shortcomings are nowhere more evident than in GM regulation. This bogus principle has been invoked repeatedly to support unwarranted restrictions on some of the safest, most intensively studied food products in human history, and in a way that reflects that the goal is protectionism, not consumerism.

In July 2003, in support of the US challenge to the EU at the WTO, Henry Miller denounced the 'EU's unnecessary, unscientific and excessive regulatory requirements for GM crops and foods'.[79]

PROFESSOR PRAKASH

Dr Channapatna S. Prakash – Professor of Plant Molecular Genetics – is known for 'working to promote acceptance of biotechnology in food and agriculture around the world, both in the scientific and marketing fields. Prakash also writes newspaper articles and delivers public lectures.'[80]

C. S. Prakash is Director of the Center for Plant Biotechnology Research at Tuskegee University, Alabama, USA, working on genetically engineering crops important to developing countries, such as sweet potato. He is a member of the USDA Advisory Committee on Agricultural Biotechnology and sits on the Commission on Biotechnology of the International Society for Horticultural Science. He is an adviser to the Department of Biotechnology of the Indian government.[81]

In 2000 Prakash started the pro-GM AgBioWorld Foundation together with Gregory Conko from the CEI (see Table 3.1) and now serves as its president. According to its own website, AgBioWorld is

devoted to bringing information about technological advances in agriculture to the developing world. Our members ... believe that recent developments in plant science, such as biotechnology, can and should be used to increase crop yields, grow more nutritious plants and reduce dependence on chemicals in order to alleviate hunger and to help preserve the environment.

The website also claims that AgBioWorld is 'an organization that has emerged from academic roots and values'.[82]

The website hosts a declaration by 'Scientists In Support Of Agricultural Biotechnology'. Of the 3,296 signatures collected by January 2002, approximately 32 per cent of signatories hold company/industry positions (9 per cent Monsanto alone), 38 per cent work in a university setting, 16 per cent are involved in private or governmental research organisations or industry organisations whilst 13–14 per cent fail to indicate whom they work for.[83]

This declaration serves a strategic purpose in the global drive to deregulate GM and further the biotech industry. Far from being scientist-led, it was conceived by CEI and Gregory Conko. In its 2000 annual report CEI states:

> CEI also took an active part in the fight against what we call 'death by regulation' – regulatory policies that threaten people's health and safety. Foremost has been the battle over biotechnology, a promising technology in danger of being stymied by a host of regulatory controls. Among other things, we played a key role in the creation of a 'Declaration of Scientists in Support of Agricultural Biotechnology', which has been signed by more than 2,900 scientists at last count, among them three Nobel Prize winners.[84]

In mid-2002, the AgBioWorld website[85] offered 34 different media interviews with Prakash, a contact list of 40 international experts in the field, a number of articles and '31 Critical Questions in Agricultural Biotechnology'. AgBioWorld also offered the AgBioView e-mail list, which has featured many attacks on environmentalists, GM opponents and critical scientists (see Chapter 4).

A keen advocate of biotechnology, Prakash takes opportunities where they arise. He states that he has 'served as a speaker on behalf of the US State Department and has travelled to European, South-East Asian and Caribbean nations to deliver public lectures and meet with the media, scientists and trade experts ....' This itinerary has included two debates in London with biotechnology critics and, according to the US embassy in London, speakers on such occasions 'are paid with US taxpayer money' as part of programmes 'to promote US government interests'.[86]

On the Equinox programme discussed above (see p. 65) he described organic food as dirty and dangerous and stated in a press release:

> There is no scientific reason to believe that genetically engineered foods are any less safe than the foods we've been eating for centuries, so we members of the scientific community felt it necessary to counter the unfounded attacks that anti-biotech activists are spreading about these products.[87]

Prakash regularly claims that GM goods have been stringently tested ('for up to eight years' in both Canada and the US, for example).[88] When asked for proof of safety and peer-reviewed papers he responded in an e-mail:

> Why don't your network sponsor some research in this direction? I am sure your researchers would find it frustrating as no safety concern will be found beyond what is already unsafe about our conventional food.

Interestingly, Professor Jose Domingo published a detailed database search in the prestigious journal *Science* showing that he could only find eight refereed journal articles dealing directly with the safety of GM foods. Only four of these were experimental feeding trials, three of which were undertaken by Monsanto teams.[89]

NOBEL PEACE LAUREATE NORMAN E. BORLAUG

Norman Borlaug, now in his late eighties, is still called upon by industry worldwide as an energetic promoter of intensive farming and biotechnology. He strongly supports Prakash and his AgBioWorld Foundation and serves on the board of directors of the American Council on Science and Health which campaigns against 'health scares' (see p. 67).

Norman Borlaug is well known as the 'father of the green revolution'. Working at the International Maize and Wheat Improvement Centre (CIMMYT) in Mexico, he developed the 'miracle' or high-response seeds that were later grown worldwide. He exemplifies the tendency for white Northern males to dominate agricultural research. Born at the beginning of the First World War, he went to university during the Great Depression. He then took a job as a microbiologist with DuPont and had the opportunity to join the first international agricultural development assistance programme through the Rockefeller Foundation in Mexico.

His main concern was to increase wheat yield in Mexico through breeding and to stay ahead of the rapidly evolving wheat rust disease. His first innovation was 'high volume crossing', where he used wheat from all around the world and made thousands of crosses, constantly watching and selecting. This approach helped to fend off the threat of wheat rust. The second innovation was an accidental one. Trying to speed up breeding, he used two different areas in Mexico, one where he could plant in May and the other where he could plant the newly selected varieties in October. Though at first wheat growing well in one region would grow poorly in the other, further selection and moving seeds back and forth between the areas achieved a type of wheat that was adapted to more than one region. This type of breeding became known as 'shuttle breeding'. It broke a basic principle of breeding at that time – that plants needed to be adapted to the area in which they grew – and has now become commonplace amongst breeders.

He then helped to transfer the varieties developed in Mexico to Asia and later worked to establish CIMMYT in Mexico, modelled on IRRI in the Philippines, with the aim of disseminating what had been learned about wheat and corn in Mexico to the rest of the world. Robert W. Herdt, Rockefeller Foundation's Director for Agricultural Sciences, says of Borlaug:

> In between times he took up the lecture circuit, hammering away at the need for constant attention to the global population problem, the need to increase food production, and the short-sightedness of misguided environmentalists who fail to see that fertiliser, pesticides and science stand between humanity and starvation.[90]

The still-active Borlaug is a major advocate of GM technology for the South. He is patron of the International Service for the Acquisition of Agri-Biotech Applications (ISAAA) (see pp. 124–7) and a senior consultant for Sasakawa–Global 2000 (see pp. 194–5 and Chapter 1).

THE HUDSON INSTITUTE AND DENNIS AVERY

The Hudson Institute (Indianapolis) is a US-based, pro-industry think tank that receives funding from biotechnology companies including Aventis (AgrEvo), Dow AgroSciences, Monsanto, Novartis Crop Protection and AstraZeneca. It is number 11 on the FAIR citation list for 1997 (see p. 63).

Dennis T. Avery studied agricultural economics at Michigan State University and the University of Wisconsin and worked as agricultural analyst (1980–8) for the US Department of State, assessing the foreign-policy implications of food and farming developments worldwide.

He is the Director of the Global Centre for Food Issues at the Hudson Institute and the author of *Saving the World with Pesticides and Plastics* and *How Poverty Won't Save the Planet*. He has made many claims about the safety and benefits of GM foods whilst proclaiming that 'people who eat organic and "natural" foods are eight times as likely as the rest of the population to be attacked by a deadly new strain of E. coli bacteria'.[91]

His website reports that 'As a staff member of the President's National Advisory Commission on Food and Fiber, he wrote the Commission's landmark report, *Food and Fiber for the Future*.' It goes on to say:

> Avery travels the world as a speaker, has testified before Congress, and has appeared on most of the nation's major television networks, including a program discussing the bacterial dangers of organic foods on ABC's 20/20.

At the Husker Feed Grains and Soybean Conference in Kearney, Nebraska in January 2000, Avery attributed intense consumer resistance to genetically enhanced crops to a well-conceived campaign by vegetarian-leaning activist groups. He also blamed poor marketing by agricultural input firms who developed 'designer' crops that could resist pressure from targeted insects and herbicides and were less expensive to grow.

However, with 'Golden Rice' in the pipeline he believes there is now a positive story that needs to be pushed (see pp. 135–40). In this climate, Avery has advised mainstream agriculturalists to go on the offensive against organic producers and consumer activist groups that spread what he calls misinformation about GMOs, crop chemicals and modern production methods.

> Advertise. You don't have much ability to get the urban media to take your [GMO] story and present it now that they have presented the other side so vigorously … but you have one avenue to reach the public and that's advertising.[92]

When the International Policy Council on Agriculture, Food and Trade – which enjoys funding support from many of the largest biotech corporations (http://www.agritrade.org/) – held its World Food and Farming Congress in London in November 2002, Avery spoke on 'The Conflict between the Affluent Consumers and the Need of the Majority'. He is quoted as saying (and his Powerpoint slide programme repeated the message):

> The activist stance on agricultural biotech is inhumane – it lacks humanity, caring, kindness, compassion, concern for people and society – it is denying the Third World equal lifespan and lifestyle choice and it is offering mainly weed-slavery in the hot sun.

Notes

1 Michael Manekin, 'PR Nation: Anti-Spin Activist John Stauber Penetrates America's Lie Machine', *Westchester Weekly* (Massachusetts, USA), September 2001. – http://www.commondreams.org/views01/0901-05.htm
2 Stuart Ewen, *PR! A Social History of Spin*, Basic Books, 1996.
3 *Ibid.*
4 Sharon Beder and Richard Gosden, 'WPP: World Propaganda Power', *PR Watch*, 2001. http://www.prwatch.org/prwissues/2001Q2/wpp.html
5 Figures and some details from Hoover's online: http://www.americasbest.com/stocks/hooversonline.htm
6 DuPont Vision Statement, January 2003. http://www1.dupont.com/NASApp/dupontglobal/corp/index.jsp?page=/overview/glance/vision/index.html
7 'Creating Shareholder and Societal Value … While Reducing Our Footprint throughout the Value Chain'. http://www1.dupont.com/NASApp/dupontglobal/corp/index.jsp?GXHC_gx_session_id_=fe2f60ec2fdef3bf&GXHC_lang=en_US&GXHC_ctry=US&page=/social/SHE/index.html
8 http://www.syngentabiotech.com/who_vision.htm (viewed December 2002).
9 Denis Staunton, 'Holocaust Survivors Protest at IG Farben Meeting', *Irish Times*, 19 August 1999. http://www.fpp.co.uk/Auschwitz/docs/controversies/deathroll/IGFarben1.html
10 'Nazi Slave Cash Dismissed as "Gesture"', BBC World Service, 15 December 1999. http://news.bbc.co.uk/hi/english/world/europe/newsid_566000/566692.stm
11 Yojana Sharma, 'Minorities – Germany: Gypsies Seek World War II Recompense', Inter Press Service, Berlin, 24 September 1998. http://www.oneworld.net/ips2/sept98/10_19_020.html
12 Quoted on website 'Justice and Awareness', http://194.247.116.119/
13 'Dow/Union Carbide Merger Could Be a Toxic Combination', Infact Press Release, 30 August 1999. http://www.infact.org/dowunion.html
14 *Ibid.*
15 Professor Allan Fels, Chairman, Australian Competition and Consumer Commission, 'Globalisation and Competition Policy', Sydney Institute, 23 April 2001.

http://www.accc.gov.au/speeches/2001/Fels_Sydney_Institute_23_4_01.htm

16 Holly Knaus, 'Ciba–Geigy: Pushing Pills and Pesticides', *Multinational Monitor,* April 1993. The text can be found on http://www.essential.org/monitor/hyper/issues/1993/04/mm0493_11.html

17 Olle Hansson, *Inside Ciba–Geigy,* Penang, Malaysia: IOCU, 1989. Dr Olle Hansson was a Swedish neurologist and paediatrician.

18 Knaus, 'Ciba–Geigy'.

19 Jed Greer and Kenny Bruno, *Greenwash: the Reality behind Corporate Environmentalism,* Penang: Third World Network, 1996, pp. 131–2.

20 D.A. Derksen and P.R. Watson, 'Volunteer Crops: The gift that keeps on giving', Poster, Expert Committee on Weeds, Ottawa: ECW, 1999 (cited in Royal Society of Canada Report, 2001); K. Topinka, J. Hoffman and Hall, 'Pollen flow between herbicide tolerant canola (*Brassica napus*) is the cause of multiple resistant canola volunteers', Poster, Expert Committee on Weeds, Ottawa: ECW, 1999; R. K. Downey, 'Gene flow and rape – the Canadian experience', in *Gene flow and Agriculture: Relevance for Transgenic Crops,* British Crop Protection Council, Farnham, Surrey, UK: pp. 109–16; Mary MacArthur, 'Triple-resistant canola weeks found in Alta', *Western Producer,* 10 February 2000. http://www.producer.com/articles/20000210/news/20000210/news01.html

21 Severin Carrell, 'GM Threatens a Superweed Catastrophe', *Independent,* 29 June 2003.

22 Manekin, 'PR Nation'.

23 Now based in Arlington, Virginia, USA.

24 Sponsors listed on website of the Biotechnology Institute. http://www.biotechinstitute.org/funding.html

25 *Ibid.*

26 Welcome letter to website viewers by President Paul Hanle, 3 November 2001. http://www.biotechinstitute.org/welcome.html

27 Novartis PR, 10 September 1999.

28 *Ibid.,* 2 February 1999.

29 *Ibid.,* 10 September 1999.

30 http://www.guerrillanews.com/stauber/stauber_transcript.html

31 *New York Times,* 8 December 1999.

32 Reported by *PR Watch.* http://www.prwatch.org/prwissues/1999Q4/monsatan.html

33 http://www.sdnetwork.net

34 Jonathan Matthews, 'The Fake Parade – under the Banner of Populist Protest, Multinational Corporations Manufacture the Poor', *Environment,* 3 December 2002. http://www.freezerbox.com/archive/article.asp?id=254

35 Greenpeace Business Conference, London, 6 October 1999.

36 Quoted in Ann M. Thayer, 'Market Dynamics, Swayed by Customers up and down the Agricultural and Food Chain, Could Hurt Ag Biotech Businesses', C&EN Houston-News Analysis, *Business,* 77, 44 (1 November 1999), http://courses.che.umn.edu/01fscn1102-1s/general_food_safety/gmo/gmo_CE News2.html.

37 Manekin, 'PR Nation'.

38 Andrew Rowell, *Green Backlash: Global Subversion of the Environment Movement,* London: Routledge, 1996.

39 *Communications Programme for EuropaBio, January 1997,* prepared by Burson–Marsteller.

http://www.transnationale.org/anglais/sources/institutions/bm_europabio.html

40 Bill McAllister, 'Burson–Marsteller Buys Va. Lobbying Firm', *Washington Post*, 14 April 1999, p. E3, as quoted in *A Clear View*, 6, 3 (11 May 1999). http://www.ewg.org/pub/home/clear/view/latest.html

41 Environmental Working Group, 1997. http://www.ewg.org/pub/home/clear/players/global.html

42 BIO website. http://www.bio.org/aboutbio/history.htm

43 'About BIO: Partner to a Dynamic Industry Coming of Age'. http://www.bio.org/aboutbio/history.asp

44 http://www.europabio.org/pages/eu_membership.asp

45 EuropaBio website, membership page, December 2002. http://www.europabio.org/pages/eu_membership.asp

46 Quote from EuropaBio presentation on BIO website. http://www.bio.org/links/Europe.asp#UK

47 'The ICC and the Environment: Mastering Corporate Environmentalism', *Corporate Europe Observer*. http://www.xs4all.nl/~ceo/icc/icc_environment.html

48 'Africabio Position Statement on Modern Biotechnology'. http://www.africabio.com

49 <http://www.aba.asn.au/>. AusBiotech Ltd.'s website address has changed to: http://www.ausbiotech.org

50 AusBiotech membership website, December 2002. www.ausbiotech.org/membwho.php

51 A list of these organisations can be found on the BIO website. http://www.bio.org/links/international.html

52 *The Ram's Horn – a Monthly Newsletter of Food System Analysis*, 126 (November/ December 2001): 8. http://www.ramshorn.bc.ca

53 http://www.fair.org/whats-fair.html

54 Michael Dolny, 'What's in a Label? Right-wing Think Tanks Are Often Quoted, Rarely Labelled'. http://www.fair.org/extra/9805/think-tanks.html

55 Dolny, 'What's in a Label?'

56 Jessica Melugin and Roger Bate, 'Natural Doesn't Mean Safe', column in *Tech Central Station*, 4 November 2002. http://www.free-market.net/rd/496119626.html

57 Ronald A. Bailey, 'GM Trade Wars', 9 August 2002. http://www.cato.org/research/articles/bailey-020809.html

58 The following list is based on data published by the *Multinational Monitor*, 22, 5 (May 2001). http://multinationalmonitor.org/mm2001/01may/may01bushcc.html

59 www.iea.org.uk/ieamain/abouttheiea.htm

60 BBC2 TV broadcast, 31 January 2000.

61 The Soil Association published a rebuttal of the 'Counterblast' arguments on its website (www.soilassociation.org).

62 C4 broadcast, 19 March 2000.

63 Quote from 'How Big Tobacco Helped Create "The Junkman"', *PR Watch*, 7, 3. http://www.prwatch.org

64 C4 broadcast, 19 March 2000.

65 'Grim up North: a Profile of Richard D. North', *Ecologist*, January 2001.

66 Marie Woolf and David Lister: 'Scruton Likely to Lose Newspaper Columnist Job after Exposure of Financial Link to Tobacco Firm', *Independent*, 25 January 2002.

67 *Ibid.*

68 George Monbiot, 'The Fake Persuaders: Corporations Are Inventing People to Rubbish Their Opponents on the Internet', *Guardian*, 14 May 2002. http://www.guardian.co.uk/Columnists/Column/0,5673,715158,00.html

69 http://www-hoover.stanford.edu/bios/miller_h.html

70 Henry I. Miller's biography on the Hoover Institution website (January 2003). http://www-hoover.stanford.edu/bios/miller_h.html

71 http://www.acsh.org/

72 Robert Vint, 'Why Do the Key GM Food Advocates Oppose the Kyoto Treaty?' 19 April 2001. rjvint@globalnet.co.uk

73 *PRWatch* investigates: 'No More Scares'. http://members.tripod.com/~ngin/ 168.htm

74 *Ibid.*

75 Short expert biography found on CEI website. <http://www.cei.org/dyn/view_ expert.cfm?expert=3&Submit2.x=10&Submit2.y=15> Longer biography found on http://www.cei.org/dyn/view_bio.cfm/3

76 http://www.healthfactsandfears.com/contributors/hmiller.html (December 2002).

77 Expert biography of Henry I. Miller found on CEI site. http://www.cei.org/dyn/view_bio.cfm/150 (December 2002). Also on Hoover Institution site http://www-hoover.stanford.edu/bios/miller_h.html (December 2002).

78 http://www-hoover.stanford.edu/bios/miller_h.html (December 2002).

79 Henry Miller, 'First salvo in transatlantic food fight is far from last word', *Nature Biotechnology* 21 (7): 737–8, July 2003.

80 Sonia Chopra, 'Biotechnology's Standard Bearer', 7 September 2000. http://www.thinkindia.com/

81 http://www.talksoy.com/Media/aBiotechExperts.htm

82 http://www.agbioworld.org/about/about.html

83 Based on the first 1,000 signatures taken as a representative sample of declaration as found on agbioworld website. http://www.agbioworld.org

84 CEI Annual Report 2000. http://www.cei.org/PDFs/2K_annual_report.pdf

85 http://www.agbioworld.org

86 E-mail from Karen Morrisey of the US Embassy in London, 23 March 2001, to Marcus Williamson, Editor, *Genetically Modified Food-News*. http://www.gmfoodnews.com/

87 See press release, 'Nobel Prize Winners Endorse Agricultural Biotechnology', *AgBioWorld* 7 February 2000. http://www.agbioworld.org/biotech_info/ pr/watson.html

88 Anne Dawson, 'Bone to Pick with GM Label', *Ottawa Sun*, 23 February 2002.

89 Jose L. Domingo, 'Health Risks of GM Food: Many Opinions but Few Data', letter to *Science*, 288, 5472 (9 June 2000): 1748–9.

90 Rockefeller Foundation website: www.rockfound.org.

91 Dennis Avery, 'The Hidden Dangers in Organic Food', *American Outlook*, Fall 1998, quarterly publication of the Hudson Institute. http://hudson.org/American_Outlook/articles_fa98/avery.htm

92 Gary Wulf, 'Farmers Urged to Stump for Ag Biotech Industry', *Bridge News*, 21 January 2000. This article is a report on the Husker Feed Grains and Soybean Conference in Kearney, Nebraska, in January 2000.

4

Consolidation, Contamination and Loss of Diversity:
the Biotech Dream Takes Hold

The last decade of the twentieth century saw the agbiotech industry con-solidate. Many of these companies also moved into the seed business, buying up companies worldwide. The increased integration of the agrochemical and seed industries into emerging biotech giants represented one aspect of the loss of diversity; the other was the dwindling of available seeds and agrodiversity, as companies dropped varieties from their catalogues. At the same time, however, biotech giants began projecting themselves as 'life science' companies – until it became clear that their new products were taking longer to come to market than had been hoped. Watching the companies merge, demerge, and create alliances is like watching poker players swap cards. Those outside the casino are entitled to wonder whether their needs are best served by this process. As the consolidation process continued, a new threat emerged, that of genetic contamination, as the constructs of the genetic engineers began to move through the food chain (see 'Starlink – GM corn', p. 92) and the environment, posing particular threats to centres of diversity. The first such incident was the discovery of GM contamination of maize in its centre of origin, Mexico. The ensuing row brought contamination of an intellectual nature, with scientists allowing their judgement to be clouded by their dependence on funding. It has become apparent that the industry can benefit from the spread of contamination, if people feel unable to maintain their resistance in the face of a tide of pollution. Monsanto has shown how companies can directly benefit from contamination by successfully suing farmers for the adventitious presence of patented genes in their crops.

The life science concept

A wholesome potato that promises consumers french fries and chips with better flavor and texture. Firm juicy tomatoes with garden-fresh flavor. Fluffy white cotton bolls on a plant

*that can fend off damaging insects without the use of chemicals. Lush healthy soybean plants
that offer growers new alternatives for controlling yield-robbing weeds.*

Monsanto leaflet (*Exploring a New World of Discovery*) on Monsanto's Life
Sciences Research Center (n.d.)

By the 1990s the big chemical companies had gained a very dirty reputation.
Events such as Union Carbide's Bhopal disaster had made them increasingly
conspicuous and unpopular. There were an increasing number of stories of
toxic chemicals building up in the food chain, appearing in mothers' milk,
forcing the greenhouse effect, opening up the hole in the ozone layer, or
being suspected of causing cancers and immune system problems. So, in the
mid- and late 1990s, as they sought to change their identities from old
chemical dinosaurs to new biotech saviours, their public relations managers
devised a new concept, the 'life sciences', which could be applied to any
company activity connected to life processes: notably crop and food production, and pharmaceuticals.

The title 'life sciences' summons up an image of benevolence. Its launch
around 1997 was accompanied by many advertisements projecting the image
of a clean and wonderful future brought by science in partnership with life.
It was more than just a PR exercise, however. The agrochemical industry had
been finding it increasingly expensive and difficult to develop new chemical
pesticides and herbicides and also faced the prospect that some of its leading
products were soon to come off patent. Moreover, their share of the revenue
from the food system was dwindling as the food retailers, processors and
distributors increased their share. The agrochemical industry found potential
solutions in biotechnology, which gave it a whole new area of science,
biology, in which to identify and patent new pesticides and technologies,
based on the DNA of organisms:

> TNCs could use biotechnology to counter generic [non-patent] competition by
> genetically engineering plants for dependence on their brand-name pesticides.
> Genetically modified (GM) crops could have the added advantage of reducing
> regulatory costs; a new pesticide costs a company between $40–100 million to
> bring through the regulatory process while it cost less than $1 million to bring a
> new plant variety to market.[1]

This explains why almost all of the early GM crops were engineered for
herbicide tolerance – and indeed still are (see Table 8.3, p. 187). It made
good business sense to do so, helping companies to keep commercial control
of products which were coming off patent through making them part of
agricultural packages containing patented seeds and tied to contracts. In
addition, the companies dreamed of using agricultural biotechnology to
create and patent new designer crops that would find ready markets in the
food and feed industry: for example, crops with additional or altered oil,
protein and vitamins.

The companies therefore sought to counter images of poisoned land, water and people with promises of crops that would need fewer applications of pesticides or that would produce their own. They borrowed from concepts such as Ayurveda, an ancient system of health and nutrition in India, claiming that they would produce crops with added vitamins and minerals or medical properties (see 'Golden Rice', p. 135). They promised new developments that are a long way from being realised and may not be amenable to genetic engineering, such as drought- or salt-resistant crops. These promises helped to intensify investor hopes for profitable synergies between the different divisions specialising in pharmaceuticals, nutrition and agriculture. Trying to find the right combinations fuelled mergers, acquisitions and spin-offs during the late 1990s. But this optimism, accompanied by grandiose name changes and advertising campaigns, proved premature.

The life science concept on hold

The unravelling of life sciences comes as no surprise to cynics who saw it less as a business strategy than a pretty label to stick on what was left of companies once they evolved by disposing of their low-margin, cyclical chemicals assets.

'Green and Dying', *Economist*, 16 November 2000[2]

During 1999, pharmaceuticals divisions commanded high premiums, mostly due to a few top-selling drugs, whilst agribusiness divisions took serious downturns. This was due partly to the general trend of depressed prices in the global agricultural commodity market, but also to campaigns in Europe against GM crops. Mid-term profits slumped and job losses were announced. Brokerage houses such as Deutsche Bank advised major players in the biotech industry to spin off their ailing agricultural divisions.[3]

By 2000 the widely trumpeted 'life sciences industry' experiment seemed to be coming apart at the seams. With the agrochemical market in a period of slow growth and the transgenic seed market still relatively small, many commentators called for the more profitable pharmaceutical sector to be separated from the agriculture sector. Companies appeared very eager to distance themselves from the stagnating agribusiness sectors, as indicated by the demerger of Aventis CropScience from Aventis or the Novartis and Zeneca spin-off of their agrochemical divisions to form Syngenta. Yet agribusiness and pharmaceuticals were still seen to have strong potential synergies, as continuing research into engineering plants to produce vaccines, antigens and increased vitamin content indicates. However, many years of development and testing are required; methods have to be found to prevent cross-contamination between crops and seeds variously required for pharmaceutical, food and industrial purposes; and it is likely that few of these promised products will actually materialise or make it through to the market.

The *Economist* reported in 2000:

> As Michael Pragnell, head of Syngenta, points out, keeping agriculture and pharmaceuticals together provides synergies in basic research, but these soon evaporate when it comes to further development and marketing. Moreover, such benefits are easily diluted by the strain of having to manage two very different businesses.[4]

Another 5–10 years to wait for the pay-off?

Some of the manoeuvring that we have seen the companies engage in since 2000 arises from the fact that they still believe that there may be huge potential profits in the life science combination of agriculture/pharmaceuticals/genetic engineering. As explained above, however, it will be some time before these are realised, so the companies have to work out how to maintain their potential stake in the gold field while retaining the confidence of lenders and investors who do not like to wait too long for good news.

A market analyst expressed it well in November 1999, although he was still premature in his forecast of the upturn in the fortunes of the life sciences, especially in view of the general downturn in the stock market in recent years:

> The agribusiness sector is, at the moment, in a turbulent state, but we believe that we are probably close to the bottom of the depression. The psychological climate cannot deteriorate much further nor can the industry's economic conditions.... The future should be brighter providing that life-sciences companies correctly manage the crucial issues .... We, therefore, believe that the timing should soon be right to invest in life-sciences companies given their current valuations. It may be sensible, however, to bide one's time for the coming wave of consolidation in order to have a clearer picture of the industry and be able to spot the future winners. It is also worth remembering that we do not expect the real economic pay-offs stemming from plant genetic engineering to filter through for 5 to 10 years. So, as far as GMOs alone are concerned, investing in life-sciences shares requires a long-term approach to investment, with each investor carefully assessing the opportunity cost of such an investment over such a long period.[5]

In addition to the tensions described above, the industry now has to deal with the fact that some of the disadvantages of the technology are emerging in the form of contamination, which has already affected Canada and the US quite seriously.

Consolidation in the agrochemical industries

We expect that only five or six major agrochemical businesses will be left by 2002; at present the top nine represent approximately 85 per cent of sales.
'Challenging Climate for Agrochemicals', Lehman Brothers analyst report,
17 January 2000

The process of corporate consolidation is complex and can be confusing. What follows is the briefest possible outline to help elucidate the tables below. Further information can be gained from corporate websites and those of organisations that analyse corporate activities.[6]

Monsanto has long been the company everyone loves to hate, boldly pushing in where others have not dared to tread and bringing hundreds of cases against farmers for alleged violation of its patented genetic traits. That is not surprising, because in 2001 Monsanto traits were present in 91 per cent of GM crops grown worldwide. Having purchased a global spread of seed companies (nearly $10 billion spent since 1996), it sought an alliance with another company, and became a subsidiary of *Pharmacia* in 2000. It was spun off in 2002, however, and could now be extremely vulnerable to market vagaries and predatory suitors.

Its patent on the best-selling herbicide ever, the glyphosate-based RoundUp, expired in 2000 and Monsanto is beginning to feel the effects. Notwithstanding its patents on GM crops tolerant to RoundUp and producing their own pesticides,[7] and despite its use of growers' contracts and its dominant position in the GM seed market, Monsanto's income was sliding by late 2002. It had also failed to make progress in Brazil or Europe and had to hold back its release of GM wheat because of opposition campaigns. It did, however, manage to achieve restricted commercial release of some varieties of Bt cotton in India and Bt corn in the Philippines in 2002.

Monsanto's agreement in April 2002 with *DuPont* means that it will share certain of its technologies with DuPont's *Pioneer Hi-Bred International Inc.* DuPont and Monsanto are number 1 and 2 in seeds and between them hold up to 40 per cent of all significant agricultural biotechnology patents. However, their agreement avoided the need for monopoly scrutiny.

In December 1999 Swiss-based *Novartis* (formerly *Sandoz* and *Ciba–Geigy*) announced plans to merge its agrochemical and seed division with *AstraZeneca's* agrochemicals division (UK) to form a combined company called *Syngenta*, which ranked number 1 in agrochemicals and number 3 in seed sales in 2001. Syngenta is a less high-profile operator than Monsanto, with a strong interest in accessing genetic resources. In December 2002 it announced a proposed biotechnology Research and Development alliance with *Diversa* to seek commercially valuable molecules. In the same month it was forced to pull out of a proposed deal with an Indian university that would have given it access to a massive rice germplasm collection. In the same year, its foundation became a member of the CGIAR (see Chapter 5).

In late 2002 Syngenta discreetly circulated in the US a report about resistance to glyphosate appearing in weeds. Although Monsanto is still dominant in glyphosate, Syngenta markets its own version of the herbicide, Touchdown. In fact, gene flow and the appearance of resistance to glyphosate looks set to increase steadily. With the added complication of multiple resistance to more than one kind of herbicide, extra agrochemicals (which Syngenta can provide) or changes in farming practice would be required.

Aventis CropScience was the result of the merger of *AgrEvo* and *Rhone–Poulenc Agro*, the agrochemical and crop-science divisions of *Hoechst* (Germany) and *Rhone–Poulenc* (France) respectively. AgrEvo was itself the result of a previous joint venture between Hoechst and *Schering*. Poor performance in the agriculture sector and the StarLink contamination incident (p. 92) meant that Aventis CropScience was placed on the market in 2000.

Bayer, an agrochemical giant in its own right, did not participate in GM crops during the 1990s. However, in April 2002, Bayer's bid to buy Aventis CropScience was cleared by the EU and US monopolies investigators. As a result, Bayer CropScience is now global number 2 in pesticides, so changing the rankings of the tables on page 84. It is particularly strong in insecticides and fungicides.

BASF has indicated that it intends to participate in the next generation of GM crops, projected to have more direct benefits for consumers, and thus, it is hoped, more likely to overcome their resistance. Its purchases of *MicroFlo* and *American Cyanamid* in 1999 and 2000 made it the world's fourth largest agrochemical company.

Dow Agrosciences has manoeuvred to become one of the top ten seed companies, with interests in multiple-trait, insect-resistant crops such as cotton and sugar cane.

> The top two companies control 34 per cent of the global agrochemical market; the top 10 control 84 per cent. The world agrochemical market was valued at US$ 29,880 million in 2000.[8]

In 2001, GM accounted for 12 per cent of the global $31 billion crop protection market and 13 per cent of the $30 billion commercial seed market.

Consolidation in the seed industry

With all the fanfare over GM crops, it is often forgotten that corporations only supply a fraction of the world's agricultural seed. African farmers utilise seeds from within their own communities for around 90 per cent of their

Table 4.1 • World crop protection

Company	Ranking			Revenue in US$ million			Share of world market
	1998	2000	2001	1998	2000	2001*	2000
Syngenta (Novartis & AZ)	—	1	1		6,100	5,385	20%
Aventis (AgrEvo + Rhone–Poulenc Agro)	1	3	2	4,676	3,400	3,842	11%
Novartis	2	—	—	4,152			
Monsanto (Pharmacia in 2000)	3	2	3	4,032	4,100	3,755	14%
DuPont	4	5	7	3,156	2,500	1,917	8%
AstraZeneca	5	—	—	2,897			
Bayer	6	6	6	2,273	2,100	2,418	7%
American Home Products	7			2,194			
Dow AgroSciences	8	7	5	2,132	2,100	2,612	7%
BASF (& Cyanamid from 2000)	9	4	4	1,945	3,400	3,105	11%
Makhteshim–Agan	10	8		801	675		2%
Sumitomo		9			625		2%
FMC		10			575		2%
TOP 7 Sales:				23,380	23,700	23,034	

* Including Cyanamid
2000 figures: ETC Group .(formerly RAFI), 'Globalization, Inc. – Concentration in Corporate Power: the Unmentioned Agenda', September 2001 (based on data provided by Allan Woodburn Associates). Cited in Agrow. http://www.rafi.org.
2001 figures: Global Pesticide Campaigner (Vol.12, No. 2) August 2002 – based on Agrow data.

Table 4.2 • Global ranking 2001 by sector: agrochemicals, seeds and pharmaceuticals, based on revenues in 2000

Company	Sales in US$ millions and global ranking (R)					
	Agrochemicals		Seeds		Pharmaceuticals	
	R	Sales	R	Sales	R	Sales
Syngenta	1	6,100	3	958		
– AstraZeneca					4	14,834
– Novartis					7	12,698
Pharmacia (incl. Monsanto)	2	4,100	2	1,600	8	11,177
Aventis	3	3,400	10	267	5	14,809
BASF	4	3,400	–	–		
Dupont (Pioneer)	5	2,500	1	1,938		1,630
Bayer	6	2,100	–	–	18	5,330
Dow	7	2,100	7	350	–	–

Source: Data researched and published by the ETC Group (then Rafi).

seed needs. In India and the Philippines, farmers are responsible for 60 and 80 per cent of the annual seed supply respectively.[9] Even in industrialised countries, farm-saved seed still constitutes a principal source of seed for a number of major crops, such as wheat and soybeans.

It was only in the twentieth century that centralised, off-farm plant breeding began to play a major role in agriculture. In northern industrial countries, especially those with colonies, such formal plant breeding was largely carried out by the public sector. Plant breeders collected and combed through the wealth of plant varieties of farmers in the South to develop varieties suited to the climatic conditions and industrial interests of their respective countries. The US soybean crop, for instance, which has become the most important crop in the US next to corn, was developed by public researchers in the post-war period working with a collection of nearly 5,000 soybean lines brought back from a 1929–31 collection mission to China.[10] The varieties developed through such public programmes served as the basis for the development of the private seed sector.

A similar process is under way in the South. The green revolution breeding programmes displaced on-farm crop development to the laboratories of the CGIAR and the national research centres. And now the private sector, through various World Bank and US Agency for International Development (USAID) seed projects, is stepping in to take over where it senses potential for profit. In Asia, for example, several companies are now pursuing hybrid rice seed markets, building on research carried out by IRRI and certain national agricultural research centres in Asia.[11] (For World Bank involvement in seed projects in Africa, see Chapter 5.)

Up until 30 years ago, most European and North American seed companies were small, family-owned businesses. Since that time, the seed industry has changed dramatically. In 2000, according to research by the Action Group for Erosion, Technology and Concentration (ETC Group) (see Table 4.3), ten seed companies controlled almost one-third of the $24.7 billion commercial seed market. Indeed, two companies – Monsanto and DuPont (with Pioneer) – controlled almost 15 per cent, and corporate market share is much higher in specific seed sectors and for certain crops. For example:

- Forty per cent of US vegetable seeds come from a single source.

- The top five vegetable seed companies control 75 per cent of the global vegetable seed market.

- DuPont and Monsanto together control 73 per cent of the US seed corn market.

- Just four companies (Monsanto, DuPont, Syngenta, Dow) control at least 47 per cent of the commercial soybean seed market.[12]

Table 4.3 · The world's top ten seed corporations

Rank	Company	HQ	Seed sales US$ millions			% change over	
			1999	2000	2001	1999	2000
1	DuPont (Pioneer)	USA	1,850	1,938	1,900	4.8	−2.0
2	Monsanto	USA	1,700	1,600	1,700	−5.9	6.3
3	Syngenta	UK &					
		Switzerland	947	958	938	1.2	−2.1
4	Groupe Limagrain	France	700	622	678	−11.1	9.0
5	Grupo Pulsar (Seminis)	Mexico	531	474	450	−10.7	−5.1
6	Advanta (AstraZeneca	UK &					
	& Cosun)	Netherlands	412	373	420	−9.5	12.6
7	KWS AG	Germany	355	332	388	−6.5	16.9
8	Delta & Pine Land	USA	301	301	306	0	1.7
9	Sakata	Japan	396		[231]		[−15.1]
10	Dow (incl. Cargill						
	N. America)	USA	350	*350	[215]	0	[16.2]
	TOTAL		7,542		7,226		

(All sales data researched and published by the ETC group.)

Concentration within the seed sector is likely to continue. Most of the largest seed companies are also the largest pesticide companies and agbiotech companies (see Table 4.2). To date, most of their research in crop development has focused on integrating their pesticide and seed businesses by genetically engineering crops for dependence on their pesticides, such as the RoundUp Ready (glyphosate) crops (Monsanto) and the Liberty Link System (glufosinate) (Aventis/Bayer), or by engineering pesticides into the crops, such as the Bt crops. The seed/pesticide conglomerates have decided to restrict the transfer of this technology and to buy up seed companies instead, in order to access germplasm and control the sale of their GM crops. Monsanto, for example, has spent more than $8 billion acquiring seed and biotech companies over the last ten years. As a result, small seed companies wanting access to the technologies have had to sell off their businesses, in whole or in part, and small seed growers have had to enter into stringent contractual agreements. Furthermore, access to germplasm of diverse domestic agricultural varieties is increasingly restricted, as they are either not grown or their seeds are not sold, often because it is no longer legal to do so.

This push towards biotechnology is the principal reason for the growing concentration in the seed sector. First, the big pesticide/seed companies (with three-quarters of the patents in agricultural biotechnology, with control over important germplasm and over the most advanced technologies through mergers and exclusive agreements with the leading genomics firms) dictate the terms under which any agricultural biotech research is done. Second, biotechnology offers the means and the incentive for these companies to move in on crops where traditionally there has been little private sector involvement. Industry analysts estimate that biotech will add 50 per cent to the value of seed markets, rescuing previously unprofitable markets such as rice or wheat.[13] Monsanto believes that the rice seed market could bring them sales of US$1,000–2,000 million a year.[14] And third, biotechnology opens the door to alliances – such as Renessen, the Cargill–Monsanto joint venture – between the upstream (pesticide/seed industry) and downstream (food and feed processors) sides of agribusiness, thus closing out competition in the seed sector and locking farmers into contract farming.

Corporate concentration is bad for biodiversity. With vegetables, where (as noted above) just five seed companies control 75 per cent of the global vegetable seed market, diversity has declined dramatically, with many old varieties disappearing forever.

> If our vegetable diversity is allowed to die out, gardeners will become ever more dependent on transnational seed companies and the generic and hybrid and patented varieties that those companies choose to offer. And that means giving up our right to determine the quality of the food our families grow and consume, and also the ability of gardeners and farmers to save their own seeds, which is the reason that much of this incredible diversity exists in the first place. (*Garden Seed Inventory*, fifth edition, p. 15, quoted by RAFI)[15]

In 2000 the Rural Advancement Foundation International (RAFI, now the ETC group) released a comprehensive report, 'The Seed Giants – Who Owns Whom?' This contains detailed information about consolidation in the seed industry and a comprehensive list of seed industry subsidiaries.[16]

Loss of agricultural diversity: Seminis and Savia

> *It's impossible to predict how much irreplaceable vegetable diversity is earmarked for extinction as a result of corporate cost-cutting and consolidation .... The seed varieties deemed obsolete and unprofitable by Seminis are now part of the company's private gene bank, and that rich diversity is lost to the public.*
>
> Kent Whealy, Executive Director of Seed Savers Exchange.[17]

The dramatic reduction of the availability of non-hybrid vegetable varieties, resulting in a wealth of seed diversity and germplasm being lost forever, is illustrated by the actions of Seminis,[18] the world's largest fruit and vegetable seed corporation, owned by the Mexican giant Savia. Seminis announced in June 2000 that it would eliminate 2,000 varieties or 25 per cent of its total product line as a cost-cutting measure.

For Seminis, the most profitable seeds are currently hybrids, because gardeners and farmers do not save seeds from hybrid plants, as they do not generally breed true. Hybrid seeds thus force farmers and gardeners to buy seed every year. New varieties can also restrict the seed saving and sharing activities of farmers and gardeners, as they are generally patented or protected by plant variety protection laws:

> most importantly, the seed corporation wants monopoly control over its varieties and that means high-tech, patented varieties. Seminis is a leader in the development of genetically engineered vegetables. The company has 79 issued or allowed patents on vegetable varieties and GE varieties, and is seeking further patents related to beans, bean sprouts, broccoli, cauliflower, celery, corn, cucumber, eggplant, endive, leek, lettuce, melon, muskmelon, onion, peas, pumpkin, radish, red cabbage, spinach, squash, sweet pepper, tomato, watermelon, and white cabbage.[19]

In California alone, Seminis has tested plots of glyphosate-resistant lettuce, peas, cucumbers, and tomatoes, plus a wide variety of fungus-, insect- and virus-resistant vegetables. One of Seminis's genetically engineered products, a virus-resistant squash, is already being grown commercially. Developed by its subsidiary, Asgrow, the first transgenic squash was approved for commercial production in 1994.[20]

Seminis established a cooperative agreement – or strategic alliance – with Monsanto in 1997 to develop GM vegetables with resistance to RoundUp or with the Bt technology. According to Sergio Cházaro, Seminis also has research and production alliances with 'Zeneca, DuPont, AgrEvo, Cornell University, John Innes, five Chinese institutions, Texas A&M University, the University of California, the University of North Carolina, the University of Jerusalem, Wageningen University and 94 other universities and research facilities'.[21]

GM contamination: plot or blunder?

Don Westfall, Vice-president of Promar International, a Washington-based food and biotech industry consultancy, said in January 2001:

> The hope of the industry is that over time the market is so flooded [with genetically engineered organisms] that there's nothing you can do about it, you just sort of surrender.[22]

Contamination of food, agricultural crops and landraces with modified genes and seeds from GM crops is rapidly growing into a global problem. There are two major pathways of contamination: one is by cross-pollination of traditional crops, native varieties (landraces) and related plants by GM crops; the other is by insufficient or careless segregation of GM materials at any stage. The issue of horizontal gene transfer – of modified genes passing from GM plants asexually to other organisms such as soil and gut bacteria and fungi – is equally problematic, but has not yet become a major public issue except maybe for the use of antibiotic resistance marker genes.[23]

The last few years have seen an increasing number of incidents, warning of what is to come if GM crops variously developed for food, pharmaceutical and industrial use continue to be pushed, not only without regard to the precautionary principle but also with inadequate separation distances, segregation and safety measures. Weak regulation and careless practice, whether in the US, Canada, Europe or Asia, are jeopardising food security and agricultural biodiversity as well as food safety and consumer choice. Contaminated seed has been found in a number of countries, including the UK, France, Italy and New Zealand Actual levels of contamination are likely to be much higher than currently acknowledged, since checking seed for low levels of contamination is difficult and not routinely carried out. There are relatively inexpensive tests available for particular proteins that are produced by the inserted GM genes – for the Bt toxin, for example. These

---

Contaminated seed

Companies themselves have failed to keep their GM lines pure. There have been several cases when seed labelled to be one GM variety was contaminated with another variety. This will only make headlines if the contaminant is an unapproved variety, as was the case in the UK in the summer of 2002. Aventis herbicide-resistant oilseed rape, planted in test trials in the UK since 1999, had an impurity of up to 2.8 per cent with an unauthorised GM oilseed rape that contained an additional gene that confers resistance to the antibiotics neomycin, kanamycin and gentamicin A and B.[24]

The *Independent* reported that the company could face prosecution with unlimited fines or five-year prison sentences if found guilty of breaching the rules.[25] Whilst sowing of winter oilseed rape was suspended, the government failed to take immediate action to clean up the fields where the unauthorised spring crops were growing. When local people tried to protect their land by removing the seed pods from the GM plants, arrests were made. Although the evidence against them was clear, nobody was charged and no prosecution followed; any case would have collapsed since the crop itself was illegal.

In a variation on the theme, European farmers planted thousands of acres with Canadian non-GM oilseed rape supplied by Advanta in the spring of 2000. This seed turned out to be tainted with GM material banned in the EU. As a result, crops were later destroyed and Advanta had to compensate the farmers.

tests will only help if one knows which particular GM crop or seed one is looking for and if the protein level is high enough to be detected. At present tests that involve testing on the DNA level, looking for the inserted DNA itself, require proper laboratory facilities and are comparatively expensive.

It is difficult to establish whether the biotech industry is concerned about GM contamination, or sees it as inevitable and non-problematic, or whether it is actually employing GM contamination as a strategy – deliberately contaminating nature and the food chain to such an extent that GM-free products become impossible and consumers apparently have no option other than to accept GM.

Suing instead of being sued

Certainly the case of Percy Schmeiser and other farmers in Canada and the US who have been sued by Monsanto for violation of the company's patent on the gene for resistance to glyphosate should serve as a warning that contamination can be a potent and profitable weapon in the hands of the companies. The judge in Schmeiser's case dismissed as irrelevant any consideration of how his canola (oilseed rape) came to contain Monsanto's resistance gene and found against Schmeiser on the basis simply of its presence in his crop. Crucially, Schmeiser and his wife had to abandon their own seed, which they had been saving for 50 years. Many countries (Argentina, for example, or most African countries) do not so far have US-style patent laws, but if they adopt them, then farmers in such countries face the prospect not only of having their crops contaminated by proprietary genes, but of then being sued for this privilege, in addition to being prevented from saving their harvested seed. This would inevitably act as an extra pressure on those farmers simply to 'roll over' and adopt the technology.

SEED SMUGGLING AND THE RUMOUR MACHINE

Another channel of contamination that has affected key regions of the South is the smuggling of GM seeds. This is often assisted by exaggerated stories about the properties of the GM seeds, so that people are persuaded to go to great lengths to get them. It is understandable that farmers should wish to buy seeds that are said to have higher yields and to need less pesticide than ordinary seed, even though this is a simplification of the real issues. GM seeds, in this case Monsanto's RR soya, have been smuggled into Brazil from neighbouring Argentina. Persistent rumours of widespread GM contamination of the soya crop added to the pressure for GM crops to be commercialised. However, Brazil continued to resist, even though the contamination has been quite serious in some regions (see Chapter 8). In

Eastern Europe, seed smuggling is a major problem: the sources appear to be mostly Monsanto's RoundUp seed being planted in Romania or Bulgaria, and US food aid which has been sent to the region on a regular basis recently (see Chapter 7).

In September 2002, Pakistan, also seriously affected by the practice of seed smuggling, decided to lift its ban on the import of GM seeds that have been legalised in their country of origin.[26] It apparently did so in order to encourage importers to obtain a certificate giving details of the nature, characteristics and origin of the seeds, so that the government would at least know what was coming into the country. The black market in GM seed had become brisk in Pakistan, because the seeds were rumoured to have higher yields and to require less pesticide. The US, China, and Australia were said to be the most likely sources and the most popular seed was cotton, genetically engineered to be resistant to Bt. It was reported that farmers in different parts of Pakistan who had planted Bt cotton had been affected by a previously unknown disease. Previous attempts to introduce biosafety regulations had stalled earlier. The fact that Pakistan decided to admit seeds that had been legalised in their country of origin reflects the ambition of the promoters of GM to set up a global system whereby recognition in one country means approval everywhere. Such a system would have extremely serious implications for the protection of biodiversity, especially in areas of origin of staple crops (see the *criollo* story on pp. 92–5).

Getting GM seed into the ground at any cost

There have been unsubstantiated reports from India, Thailand and even the US, where the seeds are legal, that farmers were not told they were planting GM seed, but simply that it was a new hybrid. The women's president of Canada's National Farmer's Union reported that heavy sales promotion was the factor most responsible for increased acreage.[27] The industry has been allowing rumours about the yields of the crops, the convenience of GM farming, and the reduction of costs and pesticide use to spread worldwide. Certainly, in countries where no technology fee is charged, for instance, there may be an initial reduction in costs. Farmers often do not have independent sources of information to which they can turn. This has fuelled the demand for the seeds. The rumour machine is also at work in India, where permission was given for the growing of certain Bt cotton varieties in 2002. Farmers heard rumours about the performance of the new seeds and were frantic to get hold of them. This made them vulnerable to bogus seed salesmen and also meant that they often did not get the right seed for their region or the right information about how to plant the seeds so as to reduce the speed of development of insect resistance.

StarLink – GM corn

StarLink has definitely set back the biotech industry, maybe five years.

Lewis Batchelder of Archer Daniels Midland to the *New York Times* [28]

Farmers in North America, where over three-quarters of all GM seeds were sown in 2000, have been growing Aventis's GM maize, StarLink, solely as animal feed. StarLink has not been approved for human consumption because the particular Bt toxin used (a protein known as Cry9C) could trigger allergic reactions in humans. Further tests still need to be carried out. Yet this GM maize illegally entered the human food chain, initially showing up in tests of corn chips and taco shells. In fact over 300 products were pulled from US grocery stores after the discovery in September 2000. Products had to be withdrawn in other countries like Japan and the UK as well, because of illegal contamination.

This contamination has had a serious effect on US grain exports and could well cost Aventis in excess of $200 million in damages.[29] When in October 2001 Bayer announced its intention to purchase Aventis CropScience for US$6.6 billion, it refused to take on any potential liabilities arising from the controversy over StarLink GM corn.

When tested for, Starlink contamination has shown up in many parts of the world, demonstrating how far and how fast contamination can spread through the food chain. Though pulled off the market altogether in the US, the StarLink Bt toxin genes seem to have contaminated other seed stock. Japanese grain importers announced in December 2002 that traces of the banned StarLink variety were found in a cargo from the United States. US corn exports to Japan - the world's biggest importer of the grain - had only started to return to normal in 2002, while South Korean food processors have continued to shun US corn for food use.[30]

Criollo – native corn

The genie is out of the bottle. What we are confronted with now is just thousands of very different genies that are still in their bottles, and the question is this: do we want to keep those bottles closed or are we opening them?

Ignacio Chapela, October 2002[31]

A shock wave ran across the globe in the autumn of 2001 when researchers found that native maize varieties (*criollo*) in the Oaxaca region of Mexico are contaminated with GM material. This region is the cradle of maize, the centre of origin of all modern varieties. It is crucial to preserve the old varieties and landraces for future food security. This is acknowledged by most who understand plant breeding.

Mauricio Bellon, the director of the economics programmes at CIMMYT in Mexico, called it 'the world's insurance policy' in an interview with the *Nation* (US) regarding the contamination of maize in Oaxaca:

> The diversity of these landraces, these genes, is the basis of our food supply. We'll have great science, we'll have great breeding, but at the end of the day, the base [of this crop] is here. We need this diversity to cope with the unpredictable.... The climate changes, new plant diseases and pests continue to evolve. Diseases we thought we had controlled come back. We don't know what's going to happen in the future, and so we need to keep our options open. And this [the growing of landraces] is what keeps our options open.[32]

Plant molecular biologist (microbial ecologist) Ignacio Chapela and David Quist from the University of California at Berkeley published their study on transgenic maize in the journal *Nature* on 29 November 2001.[33] Looking at landraces grown in the Oaxaca region, they had identified a genetic sequence in four out of six maize samples that was commonly used as part of the novel genes genetically engineered into plants, namely the 35S promoter from the cauliflower mosaic virus.

On the day their findings were published in *Nature*, a series of e-mail messages appeared on the AgBioWorld bulletin board (see pp. 70–2) asserting that Chapela could not be an objective scientist because he was an activist and on the board of directors of Pesticide Action Network North America (PANNA). In April 2002, *Nature* published a note from the editor, withdrawing the original article and stating that he had consulted with three referees before making this decision. It later emerged that only one of the referees thought the article should be retracted. The editor's note was accompanied by two letters written by people linked to the University of California who had supported a five-year 'collaborative research agreement' between Berkeley and Novartis (now Syngenta) in 1998. This agreement had generated considerable conflict at the time and Chapela had strongly criticised it on the grounds of public interest. Careful research (by Jonathan Matthews of the Norfolk Genetic Information Network, UK) revealed that some of the e-mail messages criticising Chapela were connected with the Bivings Group, a public relations firm which specialises in e-mail and Web work and which has Monsanto on its list of clients. Furthermore, some of the people alleged to have sent them did not actually exist.[34]

The University of California at Berkeley reported on Chapela's findings:

> Genes from genetically modified crops that spread unintentionally can threaten the diversity of natural crops by crowding out native plants, said Chapela. A wealth of maize varieties, cultivated over thousands of years in the Sierra Norte de Oaxaca region, provide an invaluable 'bank account' of genetic diversity, he said. Chapela added that genetically diverse crops are less vulnerable to disease, pest outbreaks and climatic changes. '*We can't afford to lose that resource,*' he said.[35]

Mexico's government seems no less concerned. In 1998 it imposed a moratorium on new plantings of GM maize to protect the centre of origin. The closest region where transgenic corn was ever known to have been planted is 60 miles away from the Sierra Norte de Oaxaca fields, where Chapela found the contamination. First rumours and then news of GM contamination caused the government to initiate an investigation into the subject and to ask its own research institutions to carry out tests for Oaxaca and the neighbouring state of Puebla. DNA tests (PCR, Southern blot and sequencing) and protein tests (strip test and ELISAs) confirmed the presence of transgenic DNA (35S promoter, for example) as well as the Bt toxin and its gene cry1A. The latter was found extensively in the landraces of Oaxaca, while cry19 was not found. In the view of Ariel Alvarez-Morales, one of the researchers, 'The changes observed are those expected when the farmers use a hybrid to "enhance" or improve their landraces, a practice that is very common among small growers in this area.'[36]

Confirming Chapela's findings of widespread contamination, the Mexican scientists sent their paper to *Nature* for publication. And once again *Nature* showed it does not know how to handle controversial scientific findings. The Institute for Food and Development Policy (also known as Food First) reported in a press release on 24 October 2002 that *Nature* had rejected the paper

> after two external peer reviewers recommended against publication for opposite reasons. One reviewer recommended rejection of the Mexican report because the results were 'obvious', while the other recommended rejection because the results 'were so unexpected as to not be believable'. A third reviewer emphasised technical issues. When asked for comment, *Nature* editor-in-chief Philip Campbell said the paper was rejected on 'technical grounds'. He added 'the conclusions of the paper could not be justified on the grounds of the reported evidence'.[37]

Yet how exactly the widespread contamination occurred remains a puzzle and nobody knows for sure what precise variety of transgenes ended up in the landraces. Dr Norman Ellstrand, Professor of Genetics at the University of California, Riverside, and a specialist on corn genetics, says that

> the corn in Capulalpan could contain any number of characteristics that have been engineered into American corn. Since corn is openly pollinated, he explains, pollen from one plant can blow or be transported in some other way to fertilise another plant. 'And if just 1 per cent of [American] experimental pollen escaped into Mexico, that means those landraces could potentially be making medicines or industrial chemicals or things that are not so good for people to eat. Right now, we just don't know what's in there.'... This year, he is researching how long transgenes will persist in native varieties – whether, in fact, they can ever be bred out of the population. This is a question that until now has not even been studied.[38]

Contamination through food aid

Chapela stated that in 2000, 5–6 million tons of corn entered Mexico from the US, while Mexico had 'exactly the same amount of domestic corn rotting away, unused'.[39] Said to be 30–40 per cent transgenic, the US corn was distributed through welfare food systems through the country, heavily subsidised by the US tax payer. In the US people distinguish between seed for growing and grain for consumption – though seed and grain might be identical. In Mexico, it is different:

> How could transgenic crops have made it into the fields in this remote location in Mexico? In Capulalpan, Olga [a Mexican subsistence farmer] herself remembers buying some corn from the local store, where imported kernels are sold by the crate (and are, legally, only supposed to be ground up for food). She didn't know about the government ban on planting, and she figured she'd try some of it out in her fields. *'I planted that corn out of curiosity,'* she says. *'I bought it at the government store and planted it to see if it was better than ours.'*[40]

This theme recurs in Chapter 8, where there is further discussion of the role of GM in food aid.

Letting out the pharma genie

A new and potentially even more alarming source of contamination arises from the development of GM crops engineered to produce pharmaceuticals. In most cases, the 'pharma-gene' has been engineered into common crop plants, especially maize (corn), a prolific pollinator. As the physical appearance of 'pharma-plants' and seeds is the same as those of conventional plants and seeds, accidental contamination cannot be easily detected. Furthermore, any cross-pollination with food crops could contaminate food sources with drugs for years to come.

The American company ProdiGene Inc. recently had a foretaste of the future. Projecting that 10 per cent of the corn crop will be devoted to 'biopharm' (pharmaceutical) production by 2010, ProdiGene has made a number of trial plantings of drug- and chemical-producing crops. Two of these tests went wrong. In the Nebraska incident in October 2002, some 500,000 bushels of harvested soybeans were contaminated by ProdiGene's pharma-corn, which re-emerged as volunteer plants after being grown on the same land in the previous season. The soybeans were seized by the USDA after harvest in October. ProdiGene was ordered in December 2002 to pay a $250,000 fine, plus an estimated $2.8 million to buy and destroy contaminated soybeans. A further $1 million must be given as a bond to the USDA to develop a compliance programme for future pharmaceutical crops.[41]

In another incident, this time in Iowa, ProdiGene was ordered to destroy 155 acres (63 hectares) in September 2002 because of potential contamination of food crops in nearby fields by the windborne pollen of the pharma-corn.[42]

Whilst ProdiGene's pharma-corn varieties were engineered to produce trypsin for diabetes and a compound to treat diarrhoea, most pharma-crops are engineered with human genes to produce specific antibodies. By the summer of 2002, the FDA had approved ten monoclonal antibodies, including the breast cancer treatment Herceptin and the rheumatoid arthritis treatment Remicade.[43] Pharma-plants are also being tested to produce human enzymes and hormones.

In the wake of the ensuing debate, in October 2002 the Biotechnology Industry Organisation (BIO) announced a 'new policy on plant-made pharmaceuticals and industrial plants' which 'excludes the planting of corn in the cornbelt. The cornbelt is defined as America's heartland in a recent map produced by the Economic Research Service of the US Department of Agriculture.' Given that StarLink corn was planted on less than 1 per cent of total US corn acreage, the resulting contamination of hundreds of food products and corn seed stock, despite the use of gene containment measures, should stand as a clear warning.

Attempting to regulate contamination – the EU battle zone

In the EU, there has been a long battle over the regulation of GM in the food chain. A major part of the struggle has been over thresholds of contamination. Industry suggested a threshold of 5 per cent while many consumers want it to be set at the level of detection and no more than 0.1 per cent. The Commission, Parliament and Council have been arguing over thresholds for GM crops according to whether they have been approved or not in the EU, settling for 0.9 and 0.5 per cent respectively in July 2003, but the process is not yet complete. At the same time the Commission tried to sidestep the vexed issue of co-existence by leaving it to member states to regulate, while many of them want EU-wide legislation to be adopted.

Industry has countered by proposing a GM-free label, while opponents point out that this would put the onus firmly on those who wish to produce GM-free products, rather than on the GM industry, and ask why those who do not want a technology should be expected to assume the burden of keeping their produce free from it. The EU has also encountered great opposition to its development of proposals on traceability, which were called unworkable by industry, including EuropaBio (see p. 60), the US and some in the EU, following the first vote in July 2002. The US warned that costs would have to be passed on to consumers. Others countered by pointing out that traceability in the meat industry following the BSE crisis was no less strict and that labelling without traceability is meaningless. Traceability is designed to enable a product to be followed right from the farm through every stage in the food chain. Without such information, it would be much more difficult to address any problems with GM products that might emerge in the future. The EU also persisted in developing proposals for labelling GM-derived products that might not any longer contain identifiable DNA.

However, although GM animal feed was included among products to be labelled, the EU stopped short of demanding that milk or meat from animals fed with GM feed should also be labelled. This is seen as a major problem by campaigners, who point out that animal feed is by far the largest use of GM products. Since much of the feed comes from countries outside the EU and since consumers are the ones with the major influence on EU legislation, this effectively means that a large part of the EU consumption of GM crops remains practically invisible to its opponents.

However, EU legislation to date demonstrates the importance of a well-informed and determined public. It also shows that the EU has accepted the inevitability of contamination to some level, and only seeks to control it. The argument has been about what level of contamination is acceptable rather than about whether any contamination should be allowed, which would actually be a debate about whether GM crops should be released at all. This is a prime example of the way industry moves debates from issues of principle to technical matters which assume that the fundamental decision about whether a technology is acceptable or not has already been made.

Meanwhile, there has been almost no real progress in developing proposals on liability.

MORATORIUM CONTINUES

Events in Europe also shows that strong public opinion can make laws unenforceable. A *de facto* moratorium on the approval or release of new GM crops has been in force in the EU for more than four years. Denounced as illegal in many quarters, it has been the object of several challenges, all of which have foundered. Even when the revised rules on the deliberate release of GMOs (Directive 2001/18/EC) were adopted, the moratorium continued to hold. In May 2003, the US complained formally to the WTO about the EU moratorium and the countries upholding it (France, Denmark, Greece, Austria, Luxembourg, and Belgium).

Is coexistence between GM crops and other crops possible?

The discussion about whether GM crops and traditional crops can actually coexist in the same region or farming system has gradually sharpened, as contamination and the inadequacy of separation distances hit the headlines. In the EU, regulators were slow to realise the problems they faced, for example, in keeping any control over levels of GM contamination of seed. Once seed stock has become GM-contaminated, the contamination level can potentially rise with each growing cycle, necessitating the addition of uncontaminated seed to remain within a given threshold. The Agriculture and Environment Biotechnology Commission, set up by the UK government to look at issues around potential commercialisation, went to the heart of the issue in its report: 'To put it bluntly, can cross-pollinating GM and non-GM crops coexist on our small islands – and if so how? Different sectors of the agricultural industry will hold different views on this fundamental question.'[43]

This is a crucial issue. Industry spokespersons insist that coexistence is possible, while organisations opposing them point to the rapid appearance of contamination even in countries where only trials have taken place. It is certain to prove a serious headache, both to regulators and to seed producers. Furthermore, to monitor and enforce the upper limits of contamination levels set by regulatory bodies is going to be costly, and is regarded as a disincentive to the commercialisation of GM crops in Europe.

Notes

1 Henk Hobbelink, *Biotechnology and the Future of World Agriculture*, London and New York: Zed Books, 1991, p. 147.
2 'Green and Dying', *Economist*, 16 November 2000. http://www.biotech-info.net/green_and_dying.html.
3 Frank J, Mitsch and Jennifer S. Mitchell, 'Ag Biotech: Thanks but No Thanks', report, Deutsche Bank/Alex Brown, 12 July 1999; Timothy Ramey, Mary Wimme and Rachel Rocker, 'GMOs Are Dead', report, Deutsche Bank/Alex Brown, 21 May 1999.
4 'Green and Dying'.
5 Pictet analyst report, 'Plant Biotech Past and Present', November 1999.
6 See Multinational Monitor, <http://multinationalmonitor.org/; e-mail: monitor@essential.org>; Corporate Watch UK, <http://www.corporatewatch.org.uk/; e-mail: mail@corporatewatch.org/>; CorpWatch US, <http://www.corpwatch.org; e-mail: corpwatch@corpwatch.org>; and Econexus, <http://www.econexus.info>.
7 Pesticide-producing GM crops means crops genetically engineered with insecticide toxins from the soil bacterium *Bacillus thuringiensis* (Bt-toxins).
8 Communiqué by ETC Group (formerly RAFI), 'Globalization, Inc. – Concentration in Corporate Power: the Unmentioned Agenda', September 2001. http://www.rafi.org.
9 R. C. Purohit, *The Hybrid Seeds Market in India*, Bombay: American Consulate-General, March 1994; and 'The Advantages and Disadvantages Between Modern Plant Varieties and Landraces', panel discussion, data set circulated at the UPOV-

WIPO–WTO Joint Regional Workshop on 'The Protection of Plant Varieties Under Article 27.3(b) of the TRIPS Agreement', Bangkok, 18–19 March 1999.

10 Q. Yang and J. Wang (2000) 'Agronomic Traits Correlative Analysis between Interspecific and Intraspecific Soybean Crosses', *Soybean Genetics Newsletter*, 27 (online journal), <http://www.soygenetics.org/articles/sgn2000-003.htm>; T. Hymovitz, 'Dorsett-Morse Soybean Collection Trip to East Asia: 50 Years' Retrospective', *Economics Botany*, 38, 4 (1984): 378–88.

11 Devlin Kuyek, 'Hybrid Rice in Asia: an Unfolding Threat', GRAIN, March 2000. http://www.grain.org/publications/hybrid-en.cfm

12 Hope Shand, ETC Group, personal communication.

13 G. Traxler, 'Assessing the Prospects for the Transfer of Genetically Modified Crop Varieties to Developing Countries', *AgBioForum*, 2, 3–4 (1999): 198–202. http://www.agbioforum.org/

14 Paul Teng, Marsha Stanton and Mike Roth, 'The Changing Private Sector Investment in Rice', in William G. Padolina (ed.), *Plant Variety Protection for Rice in Developing Countries: Impacts on Research and Development*, Makati City: International Rice Research Institute, 2000, proceedings of the workshop on 'The Impact on Research and Development of *Sui Generis* Approaches to Plant Variety Protection of Rice in Developing Countries', 16–18 February 2000, IRRI, Los Baños, Philippines.

15 Quoted in RAFI Genotypes (now ETC Group), 'Earmarked for Extinction? Seminis Eliminates 2,000 Varieties', 17 July 2000. www.etcgroup.org/article.asp?newsid=15

16 RAFI Genotypes (now ETC Group), 'The Seed Giants – Who Owns Whom?', December 2000. www.etcgroup.org/article.asp?newsid=13

17 RAFI, 'Earmarked for Extinction?'

18 *Ibid.*

19 *Ibid.*

20 'Expanding the Biotech Frontier – Seminis Vegetable Seeds', *Global Pesticide Campaigner*, December 1999.

21 Sergio Cházaro, 'Acquisitions and Strategic Alliances: a Mexican Case Study'. http://www.farmfoundation.org/acapulco/chazaro.pdf

22 Stuart Laidlaw, 'StarLink Fallout Could Cost Billions', *Toronto Star*, 9 January 2001.

23 Antibiotic resistance marker genes are bacterial genes that confer resistance to different antibiotics, such as kanamycin and ampicillin. Linked to a gene for a trait such as herbicide tolerance, they are often used in plant genetic engineering to mark where the transfer of a GM trait has been successful.

24 UK Department for the Environment, Food And Rural Affairs, 'Impurities Found in Aventis GM Rape Seed Farm Scale Evaluations', Press Release 336/02, 15 August 2002.

25 Paul Kelbie and Marie Woolf, 'Ministers Suspend GM Crop-testing', *Independent*, 16 August 2002.

26 Nadeem Iqbal, 'Pakistan Opens Doors to GM Seed', *Asia Times* (Inter Press Service), 15 November 2002. http://www.atimes.com/atimes/South_Asia/DK15Df03.html

27 Gundula Meziani and Hugh Warwick, 'Seeds of Doubt: North American Farmers' Experiences of GM Crops', report for the Soil Association, UK, 2002.

28 'Gene-Altered Corn Changes Dynamics of the Grain Industry', *New York Times*, 11 December 2000.

29 A. V. Krebs, *Agribusiness Examiner*, 103 (29 January 2001).

http://www.ea1.com/CARP/agbiz/103.htm

30 'Japan's StarLink Corn Find Could Hurt US Sales', Reuters, 31 December 2002.

31 Mark Schapiro, 'Sowing Disaster?', *Nation*, US, 28 October 2002. http://www.thenation.com/doc.mhtml?i=20021028&s=schapiro; see also archive: http://www.gene.ch/genet.html

32 *Ibid.*

33 D. Quist and I. H. Chapela (2001), 'Transgenic DNA Introgressed into Traditional Maize Landraces in Oaxaca, Mexico', *Nature* 414, 6863 (2001): 541–3.

34 *Global Pesticide Campaigner*, 12, 2 (August 2002), Pesticide Action Network North America: www.panna.org

35 Sarah Yang, 'Bioengineered DNA Discovered in Native Mexican Corn, Researchers Report', *Public Affairs*, University of Berkeley, California, 5 December 2001. http://www.berkeley.edu/news/berkeleyan/2001/12/05_corn.html

36 Ariel Alvarez-Morales, 'Transgenes in Maize Landraces in Oaxaca: Official Report on the Extent and Implications', paper presented at 7th International Symposium on the Biosafety of Genetically Modified Organisms, October 2002. http://www.worldbiosafety.net/title%20paper.htm

37 The Institute for Food and Development Policy (also known as Food First) (US), '*Nature* Refuses to Publish Mexican Government Report Confirming Contamination of the Mexican Maize Genome by GMOs', press release, 24 October 2002. http://www.gene.ch/genet.html

38 Schapiro, 'Sowing Disaster?'

39 *Global Pesticide Campaigner*, 12, 2 (August 2002), Pesticide Action Network North America: www.panna.org

40 Schapiro, 'Sowing Disaster?'

41 Christopher Doering, 'ProdiGene to Spend Millions on Bio-corn Tainting', Reuters, 9 December 2002. http://www.gene.ch/genet.html

42 *Ibid.*

43 Genetically Engineered Food Alert Coalition (US), 'Manufacturing Drugs and Chemicals in Crops: Biopharming Poses New Threats to Consumers, Farmers, Food Companies and the Environment', July 2002. http://www.gefoodalert.org

44 AEBC report, *Crops on Trial*, September 2001, paragraph 90. www.aebc.gov.uk

5

The Main International Players
and Corporate Influence

*Most of the world still lacks national laws to deal with genetically engineered organisms,
therefore we need strong international regulation to protect these countries and biodiversity
from genetic pollution.*

Louise Gale, lawyer and Greenpeace political adviser, 1999[1]

Whatever the intentions of the various international bodies – and many of
them announce that they are committed to eradicating poverty – the fact is
that there has actually been a net flow of resources, including funds and
genetic material, from South to North over the last 50 years. The Bretton
Woods institutions established after the Second World War (The International Bank for Reconstruction and Development, more commonly
named the World Bank; the International Monetary Fund; and the General
Agreement on Tariffs and Trade, now the World Trade Organisation – see
Chapter 2) were ostensibly set up to aid post-war reconstruction and to
build global economic prosperity. However, they have actually been instrumental in opening up economies and access to raw materials for the
transnationals, whose interests now dominate the agenda of the World Trade
Organisation. The United Nations institutions have also shown themselves
vulnerable to corporate delegations and tend to promote regulation which
serves corporate interests.

Corporate interests also have an increasing grip on research, partly
because the amounts of public funding available for such activities have
dwindled, often in obedience to the structural adjustment policies of the
finance institutions. In these circumstances, TNCs can often gain influence
over the whole research agenda by merely topping up funds with a small
proportion of the total. The universities then provide cheap research and
apparently 'independent' advocates for corporate interests.

Biotech corporations have carefully cultivated strong relations with
government and the public research sector. They appear to have persuaded

some governments (including those in the UK, the US, Australia and Canada) that biotechnology represents the next industrial revolution and is essential for competitiveness. Such governments have boosted public sector funding of the biotech industry. Corporate lobbying has led to, amongst others:

- legislation favourable to industry and positive testing of GM products;

- omission of a 'precautionary principle';

- insufficient sanctions for corporate misdeeds;

- massive channelling of public money to the biotech industry;

- research diverted towards profitable applications of GM technology;

- GM crops being dumped on the global South as food and humanitarian aid.

These developments are promoting the rapid, unchecked and under-regulated spread of GM technology and GM crops around the world.

The World Bank

> *They no longer use bullets and rope. They use the World Bank and the IMF.*
> Jesse Jackson addressing eleven African heads of state, Libreville, 27 May 1993 [2]

The World Bank was set up in 1944 to provide loans for post-war reconstruction and consists of five closely associated institutions:

- the International Bank for Reconstruction and Development (IBRD);

- the International Development Association (IDA);

- the International Finance Corporation (IFC);

- the Multilateral Investment Guarantee Agency (MIGA);

- the International Centre for Settlement of Investment Disputes (ICSID).

Although the Bank claims that 'Our dream is a world free of poverty',[3] the economist David Korten, former adviser to USAID, writes:

> If measured by contributions to improving the lives of people or strengthening the institutions of democratic governance, the World Bank and the IMF have been disastrous failures – imposing an enormous burden on the world's poor and seriously impeding their development. In terms of fulfilling the mandates set for them by their original architects – advancing economic globalisation under the domination of the economically powerful – they both have been a resounding success.'[4]

Korten later adds: 'They have arguably done more harm to more people than any other pair of non-military institutions in history.'

On its own website, the Bank proclaims:

The World Bank is owned by 183 member countries whose views and interests are represented by a Board of Governors and a Washington-based Board of Directors.... Under the Articles of Agreement of IBRD, to become a member of the Bank a country must first join the International Monetary Fund (IMF). Membership in IDA, IFC and MIGA are conditional on membership in IBRD. ... Member countries are shareholders who carry ultimate decision-making power in the World Bank.

The Bank's internal operating process is so secretive 'that access to many of its most important documents relating to country plans, strategies and priorities is denied to even its own governing executive directors'.[5] In practice the Bank's agenda is set by those countries that have invested most money in it. These are the United States, the United Kingdom, Japan, Germany and France.

The World Bank was a major promoter of the green revolution, funding fertilisers, herbicides, insecticides, irrigation and machinery for Southern countries, to go along with high response variety/high yield variety (HRV, HYV) seeds. Although grain yields increased, there were massive costs in terms of loss of locally adapted farmer varieties, destruction of the soil and the creation of multiple dependencies – the new HRV seeds depended on packages of inputs and the farmers became indebted. Even the Bank admits:

Large-scale farmers generally acquire knowledge of such technologies more quickly and because they have better access to the working capital needed to utilise these technologies more fully, they capture the earliest and largest gains from innovation .... At least in the short run, relative distribution of income worsens as between large-scale and small-holder farmers.[6]

Many observers fear that genetic engineering biotechnology will merely continue and even accelerate the trend towards inequitable distribution of resources and entitlements and lead to even further loss of farmer varieties. Moreover, studies show that other types of innovation, such as intercropping or variety mixes, can produce much better results: doubling yields without the use of costly, synthetic inputs.[7]

In an article published in *Nature* (2000), M. S. Wolfe explained that while fertiliser and pesticide use is expensive and may cause new problems, variety mixes have been shown to work. He continues:

Mixtures of species provide another layer of crop diversity, with half-forgotten advantages waiting to be exploited in contemporary approaches. It is widely recognised, for example, that high-yielding mixtures of grains and legumes (grass plus clover, maize plus beans, and many other combinations) can restrict the spread of diseases, pests and weeds. At the same time, such mixtures can provide near-complete nutrition for animals and humans alike, without recourse to expensive and uncertain forays into genetic engineering.[8]

Questioning the Bank's achievements

The Centre for Economic and Policy Research (CEPR) is a US-based public interest group dedicated to promoting democratic debate. In their papers 'The Scorecard on Globalization, 1980–2000, Twenty Years of Diminished Progress' and 'Growth May Be Good for the Poor but Are IMF and World Bank Policies Good for Growth?'[9] The CEPR shows that the World Bank and the IMF have failed to improve life for the poor in the last 20 years.

Using standard indicators like economic growth, life expectancy, infant mortality, education and literacy, the CEPR reveals that progress has slowed down between 1980 and 2000 compared with the period 1960–80. The average Mexican and Brazilian would have almost twice as much income if the rate of improvement in 1960–80 had been maintained.

They also show that, regardless of whether growth is good for the poor, the World Bank and IMF policies of trade liberalisation, privatisation, export promotion and cuts in government spending are failing to deliver even the promised economic growth. Moreover, they question the notion that the poor benefit from economic growth in itself. They call for a radical examination of the power of these institutions to carry on imposing failed economic models on the developing world.

The Bank and the seed sector in Africa – ISSSSA

In April 1999 the World Bank announced its Initiative For Sustainable Seed Supply Systems in Africa: Sub-regional Action Plan in Southern Africa. The Action Plan is designed to be implemented in Malawi, Mozambique, Zambia and Zimbabwe, as pilot countries in the Southern Africa region. National aspects are to be funded through currently ongoing World Bank and/or joint-donor-financed projects for agricultural and rural development: examples include the Agricultural Services and Management project in Zimbabwe, the Agricultural Services Project in Malawi and so-called Agricultural Sector Investment Programmes in both Zambia and Mozambique. The stated aim of the project is to harmonise seed-related regulation, improve competition and commercial development, and to promote the entry of 'improved varieties' with international involvement. There are key words in the Action Plan guaranteed to arouse the distrust of those who work to protect biodiversity and farmers.

Often a major constraint is national legislation that limits entry of improved varieties, constrains competition, restricts multinational involvement in African seed systems, and inhibits development of domestic seed companies. Restricting commercial development has also inhibited the formation of seed trade associations, which could provide substantial benefits to the African seed sector. Seed associations – open to public and private seed company membership – serve to lobby and influence governments, exchange information, and generally to ease barriers to efficient seed production and marketing and to the effective transfer of improved varieties.[10]

In the proposed outline for the Sub-regional Action Plan, the World Bank further states:

> This Action Plan is launched to analyse in more detail the challenges faced by seed sectors in the countries of Southern Africa region and to make a significant contribution to the exchange of information, debate, and dialogue between representatives from African governments, donors, seed companies, farmers' organisations and other associations pursuing national seed sub-sector strengthening, the harmonisation of seed regulatory frameworks and the development of regionally competitive seed supply systems in Africa.[11]

The African Seed Trade Organisation was founded in 1999 and in the following year the African Seed Network was launched. Both are highlighting the need to improve seed supply systems. While the first is to represent the interest of the seed trade, the African Seed Network is working more directly with farmers and claims that 'Seed supply systems in sub-Saharan Africa, particularly among small-scale farmers, are set to improve with the launch of the African Seed Network.' The Network is funded by the FAO (see Chapter 6), from which it derives policy guidance. The Network's views are in line with the other ongoing activities, such as the World Bank initiative and the activities of seed-trading organisations. The Network has stated:

> The unavailability of seed production technology in many African countries, lack of seed rules regulations and defining seed standards, phytosanitary requirements, protection of intellectual property and differences in seed rules were noted as some of the impediments to increasing the range and quality of seeds available to sub-Saharan farmers.[12]

There is growing fear among NGOs such as Genetic Resources Action International (GRAIN) that the current World Bank initiative, combined with pressures to adopt the most recent version of UPOV (Union for the Protection of New Varieties of Plants) will lead to a corporate takeover of the seed sector in Africa. UPOV sets out a regime to protect the interests of plant breeders. Until recently it had few members among Southern countries, but this is rapidly changing. These countries are being told that 'patents and other forms of IPR (intellectual property rights) are the key to attracting investment in biotechnology, which will uplift their economies and improve food security'. Africa's seed supply system could suffer the same fate as Europe's, with the outlawing of farmer varieties that do not fit the industrial criteria of being distinct, uniform and stable, and the imposition of F1 hybrids that do not breed true when saved for planting, driving the farmer back to the (increasingly corporate) seed salesman each year. It could also facilitate the entry of technology to prevent the replanting of saved seed through Terminator technology and other genetic use restriction technologies (GURTs). This would take the development of agriculture out of the hands of the African farmer.

The Bank, agrochemicals and genetic engineering

The Bank is reported to have financed US$250.75 million worth of pesticides in 1988–95. In 1993–5 alone, $56.9 million went to producers in G7 countries (see Table 5.1).

Table 5.1 • How the World Bank finances G7 pesticide producers

Funds acquired (%)	Country	Corporation	US$ million	Ranking according to funding
38	France	Rhone–Poulenc	18.6 (=33%)	1
		Roussel–Uclaf	1-3	4
27	Germany	BASF	6.6	2
		Bayer	1-3	4
		Air Lloyd	1-3	4
		Hoechst	1-3	4
15	UK	Zeneca	> 3	3
11	US	FMC Corp	> 3	3
		Cyanamid	1-3	4
10	Japan	Sumitomo	> 3	3

Two of the Pesticide Action Network's 'Dirty Dozen' pesticides also appear in these contracts: paraquat and DDT. Contracts to French and German companies supported the procurement of almost US$120,000 of paraquat for two World Bank projects in Nigeria.[13]

GRAIN draws attention to the fact that by 1996, according to a US Treasury report,

> in just two years (1993 to 1995), the World Bank and other multinational development banks had channelled nearly $5 billion to US firms. One major beneficiary was Cargill, the third largest food corporation in the world. Cargill's 1995–6 sales were a mind-boggling $56 billion, which is roughly equivalent to

the GNP of Pakistan, Venezuela or the Philippines. Company earnings reached almost $1 billion and profits were 34 per cent higher than the previous year. These are hardly credentials we would expect to qualify for World Bank assistance, nor does it seem like a wise investment for the Bank.

GRAIN speaks here for angry farmers in poor countries everywhere:

> Judging from the reaction of rural people around the world, supporting Cargill's operations does little to meet the World Bank's vision for rural development. The heated demonstrations against the company in 1992 attended by thousands of India's farmers (the very people the Bank is aiming to help) attest to the inappropriateness of entrusting agricultural development to agribusiness giants. The farmers were angry about the false promises made by the company of higher yields by switching to Cargill seeds, the environmental damage caused by the chemical packages required, the threat to agrobiodiversity posed by monocultures, and being robbed of their intellectual property.[14]

Partnerships with agribusiness

Agribusiness regularly take parts in the World Bank/corporate staff exchange programme or 'Share'. Started by World Bank President James Wolfensohn in 1995, the Share programme is, according to Wolfensohn, intended to 'foster closer partnerships with external organizations, particularly the private sector, so as to introduce fresh perspectives and new approaches to deliver better services to our clients'. Companies involved include Dow, Aventis and Syngenta.[15]

The World Bank has already provided hundreds of millions of dollars to develop biotechnology in countries such as Kenya, Zimbabwe, Indonesia, and Mexico. Doyle and Persley comment:

> The World Bank has lent at least US$100 million for biotechnology-related activities, while bilateral development agencies, such as those of the USA, the UK and the Netherlands, and private foundations such as the Rockefeller Foundation, have invested approximately US$200 million in biotechnology R&D over the past decade. CGIAR centres presently spend approximately US$22.4 million per year on biotechnology R&D for crops and livestock important throughout the developing world.[16]

In its 1999 Annual Report, the World Bank claims that

> biotechnology offers another option for increasing crop yields on less land. Advances in biotechnology are progressing rapidly in industrial countries, but few commercial applications exist for developing countries. Still, biotechnology holds promise for the latter in their efforts to increase productivity, conserve natural resources (especially biodiversity), and alleviate poverty.[17]

In December 2000, the World Bank met with 13 major players, including many of the largest agrochemicals companies: Aventis, BASF, Bayer, Cargill, Dow, DuPont, Emergent Genetics, Mahyco, Merial Limited, Monsanto, Rockefeller Foundation, Seminis, and Syngenta. The goal of the meeting was to get private sector perspectives on how to increase food security and agricultural productivity in an environmentally and socially sustainable manner.[18] This meeting stated that 'agricultural science and research, not limited to, but including biotechnology, is a key component in addressing food security'. It also candidly acknowledged that

> Presently, much of the world's agricultural research, particularly in biotechnology, is done by the private sector. In order to successfully continue working in this area, private companies must provide shareholder returns. As a result, they are not likely to meet most of the developing countries' agricultural research needs.

Along with funding the FAO and public scientific research institutions such as the CGIAR, the World Bank has funded public–private institutions to promote biotechnology in the South such as the International Service for the Acquisition of Agri-biotech Applications (ISAAA).

The Consultative Group for International Agricultural Research (CGIAR)

The CGIAR challenge is to create a new form of public–private partnership that will protect intellectual property while bringing the benefit of this research to the poorest nations.

CGIAR Review, 1998

The CGIAR's recent history encapsulates the wider struggle for control over genetic resources, which is critical for the future of agriculture and the seeds that underpin it. This is why considerable space is being given to it here. This struggle can be expressed in terms of two opposing movements. On the one hand there are those who call for a bottom-up approach starting with farmers and basing research on their knowledge, with wide civil society participation, taking into account the true complexity of the issues, working in the public domain for the common interest. On the other hand there is the top-down imposition of solutions produced by scientists behind desks or in laboratories, often owned by private companies – solutions increasingly composed of genetically engineered seeds protected by patents. The former approach favours decentralisation and a more regional process that will make it easier for the farmer to participate, while the latter favours centralisation. The key issue is the fate of the germplasm (genetic resources, for example in the form of seeds) developed, shared and safeguarded over millennia by farmers.

It is this germplasm which forms the basis of the global food supply. It is therefore vitally important and yet it generally draws little public attention in the North where people are already alienated from the real source of their food. Urbanisation has resulted in a widening gulf between food producers and consumers. Contempt among urbanites for those who get their hands dirty – soiled – in the earth means that farmers are held in low esteem. Ignorance makes people easy to manipulate, yet many sense the importance of the issue and the conflict around it.

The struggle continues, both inside the CGIAR and outside. The effect inside the organisation is to make it somewhat schizophrenic in its approach. Some sections participate in projects to promote bottom-up, farmer-based solutions while other sections participate in projects that are opposed to this, often promoting biotech and high-tech solutions. Farmer organisations and NGOs have lobbied passionately and tirelessly against this emphasis, yet they seldom get a sympathetic hearing.

The set-up of the CGIAR

The CGIAR's mission, as set out on its website,[19] is to contribute to food security and poverty eradication in developing countries through research, partnership, capacity building and policy support. The CGIAR was established in 1971 by the World Bank and the FAO with the help of the Rockefeller and Ford foundations. Eighteen governments and organisations attended as members, plus ten as observers, but none of them were from developing countries.

The CGIAR is an informal association of 58 public and private sector members, including private foundations, international development agencies and 50 governments, mainly from the North. They support a network of 16 international agricultural research centres, which now call themselves the Future Harvest Centres[20] and which have more than 8,500 scientists and support staff working in more than 100 countries.[21] In 2000, contributions from CGIAR members amounted to $331 million, making up its budget. Industrial countries, specifically the members of the Development Assistance Committee of the Organisation for Economic Cooperation and Development (OECD), account for more than two-thirds of CGIAR financing. The CGIAR is always short of funds. The Global Conservation Trust was launched in Johannesburg at the World Summit on Sustainable Development in September 2002. It is a public–private partnership initiative which aims to raise $260 million of extra funding to protect genetic resources. The CGIAR and the FAO are involved, as are the Gatsby Charitable Foundation, one of the Sainsbury family trusts, USAID,[22] Glaxo and Syngenta.[23]

The World Bank, the FAO and the United Nations Development Programme (UNDP) are co-sponsors of the CGIAR. The Novartis Foundation is a CGIAR partner and the Syngenta Foundation was accepted as a member in 2002 (see Chapter 8 for more on these two foundations).

Links with the World Bank have been close from the beginning. The CGIAR's chairperson is a vice-president of the World Bank, where its secretariat is based and from which it also receives funding. For instance, Ian Johnson, who became chairperson of the CGIAR in July 2000, was at the same time the World Bank President for Environmentally and Socially Sustainable Development. He helped found the Global Environment Facility of the World Bank in 1991 – a joint project of UNDP, the United Nations Environment Programme (UNEP) and the World Bank.

INTERNATIONAL AGRICULTURAL RESEARCH CENTRES (IARCs)

The network of 16 international agricultural research centres (IARCs) ('Future Harvest Centres') around the world currently overseen by the CGIAR include:

- the International Maize and Wheat Improvement Centre (CIMMYT) in Mexico;

- the International Rice Research Institute (IRRI) in the Philippines;

- the International Centre for Tropical Agriculture (CIAT) in Colombia;

- the International Food Policy Research Institute (IFPRI) in Washington;

- the International Potato Centre (CIP) in Lima, Peru;

- the International Centre for Agricultural Research in Dry Areas (ICARDA) in Aleppo in Syria;

- the International Crops Research Institute for the Semi-Arid Tropics (ICRISAT) in Hyderabad, India.

At the CGIAR, most decisions for the world's largest and most influential agricultural research projects have been made by a small number of white Northern men from a handful of agricultural colleges in Australia, Canada, Britain and the US, with no internal or external rules of governance. Since 1997, the CGIAR has attempted to redress this balance by filling more of the trustee posts with persons from the South and with women.[24]

The struggle for the heart of the CGIAR

In 1995, noting that it had been 14 years since the previous review of the CGIAR, NGOs called for a new review, focusing on bottom-up strategies for food security and livelihood systems, with the full participation of the South, not just confined to the IARCs. The results of the ensuing Third System-Wide Review were announced in October 1998. The review document, which contained language that openly promoted biotechnology and patenting, proposing what it termed an 'integrated gene management' approach, also proposed a central body for the system. This was rejected by the CGIAR members, while both suggestions were strongly resisted by NGOs and farmer organisations, and were dropped. A consultative council was established to draft CGIAR policy. The next attempt to find a direction for the CGIAR was undertaken by the Technical Advisory Committee (TAC), which presented its 'vision and strategy' at the CGIAR's mid-term meeting in May 2000 in Dresden. The vision called for a more regional approach, with a focus on Africa and South Asia.

At the same time, there was a meeting of the Global Forum on Agricultural Research (GFAR), partly spawned by the CGIAR. The CGIAR's budget only covers 4 per cent of agricultural research; 96 per cent is carried out by national agricultural research institutes, universities and (increasingly) corporations. It was therefore proposed that all those involved in agricultural research should be part of a global forum that would help to decide the priorities of the CGIAR. But the usual struggle began here too between proponents of top-down technological solutions, focusing on GM and IPR in liberalised markets, and those who sought bottom-up, farmer-based, participatory solutions. However, the statement from GFAR promoted solutions based on genetic engineering and market liberalisation rather than addressing fundamental problems of landlessness and access to resources. The 'global shared vision' produced by GFAR was therefore not shared by farmers groups and NGOs.

A Change Design and Management Team (CDMT) was set up within the CGIAR in 2000 to implement change, but the struggle between regionalism and centralisation continues, with some NGOs pointing out how shifting the governance of agricultural research to the different regions and away from the IARCs could reduce costs as well as improving the participation of farmers. The CDMT proposed a series of multi-centre 'challenge programmes' to give renewed energy and direction to research and shift from programmes focused on single centres towards multi-centre collaborations. This was adopted but there is disappointment amongst farmers and NGOs that major programmes adopted to date are on functional genomics and biofortification (food enhanced with vitamins and minerals), thus implying a strong role for biotechnology.

At the end of November 2002 the NGO Committee of the CGIAR indicated its disappointment with the CGIAR for embracing GM; for failing to call for a moratorium, especially in areas of origin of key crops such as maize in Mexico; and for failing to uphold the principle of the CGIAR that all genetic resources should be in the public domain. It said that it would review the CGIAR during 2003 and for that period of time would 'freeze' its relationship with it.[25] Meanwhile GRAIN and other NGOs have published assessments and critiques of the relationship between the CGIAR and farmers in poor countries.[26]

Benefits flow north

A major role of the CGIAR is to collect samples of germplasm from all over the world and to preserve them for humanity. Although many commentators point out that the most effective conservation is carried out *in situ* – that is, in the field, responding to evolutionary pressures, climate change and other factors – most of the collected samples are actually preserved in gene banks *ex situ*, where they may lose their capacity to germinate.

> [N]inety-one per cent of all the samples collected and distributed came from Asia, Africa and Latin America. Despite this only 15 per cent of these samples have so far gone to developing nations. Eighty-five per cent were distributed more or less equally among the northern-influenced IARCs and the industrialised countries themselves. The United States swallowed the lion's share with more than a quarter of all the samples.[27]

There is a great deal of evidence that the true beneficiaries of the CGIAR, both financially and in terms of germplasm, are the Northern industrialised countries. Their returns on their investment in the CGIAR can be substantial:

> Although the CGIAR's stated mandate is to increase food production in the South, the work of the IARCs has substantially benefited agricultural development in the North as well.
> Consider the US wheat crop. According to a 1996 study by one of the CGIAR's 16 IARCs, the International Food Policy Research Institute based in Washington, DC, germplasm from another IARC, the Mexican-based CIMMYT, which focuses on maize and wheat, can now be found in 58 per cent of the US wheat crop; its cash contribution since 1970 to US farmers is not less than $3.4 billion while that to the country's food processing companies is about $13.4 billion. The 1996 study conservatively places the economic gain for US consumers from IRRI germplasm, which now accounts for three-quarters of the US rice harvest, at about $1 billion since 1970.[28]

In a letter to the US senate in 1994, then Secretary of State Warren Christopher and two Cabinet colleagues argued that foreign germplasm contributed $10.2 billion annually to the US maize and soybean crop.[29]

Since 1974, according to a study funded by Australian and international agricultural research agencies, Australia's wheat industry has gained more than US $3 billion as a result of more than 50 durum wheat varieties provided by CIMMYT – the CG Centre based in Mexico. Between 1972 and 1996, the Australian Government contributed a grand total of US$80.1 million to the Consultative Group on International Agricultural Research.[30]

Corporate beneficiaries – privatising the germplasm heritage

In recent years [prior to 1996], three-quarters of ICRISAT's chickpea gene exchange and close to one third of CIMMYT's triticale (a cross between rye and wheat) have gone North. As much as one-third of the annual outflow of tropical seed samples from CIMMYT now ends up in the hands of transnationals like Pioneer Hi-Bred and Cargill. Pioneer Hi-Bred obtained hybrid maize from the Nigerian IITA [International Institute of Tropical Agriculture] centre, the product of research financed directly by the Nigerian government, and is now marketing it from Zimbabwe to Thailand. Cargill, meanwhile, is commercialising IITA's inbred maize lines in East Africa and Asia. At least four CGIAR varieties are 'protected' in the US or Europe under a plant-specific form of patent.[31]

Arguments over whether patents should be allowed on CGIAR resources have continued for many years inside and outside the organisation. The issue of Terminator technologies (see Chapter 8) aroused such strong resistance that in October 1998, the CGIAR banned them from breeding materials. After a long campaign by organisations including RAFI (now the ETC group) and GRAIN, the CGIAR has taken a position on intellectual property that seems fairly clear:

The terms of the agreements signed between the FAO and CGIAR Centres, stipulate that the germplasm within the in-trust collections will be made available without restriction to researchers around the world, on the understanding that no intellectual property protection is to be applied to the material.[32]

However, the reality is more complex. In 1994 the contents of the major gene banks were placed under the auspices of the FAO in a trusteeship agreement designed to protect them from biopiracy. The CGIAR holds only about 10 per cent of the 6 million genebank accessions, mostly collected during the 1960s, but its collection is crucial because it is well documented and preserved. According to its website,

The CGIAR holds one of the world's largest *ex situ* collections of plant genetic resources in trust for the world community. It contains over 500,000 accessions of more than 3,000 crop, forage, and agroforestry species. The collection includes farmers' varieties and improved varieties and, in substantial measure, the wild species from which those varieties were created.[33]

The *Ecologist* estimates that the CGIAR holds about 40 per cent of the unique farmer-bred varieties worldwide. This germplasm is vital for crop breeding globally.

There are three parts to the trusteeship system: the FAO–CGIAR Agreement, the joint FAO–CGIAR Statement and a model Material Transfer Agreement (MTA). Under the FAO–CGIAR Agreement, germplasm is to be held in trust for humanity, to be freely available (in the public domain), and not to be patented. All this sounds very laudable. However, the MTA says germplasm must not be patented 'in the form received', which could leave the way open for patenting anything derived from the germplasm that is sufficiently different from the original, and anything which is genetically engineered. Moreover, there is no obligation to monitor whether or not the material is later patented by the recipient. Under the Agreement, 60,000 samples of germplasm were transferred during 2000. This material may be commercialised, but there is no mechanism for transferring any benefits to those who originally developed it. Ironically, perhaps, the fact that the material is in the public domain makes it impossible for those (small farmers, local communities and indigenous people) who developed it to claim rights over it, including decisions as to how it is used and by whom.

The latest development is that the FAO Treaty on Plant Genetic Resources, which to date covers just 35 food crops and 29 forage crops, will soon govern the 'in trust' germplasm under its own provisions. This treaty contains those same words: patenting of germplasm is forbidden *in the form received*. The struggle over how these words are to be interpreted, whether material derived from the germbank may be patented, and, more broadly, who benefits from genetic resources, continues unabated. Other ambiguities remain in the Treaty. There may be a glimmer of hope in the fact that although farmers' rights are not recognised in the Trusteeship Agreement, Article 9 of the Treaty is devoted to them.

In the end, the truth of the matter is that the interests of the two main strands struggling within the organisation, independent farmers with their supporters and the corporations with their backers, are actually irreconcilable, in spite of constant efforts to suggest that they could be mutual.[34]

Genetic engineering: serving the corporate agenda

The struggle within the CGIAR over genetic engineering has been almost as intense as that over IPRs. A Private Sector Committee was set up in 1995 and there are two panels – the Panel on General Issues in Biotechnology and the Panel on Proprietary Science and Technology – which lobby within the organisation.[35] Although the Third System-Wide Review's recommendations for the CGIAR to develop a centralised legal entity to promote

Creeping contradictions: IPRs and the CGIAR system

The CGIAR centres and other international agricultural research centres have proven all too willing to concede to industry's IPR agenda in hopes of accessing new technologies for biotechnology and genomics. The International Maize and Wheat Improvement Centre (CIMMYT) was the first to go. Taking its cue from the recommendations of a dialogue with the private sector, CIMMYT announced a new intellectual property policy in April 2000, whereby it will selectively pursue its own IPR in order to 'defend' its research or to facilitate partnerships with industry.[36] Other research centres soon followed. In February 2001, the International Crops Research Institute for the Semi-Arid Tropics established an intellectual property policy that 'reserves to itself any and all IPR, without limitation, discovered or produced as a result of cooperation related to any research agreement'.[37] The International Livestock Research Institute (ILRI) in Kenya, which actively works in partnership with the private sector on transgenic technologies, takes a similar 'defensive' position. It states:

> ILRI recognises that IP protection on its products and technologies may be necessary: to ensure continued availability of germplasm, inventions publications and databases to ILRI clients and prevent them from being misappropriated by others for profit making; to ensure the delivery of improved products and technologies in developing countries; to negotiate access to other proprietary rights and technologies required for product development....

It could be argued that the public research centres have resisted pressures for IPRs by adopting policies that, while accepting IPRs, try as much as possible to keep research in the public domain and give farmers access to new technologies. Generally, the IARCs claim that they will only take out IPRs or enter into research alliances involving IPRs when these are necessary to give developing countries access to important new technologies. But this argument loses sight of the bigger picture. The IARCs and their national counterparts hold tremendous influence over agricultural policy in Africa and by accepting IPRs on biodiversity, they legitimise them. As the World Bank points out, 'politicians can be loath to change seed regulations without support from at least some national experts, including crop scientists and other agricultural experts'.[38] IPRs will have dire consequences for the very people that public research is supposed to help. Rather than gradually caving into industry's IPR demands, it would be more appropriate for these institutions to recognise their critical position and join others taking a stand against the privatisation of agricultural biodiversity and public research.

Devlin Kuyek (2002)[39]

patenting and biotechnology and to go for public–private partnerships was rejected, it reveals the thinking of the pro-biotechnology lobby inside the organisation. As we have seen, the CGIAR has very little funding for research and relies on joint ventures with universities and/or private sector support in the form of cash and/or technology.[40] Corporations have financial resources far beyond the CGIAR's means. For example, in 1998 Novartis (now Syngenta) decided to invest $600 million over the following 10 years in the Novartis Agricultural Discovery Institute Inc. (NADII) in San Diego, California, a wholly owned entity of the Novartis Research Foundation. The initial investment was announced to be $250 million, representing 75 per cent of the CGIAR's entire annual budget.

On the other hand, the corporations recognise that the CGIAR can act as a broker and multiplier for them. Sam Dryden, chairperson of the CGIAR's Private Sector Committee, explained that according to the private sector 'the CGIAR can help corporations move into territories where agriculture has been traditionally served by the public sector'.[41]

When investigating the influence of private sector involvement on the CGIAR and its biotech agenda, Janet Bell reported:

> The CGIAR does not have a very good record of serving poor farmers around the world. Industry's influence is likely to make it even less responsive to their needs and shift it back towards its technology focus and cash crop agenda. Henry Gorrisma of the Dutch government suggests that, 'The private sector may have a role to play in agricultural research, but the CGIAR is trying too hard to get it on board.' To this end, Gorrisma suggests, it is reorienting its research direction, at the expense of losing sight of its mandate and the poor. 'It is easy for industry to sway the CGIAR,' Gorrisma adds. 'It does not have to put up much money to exert a great deal of influence.'[42]

So far, most of industry's involvement with the CGIAR has been limited to the donation of genes and technologies. TNCs have increasingly allowed agricultural research centres as well as national agricultural research stations to access 'for free' the traits, cell lines, products and processes that they have patented. 'Monsanto has collaborative projects with CIMMYT and with the CIP, while Novartis has links with IRRI and AgrEvo with the CIP and ICARDA. In all cases, the companies donated genes and some technologies, but little direct funding appears to have been given.'[43] For example, Novartis has licensed the use of its proprietary technologies for cassava and for Bt in rice to certain IARCs free of charge on certain conditions.

In exchange, the corporations gain from access to the CGIAR gene and seed banks. Warnings were already given in 1990 by Cary Fowler and Pat Mooney:

> The danger – now being recognised by the IARCs – is that they will be relegated to the role of doing basic research for the benefit of private companies. The

companies can take IARC material and exploit it for their own commercial purposes.[44]

The CGIAR is therefore often caught up as a participant in projects which it serves without having any real control over them and to which it brings valuable germplasm resources which could end up as 'feedstock for the biotechnology industry' as the Biotechnology Advisory Center of the Swedish Environmental Institute has put it.[45]

In May 2000 an Oxfam/Friends of the Earth (Europe) conference on 'The Impact of Biotechnology on Developing Countries' brought together industry scientists and representatives, as well as CGIAR scientists and NGO representatives. From this meeting it seemed evident that some scientists within the CGIAR oppose the corporate research agenda on GM technology, although they support those genetically engineered crops that they consider beneficial to the people of the South. Many also support a different system of patent protection that allows open access to genetic materials rather than corporate ownership.

> It will be a serious, and quite probably insurmountable, challenge for the IARCs to team up with the private sector while still being responsive to the world's farmers.... The consequences of being dependent on industry's products and agenda are far more serious in the Third World, because the lack of accountability means that industry will be even less concerned about producing products that really work and are safe. In addition, Third World farmers do not have the same kind of safety nets as their Northern counterparts, and a failed crop may mean starvation.[46]

The erosion of humanity's agricultural heritage

Involvement in any way in genetic engineering biotechnology could well be seen as contrary to the mandate of the CGIAR. Farmer varieties are critical for food security, and many were eliminated by the green revolution, yet:

> The pace of biotechnological breakthroughs is so fast that one could safely say that no genetic conservation system exists which could collect the traditional varieties as quickly as they will likely be eliminated by biotechnology.[47]

Although this comment was made in 1990, it still applies. The CGIAR might respond that its gene banks are safe deposits for these varieties. However, there are many questions about the viability of the collections. Stored seeds need to be planted and harvested at regular intervals to remain viable and the preparation and storage of germplasm has not always been according to the rules.[48] A warning was sounded as early as 1979: 'It is estimated that even in developed countries such as [the] USA and Australia from half to two thirds of accessions brought in over several decades have been lost.'[49]

The precious heritage of agricultural diversity needs to be protected in the field, not only in gene banks. Agricultural biodiversity depends on people to maintain it and ensure it continues adapting and evolving in response to new challenges from pests and environmental and climatic changes.

Modern breeding is increasingly based on 'one gene' strategies. The focus is on the identification and selection or transfer of individual genes conferring a desirable trait such as resistance to a pest or disease. The problem is that a one-gene defence system can quickly be overcome by the pathogen, thus rendering the resistance gene useless. Long-term stable resistance is conferred by whole groups of genes interacting with each other and being able to alter and adapt the plant's response. Such complexes have evolved through natural ecological dynamics, helped by farmer selection and traditional breeding. Co-evolution between crops, pests, diseases and environmental factors is continuous and vital for healthy and sustainable farming systems and crop health, including pest tolerance and resistance. This is a major reason why *in situ* conservation of varieties – continuing adaptive preservation of varieties in the field through frequent planting and harvesting – is the most effective way to maintain germplasm. Genetic uniformity – as monoculture hybrids show – leads to a uniform response. Once the pathogen has adapted to the defences of one plant, it has the key to all the plants in the field. Thus genetic uniformity or reliance on single genes leaves plants vulnerable and puts the crop and those who depend on it for food or livelihood at risk.

Genetic engineering takes the process of narrowing the genetic base of crops still further. It sidesteps traditional breeding practices that at least allowed gene complexes to survive and evolve. It is likely to continue and intensify the trend of working with a single gene for resistance and planting monocultures. It will also continue the process of eliminating farmer varieties. These can be lost very quickly through using modern hybrids with high levels of inputs even for a short time, because this changes the soil ecology and the interrelationships between plants, soil micro-organisms, pests, predators and nutrients. Even if the varieties are not lost, the soil ecology may be so much altered by chemical pesticides and fertilisers as to hinder the farmer variety from growing. Soils may take a long time to regenerate if the microflora and soil structure have been seriously damaged.

From 'miracle' rice to hybrid seeds: the International Rice Research Institute (IRRI)

We are being starved to death and we've starved to death for 20 years.... We are in this predicament because of the direction which IRRI research has taken over the last 20 years ... IRRI should not only be dismantled, it should be sued by the farmers' organisations

... I think IRRI stands indicted for complete and absolute negligence, at the very least....'
Alejandro Lochauco, lawyer, at the national conference of the Philippine
peasants' organisation (BIGAS) in 1985, months after IRRI celebrated its
25th anniversary

Rice is the world's most consumed staple food grain, with half the world's
people depending on it. It is harvested on about 146 million hectares, representing 10 per cent of global arable land. The yield is reported as 535 million
tons per year and 91 per cent is produced by Asian farmers, especially in
China and India (55 per cent).[50] Rice is primarily consumed where it is
produced. In 1998 only 5.3 per cent (28.6 million tons) of the world's rice
production was traded internationally.[51]

IRRI was established in 1960 by the Ford and Rockefeller foundations
with the help and approval of the government of the Philippines.

> From its founding, IRRI was registered as a non-stock non-profit corporation
> under Philippine law. In 1979, President Ferdinand Marcos granted IRRI a
> number of diplomatic immunities and privileges through Presidential Decree
> 1620. Under PD1620, IRRI is immune from civil, administrative and penal
> proceedings in the Philippines.[52]

Rice is not just a daily source of calories – farming is intrinsically linked
to Asian lifestyles and heritage. Present indigenous and local varieties are the
product of centuries of breeding and selection by farmers to produce rice
suitable to their environment and needs. IRRI was founded with a clear
agenda to increase rice production and the mandate to preserve traditional
seeds and varieties (germplasm). However, the Institute's leaders persuaded
government officials that research on local rice varieties was no longer
necessary and this halted such research for nearly three decades.

A conference in 1985 attended by 45 farmer organisations, progressive
scientists from the University of the Philippines and development NGOs
demanded the immediate dismantling of IRRI and the launch of a national
programme on rice to respond to their needs, and to work within their
capacities and limitations. They also demanded collaboration with progressive scientists for farmer-led research on rice. The fortieth anniversary of
the Philippine-based IRRI, in April 2000, was marked by mass protests by
farmers.

THE BREEDING RACE: FROM HIGH RESPONSE TO HYBRID

In Sri Lanka as in the Philippines, the first IRRI representative urged the
government to phase out its own rice research on the grounds that IRRI
could supply all the new varieties needed. In 1966, IRRI released its first
variety of high-response rice, IR-8, the cross-breed of a Taiwanese dwarf
and an Indonesian variety. 'Despite several serious drawbacks – IR-8's grain
was of poor quality and the variety lacked resistance to common rice diseases

and pests – it was widely distributed because of its high yield potential. By the late 1960s some 25 per cent of "Third World" rice land was planted with IR-8 or similar semi-dwarfs.' By 1986, this figure had reached 55 per cent.[53]

A few years ago, the famous 'miracle strain' of rice in the Philippines, IR-8, was hit by tungro disease. Rice growers switched to a further form, IR-20, whereupon this hybrid [actually line] soon proved fatally vulnerable to grassy stunt virus and brown hopper insects. So farmers moved on to IR-26, a super-hybrid that turned out to be exceptionally resistant to almost all Philippines diseases and insect pests. But it proved too fragile for the island's strong winds, whereupon plant breeders decided to try an original Taiwan strain that had shown unusual capacity to stand up to winds – only to find that it had been all but eliminated by Taiwan farmers as they planted virtually all their ricelands with IR-8.[54]

IR-26 thus gave way to IR-36, which by 1980 was increasingly susceptible to a new strain of brown planthopper and was by 1982 replaced by IR-56. Breeders are in a constant race to stay a step ahead and hardly any of the highly inbred HRVs (high-response varieties) last more than a few years before showing declining resistance to natural stress and giving lower yields.[55]

True breeding lines versus F1 hybrids

F1 hybrids are the first generation outcome of crossing two varieties. They are of particular interest to the seed business because they give a uniform performance, while their harvested and replanted seed (F2) will not. As a largely self-pollinating crop, rice is a poor candidate for producing F1-hybrids. IRRI's HRV rice varieties are often called 'hybrids', but are actually true breeding lines, created through one step of 'hybridisation', but then made stable through multiple backcrossing (repeated crossing between a hybrid and one of the parent strains over many generations) .

Due to the difficulties of producing F1 rice hybrids on a large scale, private industry did not enter the seed business until tempted by the profits assured through intellectual property rights, mainly patents (see below) and the potential for F1 hybrids. The advent of a male sterile line, called a *maintainer line*, developed by Chinese scientists, opened the door to commercial F1 hybrid seeds, as such plants depend on the pollen of other plants, called *restorer lines*, to produce seeds.

IRRI, the FAO and the Asia Pacific Seed Association (APSA – a group including all the public and private seed companies) have entered into a collaboration entitled 'Development and Use of Hybrid Rice in Asia' – funded by the Asian Development Bank (ADB). Under the leadership of

Sant S. Virmani, IRRI has been developing hybrid rice technology since 1979. Dr Virmani recently stated:

> In 2001, more than 700,000 hectares were planted to rice hybrids in irrigated areas in Vietnam (480,000 hectares), India (200,000 hectares), Bangladesh (15,000 hectares), the Philippines (5,000 hectares), Myanmar (10,000 hectares) and the USA (10,000 hectares).[56]

F1 hybrid seeds are difficult to produce and cost ten to fifteen times more than ordinary seeds. Crops are dependent on well-irrigated land and costly inputs. Even then, yield increases have been disappointing. Furthermore, the rice is said to have a poor flavour and is vulnerable to pests. As Dr Virmani states, 'this technology is not for farmers who are still struggling at the level of two or three tons' – which is exactly where the vast majority of rice farmers in Asia are placed.[57] This makes it hard to see how developing hybrid rice fits in with IRRI's mandate. IRRI thus acknowledges that its research is primarily to encourage commercial production. Asian governments have also concentrated their support for rice production on larger farms, implementing agricultural programmes to promote biotechnology and F1 hybrid rice.[58] Judging by previous history, the development of hybrids is likely to benefit the private sector rather than the small farmer, with yield increases remaining quite small and seed prices becoming very high. In fact, hybridisation has been called 'the scam of the century'.[59]

Rice patents and genetic engineering

A number of circumstances have now come together that make it worthwhile for biotechnology companies to enter the rice seed market. These include: the increasing availability of patent and seed protection; the technological advance in the development and production of F1 hybrid rice seeds on a large scale; and the availability of networks promoting microcredit and new technologies, which sometimes work together.

In February 2000 Monsanto enthusiastically announced that it and other seed giants were pouring money into hybrid rice research. The company explained, 'With the advent of adequate intellectual property protection in several countries, private sector investment in rice has dramatically increased in the seed industry.'[60] Intellectual property regimes enable companies to charge an additional 10–30 per cent over the cost of any seed, in the form of royalties and licence payments. Furthermore the sequencing of the rice genome by Monsanto as well as Syngenta shows their keen interest in establishing leadership in the now lucrative rice seed market.

According to the Philippine Farmer–Scientist Partnership for Development, MASIPAG,[61] IRRI has field-tested genetically engineered blight- and blast-resistant rice and are also working on Bt rice. Components of the resistant rice, from the gene itself down to the markers and promoter, are patented by Monsanto, Novartis and other Northern companies or institutions.

In January 2001 the first samples of the GM pro-Vitamin A rice, known as Golden Rice, arrived at IRRI (see pp. 135–40) to be welcomed by its Director-General, Ronald P. Cantrell:

> The arrival of these initial samples at IRRI is a very significant step and allows us to finally start on the required testing processes using local rice varieties. IRRI expects to play a major role in the ongoing 'Golden Rice' research effort and its eventual introduction to the world's millions of poor rice farmers and consumers.[62]

Companies including Syngenta Seeds AG, Syngenta Ltd (Novartis & Zeneca), Bayer AG, Monsanto Company Inc., Orynova BV, and Zeneca Mogen BV have patents on technologies and gene sequences involved in Golden Rice. Syngenta was later granted the rights to commercialise Golden Rice and it was agreed that no charge would be made for 'humanitarian use' in any developing nation. Syngenta has now become a major funder of IRRI.

Bt treasure trove

Plant Genetics Systems (PGS), later owned by Aventis, which in turn has become Bayer CropScience, also worked with IRRI. In 1996, hybridisation and insect tolerance accounted for over 90 per cent of the PGS research and development budget. The primary target was to genetically engineer crops with insecticidal toxins from the soil bacterium *Bacillus thuringiensis* (Bt toxins). The PGS collection of over 12,000 strains of *Bacillus thuringiensis* was mainly obtained from IRRI in Laguna, the Philippines, as part of a two-year project funded by the Rockefeller Foundation for the isolation, identification and characterisation of Bt strains able to kill rice pests.[63] Many of these were taken from IRRI in return simply for the training of some IRRI scientists in PGS's laboratories.

International foundations

There are a number of extremely powerful international, mostly US-based foundations involved in agriculture and biodiversity projects in the South. They include the Ford, Rockefeller, MacArthur and Winrock foundations. Many of these large US foundations are built on corporate profits from major industries such as oil and automobiles from bygone days. Some of their funding assets will have been drawn from the exploitation of resources in the global South. In the 1950s the Rockefeller and Ford Foundations sent

agricultural researchers to the Third World to work alongside national institute personnel (see p. 188). Both foundations were also founders and architects,
with the World Bank, of the CGIAR system, established in 1971. Although
these foundations support projects carried out by local communities in the
Third World, the decision to grant the money and the rules about how it is
to be used are made by a US foundation. Moreover, US foundations are
obliged by statute to abide by US policy and promote US interests abroad.
The cynical could therefore be forgiven for feeling that they are just another
arm of US government, albeit indirect.

The Rockefeller Foundation[64]

The Rockefeller Foundation describes itself as a 'knowledge-based, global
foundation with a commitment to enrich and sustain the lives and livelihoods of poor and excluded people throughout the world'.[65] Founded in
1913 and endowed by multi-millionaire John D. Rockefeller, it has since
given more than $2 billion in grants worldwide. For 1999, the Foundation
had a grant-making budget of $177 million dedicated to projects that
'promote the well-being of mankind throughout the world'.[66] Its assets are
given as $3.5 billion.

The Foundation's general objectives are set out as the promotion of
scientific advancement. Its association with the science of genes began
during the 1930s, when Warren Weaver of the Rockefeller Foundation
coined the term 'molecular biology' and poured money into research. It also
began funding agricultural projects in the South during the 1930s and was
perhaps the major proponent of the green revolution. Now it is one of the
biggest funders of genetic engineering projects in the South, both directly
and indirectly through the ISAAA (see below) and other NGOs. It has a
large agricultural biotechnology programme, funding all aspects of genetic
engineering research and work on patenting with Southern agricultural
institutions.

The Foundation initiated an International Programme on Rice Biotechnology in 1983. Over the next 17 years, $105 million were spent on
furthering the development of rice varieties and capacity building, culmi-
nating in 2000 with a series of final rice grants awarded in Asia. The funding
emphasis has now begun to shift towards Africa.[67] These funds constitute a
considerable portion of overall funding for agriculture research in many
developing countries and, consequently, the Rockefeller Foundation exerts
a significant influence over the direction of national R&D.

In 1998, when Professor Gordon Conway became president, the Rockefeller Foundation moved to take a middle position in the global GM debate.
Conway distinguishes between the use of *tissue cultures*, to cross species that

would only very rarely cross in nature; *marker-aided selection*, which helps to identify a gene in normal cross-breeding; and *genetic engineering,* when discussing biotechnology.[68] He situates biotechnology within the Foundation's support of integrated pest management (IPM) – an agricultural system that moves away from using chemical pesticides and encourages the use of natural predators – and he argues that certain genetic engineering applications, such as genetically engineered pro-vitamin A rice, can contribute to food security. Conway has publicly criticised Monsanto and other companies for fast-tracking GM products in the South and developing Terminator seeds, but at the same time he supports the participation of the private sector in the expansion of biotech R&D in the South. Conway believes that the needs of the poor and the interests of the biotech TNCs can be brought together. In this spirit he has urged corporations to abandon their pursuit of Terminator seeds and to allow exceptions in their intellectual property rights to make important crops freely available to subsistence farmers.

The first agreement of this kind concerns the Pro-Vitamin A rice developed by Swiss and German researchers with funds from the Rockefeller Foundation (see pp. 135–40). Syngenta acquired the rights to Golden Rice on condition that it make the rice freely available to a segment of farmers – those earning less than $10,000 from it each year – if the rice they produce is not exported. An IPR adviser at the CGIAR says that this kind of market segmentation is a 'practical problem' in areas 'where there are both subsistence and large-scale farmers'.[69] The Public Sector Intellectual Property Resource for Agriculture (PIPRA) was launched in July 2003 to facilitate further agreements for access to patented technologies for 'humanitarian use' for the benefit of both subsistence farmers and US agriculture.

The Rockefeller Foundation also funds non-GM research, looking at natural pest and weed management as exemplified by work at the Nairobi-based International Centre of Insect Physiology and Ecology (ICIPE), where research is being carried out into termite, stemborer and tsetse fly control, and into controlling losses in maize cultivation from stemborers and *striga* weeds using napier grass and *desmodium* plants.[70]

International organisations promoting biotechnology

International Service for the Acquisition of Agri-biotech Applications (ISAAA)

> *Biotechnology offers the unique opportunity to deliver a scale-neutral and appropriate technology to subsistence farmers by incorporating one of the most sophisticated technologies known to science in the technology best known and accepted by farmers, the seed.*
>
> ISAAA mission statement

The ISAAA was set up in 1991, based on the earlier International Biotechnology Collaboration Programme.[71] It collaborates with research institutions in the South, brokering agreements to develop biotechnology projects and secure funding through other research institutions and corporate research programmes. In 2001 the ISAAA was operating in twelve countries – Indonesia, Malaysia, the Philippines, Thailand and Vietnam in Asia; Kenya, Egypt and Zimbabwe in Africa; and Argentina, Brazil, Costa Rica and Mexico in Latin America.

The ISAAA is closely linked to the CGIAR network. It was set up and is still run by Dr Clive James, former Deputy Director-General of the CIMMYT.

- The first ISAAA centre, the *AmeriCenter*, opened in 1992 at Cornell University in the US, where the ISAAA's most recent Executive Director, Anatole Krattiger, another former CIMMYT employee, was stationed.

- The *AfriCenter* is based at the regional office of the CIP, Kenya.

- The *SEAsia Center* is based at IRRI in the Philippines.

- The *EuroCenter* is based at the John Innes Centre, in the UK

- The *AsiaCenter* is based at Technova Inc., in Japan.

Donors include the World Bank, Rockefeller Foundation, USAID, the UN Environment Programme, Aventis (AgrEvo), Novartis, Monsanto, Pioneer Hi-Bred International, Cargill Seeds International, Dow Agro-Sciences, the Biotechnology and Biological Science Research Centre (BBSRC) (UK), the Gatsby Charitable Foundation (UK) and the Hitachi Foundation (Japan). Both Monsanto and Novartis have been on the board of directors. Other directors include representatives from CGIAR and the World Bank. Norman Borlaug and M. S. Swaminathan, two of the best-known scientists of the green revolution, are patrons.

As well as technology transfer, the ISAAA promotes 'capacity building' workshops and training for national policy makers and scientists. These encourage the development of national regimes of intellectual property based on the US model. Such a system of 'plant patenting' has been resisted by many Southern NGOs and scientists. ISAAA also provides fellowships and exchanges for Southern scientists to visit high-tech corporate research facilities.

ISAAA has brokered deals between Monsanto and research institutes in Mexico and Kenya (see Box, p. 127: 'Monsanto and the ISAAA'). Other ISAAA projects include the tomato spotted wilt virus project in Indonesia and the Papaya Biotechnology Network (aiming to eradicate the papaya ring spot virus or PRSV). Both diseases are prevalent and enhanced by monoculture cultivation practices that commonly go hand in hand with cash-crop planting for the export market. In this context it is unclear how these projects will be of value or affordable to small farmers; indeed, it seems that they might further the expansion of cash-crop farming at the expense of food security. One-gene defence strategies may amount to little more

Monsanto and the ISAAA

Monsanto donated genes for protection against potato viruses X and Y (PVX and PVY) to Mexican researchers for engineering into local varieties of potatoes grown for local consumption. The same genes were donated to the Kenyan Agricultural Research Institute (KARI) for sweet potatoes which can suffer from the same plant viruses. The ISAAA brokered both these deals while the Rockefeller Foundation provided funding. As part of the deal, Monsanto provided not only the genes but also training for Mexican researchers, one of whom studied field trial protocols and regulatory issues in the US.

Monsanto gained not only from familiarising Mexicans with the idea of transgenic crops, but also in managing to export industry-friendly TRIPs-style regulatory procedures to Mexico. In doing so, Monsanto managed to ease the entry of its own commercial varieties into the country.

According to the ISAAA, the deal 'helped Mexico establish regulatory procedures and a bio-safety review system.... The US companies were able to supply Mexican authorities with information on field problems, on potential risks that field testing might pose, and on how to deal with them.'[76]

The work at KARI was started by Dr Florence M. Wambugu, who trained at Monsanto and who was the head of the ISAAA's AfriCenter until October 2001. She is an outspoken supporter of genetic engineering technology, and is frequently quoted as an independent Southern scientist by Monsanto and the biotech industry as a whole. She said of her critics: 'They don't want Africa to embrace biotechnology because they know the technology has the potential to solve Kenya's famine problems.'[77]

Florence Wambugu has been engaged as a strongly pro-biotechnology speaker at international events sponsored by the biotech industry, such as the lunchtime lectures at the Biosafety Protocol negotiations during the Biosafety Convention held in Montreal in 2000.

With the engineering of one unpopular potato variety against the American strain of the virus, the KARI sweet potato project has done little to meet the needs of small farmers. Instead it helped to drive the implementation of legislation on intellectual property rights and biosafety in Kenya in exactly the same way as Monsanto's gift of potato genes achieved the introduction of a biotech-friendly regulatory regime in Mexico.[78]

than a short-term techno-fix further compounding the agricultural problems of both South and North. In short,

> ISAAA is a valuable tool for the biotech industry. On the one hand, it supports a constant stream of public relations exercises to propagate hype about humanitarian motives behind biotechnology. On the other hand, it concentrates on generating the proper business climate for the biotech industry's market expansion in important developing countries.[72]

The Citizens' Network for Foreign Affairs (CNFA)

The CNFA describes itself as a 'non-profit, non-partisan organisation dedicated to stimulating international economic growth in developing and emerging world markets'.[73] The brainchild of former US secretary of state Henry Kissinger, it was founded in 1985 just as cracks were emerging in the former USSR. Its name, suggesting a civil society organisation, is misleading. An alliance of some 250 US organisations in agribusiness and banking, it counts Monsanto and Pioneer among its members. It is closely linked with the Citizens' Network Agribusiness Alliance (CNAA) and is an industry-led initiative set up to ensure that US agribusiness gains a stronghold in these emerging markets. CNFA president John H. Costello also has links with the World Bank, as part of its 'agribusiness and markets thematic group'.

It has been working in the food and agriculture sector of the new independent states of the former Soviet Union (Ukraine, Russia, Moldova and Belarus) and in southern Africa (Zimbabwe, Mozambique and Zambia). The CNFA is expanding its model of public–private partnerships into different economic sectors and disciplines, and into other developing areas of the globe. An important part of its work has been to create a hospitable political and legal climate for US business. In the Ukraine, the CNFA has been very active in promoting Monsanto's GM potatoes (see Chapter 7). Its representative in the Ukraine, environmental lawyer Wayne Williams, worked with the Ukraine Ministry of the Environment to prepare GMO legislation.[74] Beyond this, the CNFA is involved in international lobbying:

> To protect the investments of American agribusinesses, CNFA also supports local agricultural institutions which challenge entrenched state systems that hinder the fledgling private sector. Internationally, CNFA's participation in the Gore–Chernomyrdin and Gore–Kuchma commissions helps ensure effective representation of US agribusiness in bilateral discussions.[75]

Corporate supporters and sponsors include: AgrEvo, American Home Products Corporation, ADM, Cargill Inc., Cyanamid International, Dekalb Genetics, DowAgroSciences, DuPont, Farmland Industries, Iowa Export–Import, Kraft, Monsanto, Novartis, Pioneer Hi-Bred International and Rhone–Poulenc.

THE AGRIBUSINESS PARTNERSHIPS PROGRAM

This public–private partnership is a win–win initiative. It will help US agribusiness compete and succeed in Ukraine without shouldering all the risks on their own, while USAID benefits from leverage that will provide more agricultural assistance for every US taxpayer dollar invested in the program.[79]

John Costello, CNFA president, 1995

In 1993, the CNFA was awarded $44.5 million by USAID and $109 million by US agribusiness to implement a three-year Food Systems Restructuring Program in the former Soviet Union. The aim of this programme was 'to replace ageing and inefficient state-owned communist-style enterprises with privately owned and operated commercial joint ventures'. USAID subsequently gave a further $26.5 million, while an additional $32.4 million was contributed by Russian and Ukrainian partners. The Russian programme was mainly completed by 1996, with a further $100 million in private sector assets being leveraged in 2001 to strengthen food systems in Ukraine, Belarus and Moldova.

There are currently 19 partnerships in Ukraine and Moldova. They cover the full spectrum of food production: from agricultural inputs (seed, fertiliser, pesticides), to food and feed processing and marketing. US companies that have established joint ventures through CNFA's Agribusiness Partnerships Program include Monsanto, Global Agricultural Management Enterprises, Cargill (Seed and Fertiliser), Cyanamid, Progressive Genetics, Pure Sunshine, Developed Technology Resource Inc., Kyiv-Atlantic and Food Pro.

RAISE (RURAL AGRICULTURAL INPUT SUPPLY EXPANSION)

RAISE is yet another CNFA programme – this time in Zimbabwe – to expand the market for transnational agricultural corporations. The following project description for 1999–2001, found on the CNFA website, illustrates the new interest taken by transnationals in small farmers:

Smallholder farmers in Zimbabwe will not be able to make the transition from subsistence to commercial farming without modern agricultural inputs. International farm input supply companies such as Monsanto, American Cyanamid, Cargill, Novartis, and Pioneer are active in Zimbabwe. Many see the market potential in the small-scale farming sector, but the distribution network to get agricultural inputs from the supplier to smallholder farmers is inadequate. As a result, less than 10 per cent of farm inputs sold in Zimbabwe reach small-scale farmers though they outnumber large-scale farmers 200:1.

In order to stimulate expansion of supply links to small-scale farmers, CNFA's RAISE program is working with both village-level retailers and agricultural input suppliers to build effective links between the two. RAISE will develop a commercially sustainable web of input wholesalers and retailers who can expand their markets and sell inputs to smallholder farmers.[80]

Other current programmes of the CNFA

The following programme descriptions are taken directly from the CNFA website:

Development Education – The CNFA engages public and private sector leaders throughout the United States in unique dialogue on the US stake in promoting economic growth and sustainable development in the world's emerging economies.

Citizens' Network Corporate Sponsor Program – The CNFA offers a special programme to US food and agribusiness executives and other interested parties to keep them abreast of new investment opportunities in emerging economies, particularly those of the former Soviet Union. Through the voluntary contributions of its sponsors, the CNFA can continue to foster the development of market-based economic systems, democratic structures, and trade and investment opportunities in emerging markets around the globe.

Citizens' Network Agribusiness Alliance (CNAA) – More than 250 businesses, organisations and individuals participate in the CNAA, which harnesses the creativity and technical know-how of its members to redesign food and agriculture systems and build markets in developing and emerging economies.

Agribusiness Volunteer Program – This programme sends US agribusiness professionals and farmers on short-term overseas assignments to provide direct, hands-on assistance to their counterparts in emerging economies and developing nations.

RAISE is now expanding to Malawi. In June 2002 CNFA received a Rockefeller Foundation grant of $2 million for rural development in southern Africa. The main aim is stated as:

> Development, in partnership with farm input supply companies, of a financially sustainable business management training program for Malawi designed specifically to enable village-level shopkeepers to qualify as farm input distributors and receive inventory credit from supply companies.... Creation of a guarantee fund to stimulate an increase in farm input supplier credit to village retailers and thereby improve and expand the flow of inputs to disadvantaged smallholder farmers in Malawi.[81]

In contrast, the organisation UBINIG (Policy Research for Development Alternatives) of Bangladesh believes that closing down shops that sell agricultural inputs is one of their major achievements.[82] It highlights the degree to which Africa is being targeted as a new frontier by the corporations and their networks. They may hope to meet with less resistance in Africa than in Asia, just because the green revolution failed to take root in Africa and people are less aware of the likely impacts than they are in Asia (see Chapter 8; see also World Bank, this chapter, pp. 104–6).

Universities and research institutes

> *The universities are cheering us on, telling us to get closer to industry, encouraging us to consult with big business....We can't help but be influenced from time to time by our desire to see certain results happen in the lab.... All of these companies have a piece of me. I'm getting checks waved at me from Monsanto and American Cyanamid and Dow, and it's hard to balance the public interest with the private interest. It's a very difficult juggling act, and sometimes I don't know how to juggle it all.*
>
> John Benedict, former Texas AM University entomologist[83]

There are a number of reasons for the influence that biotechnology companies exercise over universities and research institutes. Biology used to be of little interest to industry; now it has become a major field for identifying profitable applications and technologies. At the same time the equipment and materials needed for research, especially in molecular biology, are very expensive, requiring high-grade chemicals and facilities. Governments eager to participate, such as the UK, Canada, Australia and the US, have contributed funds to promote partnerships between universities and industry. Such high costs put biotech research beyond the reach of many Southern governments, especially where they are cutting back expenditure due to structural adjustment programmes. Moreover, private research money is not currently going to Southern countries. In addition, the General Agreement on Trade in Services, one of the World Trade Organisation agreements, facilitates companies seeking to access and exploit university resources and set up whole departments within universities worldwide. The agrochemical industry offers lucrative research contracts and grants to training colleges, universities and research institutes to carry out particular research. However, it should not be forgotten that these companies benefit in return from public funding in the form of university infrastructure and other resources, such as intellectual capital and reputation. This diversion of public resources to private ends does not take into account the fact that most of these institutions were set up with public money for the common good, not to generate private profit. Industry is keen to promote its interests as being identical with the public interest, but there is considerable disquiet about the impact of corporate sponsorship on the independence of universities and the direction of research.

The increasing corporate colonisation of universities is another example of the appropriation of public assets that we are now experiencing in so many spheres, whether it is the water supply or traditional knowledge about medicinal plants. In the UK, organisations such as the Council for Academic

Autonomy and the Council for Academic Freedom and Academic Standards are concerned to raise awareness of the issues.

Many educational and research establishments are now shaping academic courses towards winning corporate funding. Increasingly, scientific research is directed to areas with an industrial application, as companies seek to recover costs by bringing products to market quickly. Science and industry have come to be seen by politicians and university presidents as one and the same. Across most of the OECD countries, science policy is now the domain of government departments of industry.

Genetic engineering is an obvious example of a highly 'bankable' subject, offering the potential for big returns, so long as products can be developed. Indeed, the Biotechnology and Biological Science Research Council (BBSRC) reported that in the US, as closures and rationalisation plans dogged other university sectors, 'life sciences' was one of the fastest-growing university disciplines with 20 per cent growth between 1995 and 2000.[84] This makes it very difficult for scientists to remain independent – and objective. It also makes it hard for them to speak out, since they risk compromising their ability to work if they criticise the system or the priorities imposed by company funders. The threat to the future of independent science is clear, as already documented in 1990 by Henk Hobbelink:

> Monsanto has donated $23.5 million to Washington University for biotech research; Bayer is contributing to the Max Planck Institute in Cologne for the same purpose; and Hoechst built an entire $70 million biotech research laboratory for the Massachusetts General Hospital where research on crop genetics is also carried out.... Of the Hoechst grant for a biotech lab, one researcher has commented: 'Essentially, everyone in that lab is an indentured servant to Hoechst.' In most contracts, the TNC has the right to the first look at the results and can delay publication of them until patent possibilities are investigated.[85]

In other cases, companies and corporations contract out work to universities. To decode the rice genome, Monsanto relied on a new gene sequencing approach producing the data primarily in the laboratories of Dr Leroy Hood, at Washington University in Seattle under contract to the company.

Another approach is to sponsor high-level posts at universities. The Pioneer Hi-Bred Agronomy Professorship and the Pioneer Hi-Bred chairs in Agribusiness, Molecular Biology and Science and Technology Policy have all helped Pioneer Hi-Bred's cause at Iowa State University. As Steven Rose, Professor of Biology at the UK's Open University, has remarked,

> the old idea that universities were a place of independence has gone. Instead of which one's got secrecy, one's got patents, one's got shareholders.[86]

Corporate funding of US universities and patents

It is reported that in the US corporate funding of universities has multiplied sevenfold since 1970. It is still less than 8 per cent of the grand total but it is having a marked impact on the direction of research and on the manner in which it is undertaken.

Examples of partnerships include:

- Novartis, 1998: $25 million over five years to the University of California at Berkeley in return for being allowed to sift through plant and microbial biology research.

- Washington University in St Louis has had a funding deal with Monsanto for 20 years.

- Ribozyme Pharmaceuticals gave the University of Colorado a five-year, $500,000 unrestricted research grant in exchange for university research.

Nelson Kiang, professor emeritus at the Massachusetts Institute of Technology, has seen this kind of sponsorship increase massively over the years and believes that the university ethos of the free exchange of ideas is coming more and more into conflict with the corporate desire for business secrecy. The *Christian Science Monitor* reported in 2001:

> In fiscal 1999, more than 120 US research universities filed a total of 7,612 patent applications, according to the Association of University Technology Managers. Licenses to industry generated $641 million in gross income for the universities – and about $40 billion in economic activity overall.
>
> 'You used to have big corporations with labs that would do their own basic research,' Mr Kiang says. 'But ... it's much more effective to turn the universities into R&D labs for them. By sprinkling money around ... they don't have to compete for the best brains in the academic world, they simply buy them at low cost.'[87]

Unfortunately patent possibilities and financial interests in the outcome of research are reported to lead to delays in revealing breakthroughs. Corporate funding of university research is also reported to lead to less sharing of research information (a traditional academic freedom), the blocking of reports critical of new projects, and legal action against the reporters. Researchers may have a financial interest in the success of their research and be tempted to 'talk up' the results or suppress bad ones. It has also been found that many researchers receive research-related gifts. And these interests are not usually disclosed, leading to calls for more rules about disclosures of interests (see also Chapter 2, pp. 24–5).

Biotechnology and Biological Science Research Council (BBSRC) UK[88]

The BBSRC is Britain's leading funding agency for academic research and training in the biosciences. It was established in 1994 and according to its own mission statement its purpose is 'to sustain a broad base of inter-disciplinary research and training to help industry, commerce and government create wealth'.[89] It replaced the Agriculture and Food Research Council (AFRC) and also took over some of the research funded under the Science and Engineering Research Council (SERC). The BBSRC is pre-dominantly funded by taxpayers through the Science Budget. This is controlled by the Department of Trade and Industry via the Office of Science and Technology – at present under the auspices of Lord Sainsbury.

In 1998, the Labour government's white paper on competitiveness launched a 'reach-out' fund to encourage universities to 'work more effectively with business'. The role of Higher Education Funding Councils, which provide the core money for universities, was redefined 'to ensure that higher education is responsive to industry'.

The chairman of the BBSRC from May 1998 to 2003 was Peter Doyle, the former chief executive of Zeneca. The BBSRC's strategy board has featured representatives of many companies over time, including Syngenta, GlaxoSmithKline and Genetix plc. in 2002. The Council has seven specialist committees, each overseeing the funding of different branches of biology. Zeneca is represented on all of them.[90]

In all, BBSRC funding has supported 98 UK research establishments and university departments. Representatives from some of these advise government, sit on regulatory committees and often get a public hearing.

- The BBSRC sponsors many of the key players in genetic engineering such as the Institute of Arable Crop Research, which is involved in assessing the GM farm scale trials, and the Institute of Food Research.

- In January 1999 the BBSRC set aside £15 million for 'a new initiative to help British researchers win the race to identify the function of key genes'. During 1999, further grants for £19 million and £11 million were announced.

- The BBSRC also funds the secondment of academics to corporations where they 'influence basic research relevant to company objectives'.

- The Council launched a Biotechnology Young Entrepreneurs Scheme aimed at encouraging more enterprise in the biosciences.

- The BBSRC has paid for researchers to work for Nestlé, Unilever, Glaxo Wellcome, SmithKlineBeecham, Aventis, Dupont, Rhone–Poulenc and Zeneca.

The John Innes Centre (JIC), UK

The BBSRC is the main public funding body of the John Innes Centre (JIC), UK, – contributing 47 per cent (or about £12.1 million) in 1999–2000, for example. It also funds the Sainsbury Laboratory, which is on the same site near Norwich in Norfolk, and which also receives about £2.4 million annually from the Gatsby Charitable Foundation (one of the Sainsbury trusts). Both the JIC and the Sainsbury Laboratory are companies limited by guarantee. The Centre is world renowned for its plant research and is often perceived as an independent public institution. The JIC presents itself as essentially publicly and charitably funded. According to its own annual report, in 1999–2000 it received funding from AstraZeneca, Aventis (AgrEvo), Monsanto, Unilever, Novartis Crop Protection, DuPont and the International Atomic Energy Authority.

The JIC also had a 10-year research agreement with AstraZeneca worth about £60 million (US$86.3 million) to establish the Zeneca Wheat Improvement Centre, later called simply the Syngenta Laboratory, in the Genome Centre on the Norfolk site. In September 2002 Syngenta announced that it would pull out of the project, citing the need for rationalisation following the merger of Novartis and AstraZeneca's agricultural research divisions. The JIC and the BBSRC announced their regret but insisted that this would not damage their commitment to wheat research.[91]

Although direct commercial sponsorship is less than 10 per cent of the overall annual funding, corporate influence extends to the whole culture within which the JIC operates.[92] In this way corporations gain an influence disproportionate to their contribution. Furthermore, the GM policy the JIC promotes appears to originate from a public institution, which gives it more respectability than if it came clearly from industry. It is worth noting that public funding for the Centre, via the BBSRC, was heftily increased by Lord Sainsbury as Parliamentary Under-Secretary of State for Science. A strong GM proponent, he also has a more pervasive influence on UK government policy. Until 1998, he was chairman of J. Sainsbury plc, the supermarket chain which contributes significant funds to the Labour Party.

The director of the JIC, Professor Chris Lamb, rounded off a reply (27 March 2000) to a letter of concern about the industrial linkages to the Centre's research with the following statement: 'I'm fighting the good fight for GM foods.'[93] The JIC has its own intellectual property company, Plant Biosciences Limited, and pursues a strong policy of patent protection.

On the educational front, the Centre organises pro-GM school projects and CD-Roms. It hosts the Teacher–Scientist Network, and with that body has commissioned a play about GM to tour UK secondary schools.

Golden Rice – and the Swiss Federal Institute of Technology

I share Greenpeace's disgust about the heavy PR campaign of some agbiotech companies using results from our experiments, which were exclusively done within public research institutions, and using exclusively public funding.

Ingo Potrykus, co-inventor of Golden Rice[94]

Vitamin A deficiency (VAD) affects 100–140 million children worldwide and causes 250,000–500,000 vitamin-A-deficient children to become blind every year, half of them dying within 12 months of losing their sight.[95] With its promise to combat VAD, Golden Rice was quickly identified and adopted as the long-awaited saviour for the beleaguered biotech industry. Overnight it became their symbol of genetic engineering's promise.

However, for others Golden Rice symbolises 'application-driven' science with a narrow focus and a top-down approach, characterised by a failure to consider the broader implications of the proposed development. Like the green revolution, it seeks to substitute technical solutions for necessary political and social change. Golden Rice demonstrates the use of patents and the barriers they create, the cost and complexity of dealing with multiple owners of intellectual property, and the use of public relations to persuade the public to accept genetic engineering 'solutions' in general. It also demonstrates the complexity of the relationship between 'independent' research and corporate interests, and provides an example of how publicly funded research can be co-opted by private interests.

In January 2000, an article in *Science* announced the creation of a genetically engineered rice containing pro-vitamin A (beta-carotene).[96] As the beta-carotene colours the grain orange, the rice was named Golden Rice. A pre-print of the article was sent to journalists around the world, ensuring global coverage of the news.

EXCLUSIVE RIGHTS FOR INDUSTRY

In May 2000, AstraZeneca (now Syngenta) and Germany-based Greenovation[97] acquired exclusive rights to commercialise Golden Rice. The inventors say that this deal will give poor farmers in developing countries free access to the genetically engineered rice (see above), while allowing the life sciences company to sell it commercially in the developed world: what is called market segregation. Zeneca itself admits that the two-tier system will be hard to police. The Peasant Farmer Movement of the Philippines (Kilusang Magbubukid ng Pilipinas or KMP) made the following statement:

Why should Zeneca have the right to patent for its own profit the results of publicly funded research? And why should anyone believe that this is for the poor when Zeneca has made it clear that their motive is to make money from the technology in the North?[98]

On 2 June 2000 BIOTHAI, KMP and MASIPAG (Farmer–Scientist Partnership for Development) issued a statement saying moves like Zeneca's 'are clouding the real issues of poverty and control over resources'.[99] And Gordon Conway, president of the Rockefeller Foundation, said in an interview:

> I agree ... that the public relations uses of Golden Rice have gone too far. The industry's advertisements and the media in general seem to forget that it is a research product that needs considerable further development before it will be available to farmers and consumers.[100]

WHAT'S LIES BEHIND THE PATENT ISSUE?

The research was presented publicly as the work of the independent Zurich-based Swiss Federal Institute of Technology, led by Dr Ingo Potrykus, in collaboration with Peter Beyer (University of Freiburg, Germany). Potrykus had spent the last 10 years working on this technology, transferring three genes from daffodils and bacteria into rice. His research was mostly funded by the Rockefeller Foundation and for shorter periods by (amongst others) the European Union, the Swiss Federal Office for Education and Science and (through the contribution to the carotinoid sub-project in the EU Biotech Programme) the company AstraZeneca.[101]

The *Scientist* reported in 2001:

> Potrykus maintained that 'from the beginning' he wanted to make golden rice available free of charge. Still, he couldn't turn his research into a product as a 'freedom-to-operate' study [carried out by ISAAA] revealed that 70 patents belonging to 32 holders covered technology used in the process. He convinced AstraZeneca to help tackle the problem, and together they agreed on a definition of humanitarian use that could circumvent patent obstacles: 'Everything which leads to a less-than-$10,000 annual income to farmers should be considered a humanitarian use,' Potrykus stated. The public/private compact paved the way for patent waivers.[102]

Co-inventor Peter Beyer stated in an interview with the *Hindu* newspaper on 7 November 2002:

> Farmers can produce and sell Golden Rice to the tune of $10,000 a year. But they can only sell it within the country and not export it.

There are at least three issues here. The first is the breeding of Golden Rice transgenes (engineered genes) into local rice varieties – the inventors' preferred option. 'Local varieties' might mean farmers' varieties but, in view of their widespread replacement by high-input varieties, could equally mean varieties like the widely grown IR64 rice developed by the Philippines IRRI. Harmut Meyer of GENET (European NGO Network on genetic Engineering) comments on the potential consequences:

[E]ach rice variety that carries the Golden Rice transgenes seems to be barred from export by patents and contracts. If that is really true, the Golden Rice story gains a completely new dimension. The celebrated licence agreement in which biotech companies allow the use of patented technology for humanitarian use could have the potential to serve as means to control the rice economy of a whole country. One central demand to the inventors and owners of the Golden Rice is to disclose all licence agreements.

The second issue is potential patent infringement claims arising from unintentional cross-pollination of rice with the Golden Rice transgenes – as has been the case for Canadian farmer Percy Schmeiser, successfully sued by Monsanto for having their patented gene in his oilseed rape crop.

The third is whether the patent dilemma has been exaggerated or used as an excuse to hand all the rights to Syngenta. GRAIN noted that:

> of the 60 countries with Vitamin A deficiency – which Golden Rice is supposed to address – only 25 could possibly honour any of the patents involved. And in these countries, only 11 of the patents could constrain the project locally. Seven of those are held by four transnational corporations (Syngenta, Aventis, Monsanto and DuPont), two of which have expressed their interest to make the technology freely available to the poor. The other patents are held by public institutions. Furthermore, ISAAA's study looked at patent *applications* filed through the World Intellectual Property Office [sic], without confirming whether the patents were actually granted or not in the different countries.[103]

On the subject of patents Potrykus had strong words: 'So many fields of research are blocked by corporate patents. I had to ignore them or I couldn't move at all.' Scientists should simply break the law, he said. 'What company wants the negative publicity of putting me in jail for fighting poverty?'[104] On a similar note he observed in 2001 that 'industry cannot be expected to be bothered about problems of people and well-being of the poor as its interests are different'.[105]

However, Ingo Potrykus used to work at the Novartis-owned research institute, FMI, and he still has very close connections to this company. According to the Blueridge Institute,

> database research revealed that Ingo Potrykus is named as 'inventor' and thus has interest in 30 plant-related patents, most of them belonging to Novartis [now Syngenta]. The latest Novartis patent with Potrykus as inventor was issued in February 1999 (No. US 5976880). Furthermore Potrykus admits himself that they filed a patent application for the transgenic rice ('before others do it').[106]

ACCESS TO VITAMIN A AND OTHER MICRONUTRIENTS

The biotech industry seems to suggest that Golden Rice is the only way to save children from VAD and blindness. So what happened to the natural sources of vitamin A, foods of animal origin such as eggs, dairy products, liver, meat or salt-water fish? The human body also produces vitamin A from pro-vitamin A (beta-carotene), which can be found in many plants, especially in carrots, yellow cassava, yellow sweet potato, mango and apricots (also in dried form), leafy greens such as spinach, coriander, curry and radish leaves, and, most of all, red palm oil.

The problem is not a lack of foods containing vitamin A and beta-carotene, but a lack of access to these foods. It is 'hidden hunger', including the loss of knowledge about the relation between diet and health, and the consequences of eating only rice. Furthermore, vitamin A and beta-carotene are fat-soluble nutrients and can only be properly absorbed in the presence of oil and other components. Children who suffer from diarrhoea due to dirty water and poor hygiene conditions will not be able to take up or retain nutrients like vitamin A from their food.

Consequently, the most effective international programmes targeting Vitamin A deficiency take into account cultural and economic considerations, with socially based strategies such as dietary diversification, schooling for girls and improved sanitation. In the assessment of the World Health Organisation,

> These strategies will include promoting breast feeding, dietary diversification to increase intake of vitamin A-rich foods, agricultural reform and food fortification. Public health measures to deliver vitamin A supplements, via immunisation programmes, and infection control will also contribute in appropriate situations; for example, the relative importance of each intervention which will be country-specific. The delivery of vitamin A supplements is intended as a temporary solution to VAD until other more natural methods of raising vitamin A status have been found.[107]

Through existing programmes of food fortification – and without GM crops – VAD figures are already on the decline.

Food-based projects are in progress across Africa and South-east Asia. In Bangladesh, for example, families were helped by the FAO and others to grow vitamin-rich vegetables and fruits in small home gardens or vines up the sides of their houses, and to plant beans, pumpkins and bottle gourds in the vines – all of these have leaves which are commonly eaten. Health conditions improved and it was shown that small plots of land are enough to provide sufficient vitamin A. Scientific evaluation also showed that the uptake of pro-vitamin A (beta-carotene) increased with the number of varieties of vegetable and fruit eaten by a person, independently of the quantity eaten.[108] The highest levels of pro-vitamin A are found in natural food items such as the livers of animals, carrots, red palm oil, and certain green vegetables and fruits. Most palm oil has the red colour removed from it for marketing purposes, but this also removes the pro-vitamin A. Palm oil is used throughout Asia and Africa. Leaving palm oil with its original red colour and persuading people to cook with it might be a far more useful action than trying to persuade them to accept Golden Rice.

Given all the above, the glow of Golden Rice fades rapidly, not least because Golden Rice is a single-nutrient, single-plant approach. But there are other reasons for the gold to tarnish.

WHAT HAS GOLDEN RICE TO OFFER?

Golden Rice does not exist yet in any usable form. First, pro-vitamin A is in the 'wrong' type of rice and still needs to be crossbred into varieties grown or consumed in the VAD-affected countries – this is probably the smallest of the hurdles. Second, no safety tests have yet been performed, either for human and animal consumption, or for impacts on the environment and biodiversity. Such crucial tests will take at least four years once the right variety has been developed. Third, no tests have been conducted to find out whether the beta-carotene present in Golden Rice can be absorbed when eaten and converted into Vitamin A. There is still a lack of understanding of the factors influencing this conversion and recent scientific data suggest that the conversion ratio is not 6:1, as previously thought, but rather 12:1 or even 21:1. This means that 6–21 micrograms of beta-carotene are needed to produce 1 microgram of vitamin A.

Another serious problem was first pointed out by Vandana Shiva:[109] could Golden Rice, in its current or its planned form, provide the amount of beta-carotene needed to achieve the recommended daily allowance of 400 (children aged 1–3) to 1,000 (males of 11 years and upwards) micrograms of vitamin A?[110] Whilst the current Golden Rice produces less than 1.6 micrograms of beta-carotene per gram of rice, the inventors of the pro-vitamin A rice stated that their ultimate goal was to achieve a rice that produces 2 micrograms per gram.[111] One hundred grams of rice would thus contain enough beta-carotene to produce 9.5 micrograms of vitamin A or 33.3 micrograms at best, using the old conversion ratio of 6:1 (see above). A small child would thus have to eat 1.2 to 4.2 kg of uncooked rice per day, which swells to 3.6–12.6 kg when cooked, which no child aged between 1 and 3 years could possibly do.

In comparison, one carrot, whether eaten cooked or raw, will cover the whole daily requirement, and 100–200 grams of spinach, dandelion, kale, coriander leaf or amaranth will suffice, especially when a few drops of red palm oil are added.

Golden Rice thus stands accused of being either a fraud or an intentional diversion from relatively low-cost but effective initiatives that can help people to achieve a better diet almost immediately. Furthermore, the experience of Southern farmers is that intensive rice production with the use of high chemical inputs ended their integrated farming systems that included other food sources such as fish, snails, water fowl and green leafy vegetables to provide a wide range of essential nutrients, including vitamin A.

Meanwhile, new breeds of vitamin A-rich grains have been announced, namely millet (Golden Millet – ICRISAT)[112] and rice (Dream Rice – IRRI),[113] neither of which has been genetically engineered. Even so, as with Golden Rice, those grains cannot answer the problem of hidden hunger and malnutrition, which need a far more integrated solution.

Commonwealth Scientific and Industrial Research Organisation (CSIRO)

Australia has shown itself to be a keen proponent of biotechnology. It was a member of the US-led Miami Group that sought to prevent the development of a meaningful Biosafety Protocol, and in 2003 it supported the US challenge to the EU at the WTO over GMOs. Australia's climate, the nature of its soils and the adoption of colonial agricultural practices unsuitable to its conditions have helped to cause numerous problems. It was one of the first countries where glyphosate resistance was reported in ryegrass and it has been involved in biopiracy cases, for instance appropriation of chickpea germplasm (see p. 113). As an important producer of agricultural commodities, Australia has committed itself to the search for technical solutions to its problems.

CSIRO is Australia's publicly funded national research organisation, often referred to as a government agency. It was founded in 1916 as the Advisory Council of Science and Industry by the Australian government as a step towards creating a national laboratory, so giving national standing to scientific research. After several name changes it became CSIRO in 1949 and

> gradually expanded its activities so that its research was related to almost every field of primary, secondary and tertiary industry. Many other areas affecting the community at large were also covered – such as the environment, human nutrition, conservation, urban and rural planning, water supplies. In 1971 CSIRO moved its headquarters from Melbourne to Canberra as part of a government initiative to bring the heads of its agencies closer to the daily workings of the Ministers they served.[114]

According to ecologist Richard Hindmarsh, Australia's plant breeding research has a 15 per cent involvement from the seed companies, which concentrate on particular crops for which hybrid seed can viably be developed.

> The other 85 per cent is done by CSIRO, state departments of agriculture and a number of university departments. CSIRO's R&D agenda embraces the release and widespread usage of genetically engineered plants, animals and other organisms.[115]

CSIRO is Australia's major cotton breeder, while the cotton seed market is monopolised by CSD (Cotton Seed Distributors) and its wholly owned subsidiary Cotton Seed International. Over 95 per cent of CSD's seeds are supplied by GSIRO in return for royalties.

> Both CSD and CSIRO access élite lines of seed from two US companies – Delta and Pine Land Co. and Cokers Pedigree Seed – for cross-breeding purposes.... What all these developments highlight is that, similar to the US trend, a convergence is occurring in Australia between the private and public plant breeding and seeds sectors under the impact of PBR [plant breeders' rights] and genetic engineering R&D. There is also a noticeable trend towards concentration of the private seeds sector. With regard to genetic engineering, already on the market is CSIRO-developed transgenic cotton – where the natural biopesticide gene inserted, that confers resistance to caterpillars, is licensed to CSIRO by Monsanto.[116]

CSIRO is actively developing genetic use restriction technology (GURT) applications for its patented gene switch ('pPLEX') technology. To this purpose it entered into a joint venture in 1999 with RhoBio (a Rhone–Poulenc and Biogemma venture specialising in the plant biotechnology of field crops), who will develop this technology for major crops, especially the cereal crops corn, wheat, rice and barley (see Chapter 8).[117]

Concerning biotechnology in the field crops sector, CSIRO states on its website that it has

> entered strategic alliances with R&D providers and funders, and industry. The aim is to help position the Australian industry with its own valuable intellectual property, enabling it to negotiate positions which give the freedom to operate in its own right or on appropriate terms in joint ventures with the multinationals.[118]

CSIRO finds a market for its own intellectual property (germplasm) and particular technologies, or accesses those of others, through alliances. Allies have included agbiotech corporations such as AgrEvo (Aventis) or Rhone–Poulenc Agro; national bodies such as the Australian National Insect Collection, the Australian National University; and Australian companies such as BioDiscovery and several grain companies.

A key alliance for insect bioprospecting, for example, was formed between CSIRO and BioDiscovery in 1997, with CSIRO creating a library of extracts obtained from insects collected across Australia and BioDiscovery screening the library for pharmaceutical or crop protection leads. In November 1998 Rhone–Poulenc Agro joined with an AU$1.5 million three-year agreement in order to find 'new natural products which are active in crop protection'.[119]

Notes

1 Greenpeace, 'Monsanto's GE Potatoes on the Loose Again', press release, 17 September 1999.

2 Quoted in David Korten, *When Corporations Rule the World*, London: Earthscan, 1995, p. 159.

3 www.worldbank.org.

4 Korten, *When Corporations Rule*, pp. 171–2.

5 *Ibid.*, p. 160.

6 T. J. Goering and World Bank, 'Agricultural Research: Sector Policy Paper', Washington, DC: World Bank, 1981, pp. 21–2.

7 Jules Pretty, *Regenerating Agriculture*, London: Earthscan, 1995.

8 Martin S. Wolfe, 'Crop Strength Through Diversity', *Nature* 406 (2000), 681–2.

9 Mark Weisbrot, Dean Baker, Egor Kraev and Judy Chen, 'The Scorecard on Globalization, 1980–2000: Twenty Years of Diminished Progress'; Mark Weisbrot, Dean Baker, Robert Naiman and Gila Neta, 'Growth May Be Good for the Poor but Are IMF and World Bank Policies Good for Growth?' Papers by the Centre for Economic and Policy Research, May 2001, http://www.cepr.net

10 David Gisselquist, Jacob Kampen, J. Trevor Sykes, and Gary Alex, 'Initiatives for Sustainable Seed Systems in Africa', paper prepared for the World Bank by the Sub-Saharan Africa Seed Initiative (SSASI) Team, Washington, DC: World Bank. http://www.fao.org/ag/AGP/AGPS/abidjan/Paper12.htm#Initiatives

11 World Bank, 'Initiative for Sustainable Seed Supply Systems in Africa', proposed outline for Sub-regional Action Plan in Southern Africa, April 1999. http://www.fanrpan.org/news1.htm

12 'African Seed Trade Organisation Established' and 'Seed Supply Systems Set to Improve', *Local Seed Systems News*, 5, 2 (December 1999/January 2000), published by the Southern African Development Community, Food, Agriculture and Natural Resources Development Unit, Harare, Zimbabwe. http://www.sadc-sfanr.org.zw/sssd/lssnews/aseed.html

13 Mimi Kleiner and Marcia Ishii-Eiteman, 'Poison Profits – the G7 Pesticide Industry's Stake in the World Bank', briefing for the Pesticide Action Network, North America, 1997. http://www.50years.org/factsheets/pesticide.html

14 Janet Bell, 'Investing in Destruction – the World Bank and Biodiversity', GRAIN, November 1996. www.grain.org/publications/reports/bio8.htm

15 *Multinational Monitor*, 21, 6 (June 2000).

16 J. J. Doyle and G. J. Persley, 'New Biotechnologies: an International Perspective', 1998. Summary of an Investment Strategies study sponsored by organisations including the World Bank. http://wbln0018.worldbank.org/essd/susint.nsf/eaa8ca64a90ff8ff852569ff005fd078/b78e02e28f6f4870852569d800780b80

17 World Bank, *Thematic Perspectives and Development Effectiveness*, Annual Report, 1999. http://www.worldbank.org/html/extdr/extme/033.htm

18 World Bank, 'Agricultural and Science Roundtable with the Private Sector', press release, December 2000.

19 http://www.cgiar.org/

20 http://www.futureharvest.org

21 http://www.cgiar.org/ (December 2002).

22 http://www.startwithaseed.org

23 http://www.johannesburgsummit.org/html/sustainable_dev/p2_managing_resources/global_conservation2606.pdf

24 'CGIAR: Agricultural Research for Whom?' *Ecologist*, 26, 6 (November/December 1996): 259–70.

25 Statement by the NGO Committee of the CGIAR, 1 November 2002. www.ngoc-cgiar.org

26 See Susanne Gura, 'Change and the CGIAR: a Contradiction in Terms?', *Seedling*, September 2001, <www.grain.org/publications/seed-01-9-1.cfm>; GRAIN, 'The CGIAR System-wide Review', December 1998, <www.grain.org/publications/dec981-en.cfm>; Patrick Mulvany (ITDG and member of the CGIAR NGO Committee), 'Global Agricultural Research for Local Food Sovereignty: Can the CGIAR Respond to the Demands and Aspirations of Poor Farmers?', <www.uk abc.org & www.itdg.org>.

27 Cary Fowler and Pat Mooney, *The Threatened Gene: Food, Politics, and the Loss of Genetic Diversity*, Cambridge: Lutterworth, 1990, p 189.

28 'CGIAR: Agricultural Research for Whom?'

29 Pat Mooney, 'The Parts of Life: Agricultural Biodiversity, Indigenous Knowledge and the Role of the Third System', *Development Dialogue,* special issue, 1996.

30 Rural Advancement Foundation International (RAFI), press release, 1 June 1998.

31 'CGIAR: Agricultural Research for Whom?'

32 http://www.cgiar.org/whatis.htm

33 *Ibid.*

34 GRAIN, 'Biopiracy by Another Name? A Critique of the FAO–CGIAR Trusteeship System', *Seedling*, October 2002. www.grain.org/seedling/seed-02-10-6-en.cfm

35 Susanne Gura and Rüdiger Stegemann, 'Public–Private Partnership ·for Global Food Security? The Cooperation between the CGIAR and the "Life Sciences" Industry', published by the German NGO Forum on Environment and Development, 1999. www.oneworldweb.de/forum

36 *Nature*, 404 (2000): 594. http://www.orgchange.org/cimmyt.htm

37 ICRISAT, 'Policy of the ICRISAT on Intellectual Property Rights and Code of Conduct for Interaction with the Private Sector', approved by the Governing Board of ICRISAT, Bulawayo, 21 February 2001.

38 Gisselquist *et al.*, 'Initiatives for Sustainable Seed Systems'.

39 Devlin Kuyek, 'Intellectual Property Rights in African Agriculture: Implications for Small Farmers', August 2002. http://www.grain.org/publications/africa-ipr-2002-en.cfm

40 Janet Bell, 'A Greener than Green Revolution?', *Seedling*, December 1998. http://www.grain.org/publications/dec98/dec982.htm

41 *Ibid.*

42 *Ibid.*

43 *Ibid.*

44 Fowler and Mooney, *The Threatened Gene,* p. 186.

45 http://www.sei.se/biotech/bioearn.html (January 2002).

46 Bell, 'Greener than Green?'

47 Fowler and Mooney, *The Threatened Gene*, p. 142.

48 *Ibid.*, pp. 162–4.

49 International Board on Plant Genetic Resources, 12–13 May 1979 (AGP: IBPGR/79/49/p. 4), quoted in Fowler and Mooney, *The Threatened Gene.*

50 IRRI, 'World Rice Statistics', World Resources Institute website (2003). http://www.wri.org/statistics/irri.html

51 IRRI, WARDA and CIAT, 'Rice Trade', RiceWeb website: http://www.riceweb.org/ricetradeeurope.htm

52 GRAIN, 'Roundup Ready or Not', *Seedling*, March 1997.
    http://www.grain.org/publications/mar97/mar973.htm
53 'CGIAR: Agricultural Research for Whom?'
54 Norman Myers, quoted in Fowler and Mooney, *The Threatened Gene*, p. 70.
55 Derek Tribe, 'Feeding and Greening the World: the Role of International Agricultural Research', 1994.
56 IRRI, 'Vietnam Is Venue for 4th International Symposium on Hybrid Rice', news release, Los Baños, Philippines, 10 May 2002.
57 'Feeding Asia's Hungry? An NGO View on Hybrid Rice', *Suhay*, April 2000, special edition (*40 years of Unfulfilled Promises*), published by MASIPAG.
58 Devlin Kuyek, 'Hybrid Rice in Asia: an Unfolding Threat', published by BIOTHAI, MASIPAG, KMP, GRAIN, PAN Indonesia and UBINIG, March 2000.
    http://216.15.202.3/publications/hybrid-en.cfm
59 Jacques Laigneau, 'La Guerre des semences fermières', *Coordination Rurale*, December 1999, quoted in Kuyek, 'Hybrid Rice in Asia'.
60 'Feeding Asia's Hungry?'
61 *40 years of Unfulfilled Promises*, special edition of *Suhay*, April 2000, published by MASIPAG.
62 IRRI, Rockefeller Foundation and Syngenta AG, '"Golden Rice" Arrives in Asia', jointly issued press release, 22 January 2001.
    http://www.cgiar.org/irri/pa/line2001.htm#GoldenRice
63 Jos Bijman, 'Plant Genetic Systems', *Biotechnology and Development Monitor*, 19 (1994): 19–20. http://www.biotech-monitor.nl/1908.htm
64 Rockefeller Foundation website: www.rockfound.org
65 *Ibid.*
66 *Ibid.*
67 'The Rockefeller Foundation', *Biotechnology and Development Monitor*, 44–45 (March 2001): 17.
68 'Biotechnology in the Rockefeller Foundation's New Course of Action', *Biotechnology and Development Monitor*, 44–45 (March 2001): 15–18.
69 Personal communication, John Barton to Devlin Kuyek, 18 January 2001.
70 PIPRA website; www.pipra.org; ICIPE website: www.icipe.org
71 In the 1980s the Rockefeller Brothers Fund brought together several other financiers to found the Resources Development Foundation in New York. This Foundation subsequently set up the International Biotechnology Collaboration Program in cooperation with the Hitachi Foundation, with a mission to transfer biotechnology research to the Third World.
72 Devlin Kuyek, 'ISAAA in Asia: Promoting Corporate Profits in the Name of the Poor', published jointly by Biothai, GRAIN, KMP, MASIPAG, PAN Indonesia, Philippine Greens, UBINIG and Drs. Romeo Quijano and Oscar B. Zamora, October 2000. See www.grain.org/publications/isaa-en.cfm
73 CNFA website: http://www.cnfa.org
74 Iza Kruszewska (ANPED – Northern Alliance for Sustainability), 'Ukraine and Bulgaria – Monsanto's European Playground for Genetic Engineering', presentation to the Permanent People's Tribunal on Global Corporations and Human Wrongs, University of Warwick, 23 March 2000.
75 CNFA website.
76 ISAAA, 'The ISAAA Biotechnology Fellowship Program', Ithaca, New York.

www.isaaa.cornell.edu/FellowR.htm

77 John Mwaura, 'Kenya Joins War On Biotech Products', Pan-African News Agency, 29 November 2000.

78 Devlin Kuyek, 'Genetically Modified Crops in Africa: Implications for Small Farmers', GRAIN, August 2002.
http://www.grain.org/publications/africa-gmo-2002-en.cfm

79 'USAID and US Companies Announce Export Financing for Ukraine', Business Information Service for the Newly Independent States (BISNIS) Agribusiness Report, 21 March 1995.
www.friendspartners.orgoldfriends/economics/nis.fis.bus.docs/export.financing ukraine.html

80 http://www.cnfa.org/raise.htm (November 2001).

81 CNFA, 'Rockefeller Foundation Awards $2 Million to CNFA for Rural Development in Southern Africa', press release, 4 June 2002. http://www.cnfa.org/

82 GRAIN, Interview with Palash Baral, Seedling, July 2002.

83 http://motherjones.com/mother_jones/ JF97/biotech_jump2.htm

84 Lee Elliot Major, 'Commercial Potential Has Helped Boost Grants For Life Sciences', Guardian, Education Supplement, 7 November 2000.

85 Henk Hobbelink, Biotechnology and the Future of World Agriculture, London and New York: Zed Books, 1991.

86 BBC World Service: 'Science Fact or Fraud?', 15 September 2000. http://www. bbc.co.uk/ worldservice/sci_tech/highlights/000914_whistleblowers.s html

87 Mark Clayton, 'Corporate Cash and Campus Labs', Christian Science Monitor, 19 June 2001. Also available at GENET archive: http://www.gene.ch/genet.html

88 For more information see George Monbiot, Captive State: the Corporate Takeover of Britain, London: Macmillan, 2000.

89 http://dataserv.bbsrc.ac.uk/oasintro.htm

90 See also Monbiot, Captive State.

91 BBSRC, 'John Innes Centre Loses Research Partner as Company Restructures', press release, 18 September 2002.
http://www.bbsrc.ac.uk/news/pressreleases/02_09_18_jic.htmlm

92 See excellent articles on the John Innes Centre on the Norfolk Genetic Information Network (NGIN) website.
http://members.tripod.com/~ngin/biospin

93 NGIN, 'Biospinology in our Science Communication? Report on the Science Communication Activities of the John Innes Centre (JIC)', briefing, updated April 2001.

94 Quoted in GRAIN, 'Sprouting Up: Grains of Delusion', Seedling, March 2001.
http://www.grain.org/publications/mar01sp1-en.cfm

95 See website of the World Health Organisation: http://www.who.int/nut/vad.htms

96 Ye et al., 'Engineering the Provitamin A (Beta-Carotene) Biosynthetic Pathway into (Carotenoid-free) Rice Endosperm', Science, 287 (14 January 2000): 303–5.

97 Press release, 16 May 2000: http://www.greenovation.com/news1.htm

98 BIOTHAI, KMP and MASIPAG in cooperation with VIA CAMPESINA and GRAIN, 'Genetically Engineered Rice Is Good for PR, Not the Poor Say Southeast Asian Farmers' Groups', joint statement to the press, 2 June 2000.

99 Kelvin Ng, 'To Critics, "Golden Rice" Has No Shine', Asia Times, 22 June 2000.
http://www.atimes.com/se-asia/BF22Ae01.html

100 Paul Brown, environment correspondent, in Guardian, 10 February 2001.

101 Antje Lorch, 'Is This the Way to Solve Malnutrition?' *Biotechnology and Development Monitor*, 44–45 (2001): 18–22; see also Zeneca (Syngenta), '"Golden Rice" Collaboration Brings Health Benefits Nearer', press release, 16 May 2000. http://www.syngenta.com/en/media/article.asp?article_id=38

102 Barry A. Palevitz, 'Society Honours Golden Rice Inventor', *Scientist* 15 [16], 8 (20 August 2001). http://www.the-scientist.com/yr2001/aug/palevitz_p8a_010820.html

103 www.grain.org/publications/asiaipr-en.cfm

104 Peter Downs, 'Food Gene Fixers Split Over Corporate Control', *Progressive Populist*, 5, 9 (September 1999), St Louis. http://www.populist.com/99.9.downs.genefixers.html.

105 Said at a panel discussion on 'Opportunities for and Threats to the New Indo–Swiss Collaboration in Biotechnology Programme', 13 February 2000.

106 Florianne Koechlin, 'The "Golden Rice" – a Big Illusion?', Blueridge Institute, February 2000. http://www.blauen-institut.ch/

107 http://www.who.int/vaccines-diseases/diseases/vitamin_a.shtml

108 A 1996 report by M. W. Bloem and his team from Helen Keller International, produced for India Together and discussed by Koechlin in 'The "Golden Rice"'. http://www.indiatogether.org/reports/goldenrice/science4.htm

109 Vandana Shiva, 'The "Golden Rice" Hoax – When Public Relations Replaces Science', Research Foundation for Science Technology and Ecology, India, September 2000. GENET archive: http://www.gene.ch/genet.html

110 375 micrograms for infants; 400, 500 and 700 micrograms for children aged 1–3, 4-6 and 7–10 years; 800 micrograms for females (11 years and upwards); 1,000 micrograms for males (11 years and upwards) and 1,050 micrograms for nursing mothers. Food and Nutrition Board, National Academy of Sciences, National Research Council.

111 Ye *et al.*, 'Engineering the Pathway'.

112 K. S. Jayaraman, 'Natural "Golden Millet" Rivals "Golden Rice"', 25 June 2002, http://www.scidev.net/scidevnetemailreturn.asp?id=2506200215520627 Archive: http://www.gene.ch/genet.html

113 Pallava Bagla, 'Dream Rice to Curb Malnutrition', *Indian Express*, 30 January 2003. http://www.indianexpress.com/full_story.php?content_id=17506 Archive: http://www.gene.ch/genet.html

114 http://www.csiro.au/index.asp?id=/aboutCSIRO/history.xml

115 Richard Hindmarsh, 'PBR, Genetic Engineering, and Seeds: a New Form of Colonisation'. http://www.mp.wa.gov.au/jscott/sow_seed/ss_pbr1.html

116 *Ibid.*

117 CSIRO, 'Expanding Global Agribusiness for Australia', press release, 28 September 1999. <http://www.biotech-info.net/expanding_agribus.html> See also *Agrow*, 338 (15 October 1999).

118 CSIRO website: http://www.csiro.au/csiro/connections/case/cs5.html.

119 CSIRO, 'Australian Farmers to Benefit from Biotechnology Deal', media release 98/276, 26 November 1998. http://www.csiro.au/index.asp?type=mediaRelease&id=AustralianFarmersToBenefitFrom.

6

Corporate Influence on International Regulatory Bodies

It is hard to arouse public interest in bodies such as Codex Alimentarius or the Transatlantic Business Dialogue, yet what they decide has profound implications for us all. Corporations, on the other hand, put much energy into lobbying international regulatory bodies to remove barriers to corporate globalisation.

Corporate influence at the World Trade Organisation (WTO)

The World Trade Organisation was born out of the highly contentious and lengthy Uruguay Round of the General Agreement on Tariffs and Trade (GATT) in 1995, at the strenuous insistence of the US and the TNCs (see Chapter 2). It is the international body that regulates international trade and enforces trade rules. Member countries that do not open up to this forced 'right to trade' may be taken to the Dispute Resolution Mechanism of the WTO, which makes the WTO the only international agreement with the power to inflict punishments for non-compliance.

Corporations have penetrated the whole process of the WTO with well-organised and well-resourced lobbying groups. WTO rules give large transnationals a similar status to that of nations, which is perhaps hardly surprising since several of them are larger in financial terms than many countries (see Table 6.1). Over 500 corporate delegates attend the biennial WTO Ministerial Conferences as 'trade advisers', whilst some poor countries may have a single delegate trying to cover all the issues.

At the Seattle WTO Ministerial in December 1999, the US, Canada and Japan hoped to move the regulation of GMOs out of the Convention on Biological Diversity (CBD) and place it under WTO jurisdiction. This would have negated all the work of years of negotiation for an international Biosafety Protocol to the CBD. However, the breakdown of the Seattle talks, as well as the immediate reaction by Europe's environment ministers against the proposal, foiled this attempt, and the text for the Biosafety Protocol (the Cartagena Protocol) was finally agreed in January 2000. At the 2002 World Summit on Sustainable Development, however, an attempt was made by the US to put trade considerations ahead of international environmental agreements, including the Biosafety Protocol. The Ethiopian delegation led a Southern revolt against the proposal at the last moment and the attempt was foiled.[1]

Table 6.1 • Revenues of largest TNCs compared with country GNPs in 2000

Global rank (according to revenue)	Company	Revenue (US$ billion)	Global rank (according to GNP)	Country	GNP (US$ billion)
1	Exxon Mobil	210.392	21	Austria	228.140
			22	Turkey	210.811
2	Wal-Mart Stores	193.295	23	Denmark	185.238
3	General Motors	184.632			
4	Ford Motor	180.598	24	Russia	179.325
			25	Poland	175.207
			26	Indonesia	169.295
			27	Hong Kong (as part of People's Republic of China)	165.956
5	DaimlerChrysler	150.069			
6	Royal Dutch/ Shell Group	149.146	28	Norway	147.936
7	BP	148.062	29	Finland	146.030
			30	Thailand	142.654
			31	Greece	136.889
8	General Electric	129.853	32	Saudi Arabia	133.752
9	Mitsubishi	126.579			
10	Toyota Motor	121.416	33	Portugal	120.932
			34	South Africa	120.693

Source: Data from Global 500 and IMF/WEO.[2]

Revolving doors at the WTO

The following examples indicate the lobbying power of US TNCs and the people who 'revolve' between government and TNC roles.

• The US Intellectual Property Committee is made up of 13 major US corporations including DuPont, Monsanto and General Motors. These corporations were instrumental in developing the Trade Related

Intellectual Property Rights (TRIPs) agreement which was included in the Uruguay round of the GATT (1985–94).[3]

- Monsanto has very close links with the US government. For example, when Robert Shapiro was chair of Monsanto, he was also the chair of the President's Advisory Committee for Trade Policy and Negotiations.

- Micky Kantor, US trade representative for much of the Uruguay round of GATT trade talks, is now a board member of Monsanto.[4]

- Marcia Hale, former assistant to President Clinton and Director for Inter-governmental Affairs was then director of international government affairs for Monsanto.

- Claydon K. Yeutter, former Secretary of USDA, former US Trade Representative who led the US team in negotiating the North American Free Trade Agreement (NAFTA) and helped launch the Uruguay Round of the GATT negotiations, was as of February 1999 a member of the Board of Directors of Mycogen Corporation, whose majority owner is Dow AgroSciences, a wholly owned subsidiary of the Dow Chemical Company.[5]

Transatlantic Business Dialogue (TABD)[6]

The TABD is much more than just another example of a corporate lobby group influencing and manipulating the political environment on behalf of its member companies – it has the advantage of having been initiated and nurtured by governments. Through the TABD, EU and US-based corporations develop policy demands which (parts of) the European Commission and the US government then attempt to implement.

Open letter sent to EU Trade Commissioner Pascal Lamy, by 20 groups from 11 European countries, 26 September 2001

Some 150 corporate leaders are involved in the Transatlantic Business Dialogue established in 1995 between big businesses in the USA and the EU. They develop common strategies that are then communicated directly to high-level government officials, as the TABD enjoys close links with governments. It is well known for promoting the 'public–private partnerships' that have recently become an international bone of contention.

The TABD has proven itself very apt in predicting the course of policy making in the EU and US, and has successfully diverted the flow of any policy discourse that would have posed a threat to its ultimate goal of no barriers to trade and investment in the transatlantic marketplace and beyond.[7]

TABD seeks to harmonise regulation in the EU and the USA with the aim of securing 'mutual recognition', or the acceptance by the EU of US rules developed on an issue, and vice versa. This would speed up the develop-ment of TNC-friendly legislation. According to the TABD's newsletter, its priority issues for 2001 included the WTO agenda, and targeting

> regulation's impact on business, including sector-specific concerns, the goal of 'Approved Once, Accepted Everywhere', and promotion of international stand-ards and harmonisation in EU/US systems and procedures, such as transatlantic merger review.[8]

The TABD lobby in action

Following TABD proposals, a US–EU Summit in June 1999 agreed on a set of principles that established an Early Warning Mechanism for potential trade disputes. The Early Warning Mechanism is one of the routes that institutionalises TABD lobbying through existing transatlantic government structures, and the TABD is using it to attempt to obstruct or delay policies which its member businesses dislike. At its annual conference in Berlin in 1999, the TABD used the Early Warning Mechanism to attack the pre-cautionary principle in trade, the EU Take-Back Directive, EU proposals to phase out hydrofluorocarbons (HFCs), proposals to phase out animal testing, and the draft of the Biosafety Protocol.[9]

In efforts to further tighten corporate control, the TABD is calling for trade interests to be upstreamed in the decision-making process, for instance through 'trade impact assessments' for all regulatory and legislative proposals.[10]

- The TABD also seeks to establish rules for investment that would be applied globally.

- It warns against the use of science to block trade, calling for a convention to regulate this.

> Appropriately, governments will continue to have the duty to protect the health and safety of their citizens. But scientific facts are just that – facts. Unless conventions are adopted on the regulation of science, varying systems could create unintentional trade barriers. Worse, others may use scientific standards intentionally to frustrate free trade.[11]

- It tries to block the introduction of any environmental protection initia-tives that would interfere with international trade and seeks an agreement that would prevent multilateral environmental agreements (MEAs) and labelling regimes from interfering with the free flow of goods and services.[12]

- It has also called for the EU and the US to enforce implementation of the WTO's TRIPs agreement in developing countries.[13]

If the TABD were to succeed in its aims, Europe would not be able to refuse US GM products. However, the TABD's strong efforts to advocate acceptance of biotech crops and food in Europe have so far met with little success in the face of strong public opposition. In the summer of 2001, the US government indicated its intention to step up the pressure.[14]

The Food and Agriculture Organisation (FAO)

The FAO is a large United Nations organisation that represents a plethora of different viewpoints and interests on agricultural production and policy. It consequently displays a rather schizophrenic approach to genetic engineering. Its website shows an alarming juxtaposition between, on the one hand, an in-depth understanding of the problems that small farmers face (citing the green revolution as the cause of many of these problems), and, on the other hand, uncritical support for genetic engineering.

In the run-up to the World Food Summit in Rome, November 1996, and at the Summit itself, it became evident that industry and US-led lobbies were pushing for genetic engineering of crops as the best option to solve world hunger. The impact of this was not reflected in the Summit's official papers. Yet polarisation within the FAO remained. Speaking prior to the G8 Summit in Japan in June 2000, the FAO Director-General, Jacques Diouf, gave GM organisms his backing, saying new plant and animal varieties were needed to feed a burgeoning world population. He predicted that a shortage of land available for cultivation would make it impossible to feed the global population, expected to peak at 9 billion in 2050, without recourse to genetically engineered plants and animals.

However, just over a month later, FAO research contradicted his arguments. In July 2000, the FAO's Global Perspective Studies Unit published *Agriculture: Towards 2015/30*,[15] a report showing that, contrary to usual pro-biotech claims, there *would* be enough food to feed the world over the next half-century. The report specifically did not allow for future technological developments in crops, in particular GM crops, because of the ongoing uncertainties regarding the technical performance, safety and acceptability to consumers of GM crops.

The FAO was excited by the announcement of the mapping of the rice genome in January 2001, claiming it would 'provide us an additional tool to increase food production in the next 20 years as the population rises' – though such optimism was tempered by Devinder Sharma, a food and trade policy analyst from India, who cautioned that 'rice genome mapping cannot address the real issues of access and distribution that result in hunger'.[16]

Jacques Diouf seems to have come to similar conclusions when stating on 17 February 2001: 'Faced with the needs of the 800 million people who are suffering from hunger, we don't need GMOs.'[17] He referred to Indonesia where pesticide use had been reduced by 65 per cent while rice production had increased by 25 per cent between 1987 and 1992.[18]

The FAO postponed its Hunger Summit 2001 – also named World Food Summit: Five Years Later – until June 2002 in Rome. The Summit was meant to review the limited progress and achievements since the 1996 Food Summit and to make decisions for actions to be taken. As at the 1996 Summit, heavy agro-industry and business lobbying took place. This time it had clear results. Chapter 1, Paragraph 25 of the statement of the 2002 Summit reads:

> We call on the FAO, in conjunction with the CGIAR and other international research institutes, to advance agricultural research and research into new technologies, including biotechnology. The introduction of tried and tested new technologies including biotechnology should be accomplished in a safe manner and adapted to local conditions to help improve agricultural productivity in developing countries.[19]

Codex Alimentarius: UN body for food standards

The volume of world food trade is enormous and is valued at between US$300 billion and $400 billion.

Codex website

The Rome-based Codex Alimentarius Commission is a body jointly administered by the FAO and the WHO. Established in the early 1960s, it is responsible for setting internationally harmonised minimum standards on food safety and quality. 'The publication of the Codex Alimentarius is intended to guide and promote the elaboration and establishment of definitions and requirements for foods to assist in their harmonisation and in doing so to facilitate international trade.'[20]

Codex is powerful in that it is widely recognised, providing the basis for food safety standards in regional trade blocs such as NAFTA, the EU and the Asia–Pacific Economic Cooperation (APEC) Forum. Above all, the WTO explicitly recognises the standard-setting role of Codex. During the Uruguay Round of trade agreements in the lead-up to the establishment of the WTO, agriculture and food were for the first time incorporated under world trade rules. At the final talks in Marrakesh in 1994, two new agreements were added in order to prevent countries from adopting measures that could operate as discriminatory barriers to trade:

- The Application of Sanitary and Phytosanitary Measures (SPS) Agreement allows governments to take sanitary and phytosanitary measures necessary for the protection of human health but seeks to prevent them from discriminating against any other party.

- The Technical Barriers to Trade (TBT) Agreement is designed to ensure that regulations and standards, including labelling requirements, do not create 'unnecessary obstacles to trade'.

Codex plays a major role in defining and harmonising SPS and TBT standards for food safety and quality at international level (it has 169 member countries). It has also updated its own standards to reflect these WTO rulings.[21]

Codex has statutes, rules of procedure and two kinds of committee. There are five coordinating committees, one for each major region of the world. Subject committees are subdivided into two kinds: nine general subject committees (including pesticides, food additives, labelling) and sixteen commodity committees (including pulses, sugars, oils and fats, fresh fruits and vegetables).

The Codex Commission also publishes the *Code of Ethics for International Trade in Food*, which is meant to stop the dumping of poor-quality or unsafe food on international markets.

As the primary reference for the WTO in SPS measures, Codex has significant influence over national policies across the globe. Industry recognises its importance and is heavily involved in negotiations. Northern government delegations to Codex have included representatives of the largest corporate interests, among them Nestlé, Coca-Cola, Pepsi, Cargill and SmithKlineBeecham.

Looking, for example, at the Codex Committee on Pesticide Residues (CCPR) – establishing maximum residue limits (MRLs) for pesticides in food – industry presence is striking. Lisa Lefferts of Consumer International reported:

> The Global Crop Protection Federation delegation, which represents the pesticide industry, included 30 members at the 1998 meeting. Three of the four members of the Swiss delegation represent industry (Novartis and Nestec/Nestlé). Mingled into other delegations are representatives from Dow, Monsanto, and a multitude of multinational companies, from Avcare to Zeneca.[22]

After a long process, Codex formally adopted the 'Principles and Guidelines on Foods Derived From Biotechnology' on 9 July 2003. It sets out principles for risk analysis of GM foods and guidelines for the safety assessment of foods derived from recombinant DNA plants and microorganisms, including allergenicity and unintended effects.

The Convention on Biological Diversity (CBD)

In 1972, the United Nations Environment Programme (UNEP) was founded and in 1987 the World Commission on Environment and Development (the Brundtland Commission) produced the report, *Our Common Future*, which called for economic development to be balanced against the environment and the needs of future generations. Work to develop the Convention on Biological Diversity and the Convention on Climate Change (which targets industrial and other emissions of greenhouse gases such as carbon dioxide) culminated in the largest-ever meeting of world leaders, which took place at the Earth Summit – the United Nations Conference on Environment and Development in Rio de Janeiro in 1992. At this summit, the CBD was signed by more than 150 governments.

The CBD calls for the balancing of conflicting requirements: conservation of biodiversity, its sustainable use, and equitable sharing of the benefits. It calls for the protection of the interests of indigenous peoples and local communities, yet refers to patents and biotechnology as means for exploiting biodiversity.

The CBD is legally binding and has 181 parties which are the nations that not only signed but also ratified it, accepting it as an internationally binding agreement. The US is not a party to the CBD, as it has not ratified this agreement. However, it is always present at the meetings with its hand-picked delegations, which always include a large number of corporate representatives. Other countries have so far not challenged its right to intervene in the business of the Convention, although they have more than once prevented the US from subordinating the international environmental agreements to the trade agreements.

Industrial lobbying of the CBD

Industrial lobbying of the CBD has been prolific. Composed of many of the leading global corporations, the Business Council for Sustainable Development (BCSD) had unparalleled access to the conference secretariat of the Earth Summit in 1992.[23] That conference was completed with hardly a single reference to the responsibility of the multinationals for environmental degradation and social injustice, or to the need to limit their rights, except in the statements made by NGOs.

The BCSD has now acquired the grandiose title of the World Business Council for Sustainable Development (WBCSD), which 'aims to develop closer cooperation between business, environment and sustainable development.'[24] It has 125 corporate members including Monsanto, Novartis and DuPont as well as Shell International, BP, General Motors and Rio Tinto.

The Rio Plus 10 meeting in Johannesburg in 2002 was predictably a major disappointment. Concentration of corporate power has increased considerably since 1992, with many takeovers, makeovers and mergers. Industry has managed to evade any major attempt to control its activities during the intervening decade. However, proposals were presented by a broad group of NGOs in Johannesburg for binding rules on corporate accountability. In addition, African networks used the summit as an opportunity to come together and build their strength.

The Cartagena Protocol on Biosafety

The Biosafety Protocol is designed to protect biodiversity and its sustainable use from the potentially negative effect of the transboundary movement (i.e. trade) of genetically modified organisms (GMOs) which are defined as LMOs (living modified organisms). The Protocol also refers to human health and socio-economic impacts. It allows countries to invoke the precautionary principle and prevent the import of GMOs in certain cases.

Justifying US opposition to a strong Biosafety Protocol, Rafe Pomerance, US Deputy Assistant Secretary of State for Environment and Development and head of the US delegation at the negotiations in 1999, stated simply: 'This is about a multimillion dollar industry.'

The Protocol should have been finalised in 1999 in Cartagena, Colombia. But for once the US and its friends – having come together as the Miami Group of the three major GM-exporting nations and their allies (the US, Canada and Argentina, supported by Australia, Uruguay and Chile) – had drastically miscalculated the strength of the South, where national negotiators had created the Like-Minded Group. In an effort to exclude almost every key issue from the Protocol, the US 'over-bullied' not only the South but all delegations, including the EU. The South did not give way and the talks finally collapsed when the Like-Minded Group stood firm.

> Their belittling us gave us a headstart in getting unobtrusively united. By the time they knew that we really knew what we were saying, we had cemented an African unity of purpose, and blackmail and intimidation directed at individual delegations in order to break up our unity always backfired.
>
> Tewolde Egziabher, biologist and chief negotiator, Like-Minded Group[25]

Following the collapse of talks in Cartagena and the failure of the WTO talks in Seattle in November 1999, there was hope that despite opposition from the Miami Group – at that time already without active support from Chile – a strong Biosafety Protocol could be established to ensure that environmental and health concerns could take precedence over free trade rules.

In January 2000, after five years of negotiations, 134 countries met in Montreal, Canada, under the auspices of the UN Convention on Biological Diversity (CBD), in a final effort to establish an internationally binding Biosafety Protocol. This Protocol – officially to be called the Cartagena Protocol on Biosafety – establishes an international framework of regulation for the safe handling, transfer and use of GMOs across national boundaries. Adopted on 30 January 2000, the Cartagena Protocol entered into force in September 2003, ninety days after the fiftieth country had ratified it.[26] This was in the same month as the WTO's Cancun ministerial, as if to underline the ongoing struggle for precedence between the two, which is set to intensify now the Protocol is actually in force.

The Protocol has set a new landmark in the development of multinational environmental agreements but it has also made history for other reasons. It was the first time in the history of negotiations for international treaties and agreements that the North had failed to dominate, while the South maintained a solid unity and refused to be bullied into submission.

The biotech industry lobbied heavily at the Biosafety negotiations. For example, in May 1997 at least 28 agrochemical/life sciences companies or company associations were present at the negotiations in Montreal. Of these, 22 were from the US and Canada. Monsanto alone sent 6 representatives to the meeting. Pro-industry lobbyists also attended meetings under the guise of anonymous-sounding political institutes and universities. Most African countries could only afford to send one delegate each. Thirty-one different industry groups were present in Montreal in January 2000 when the Biosafety Protocol was finally adopted.[27]

What has been achieved?

The Biosafety Protocol agreed in Montreal is only a beginning. Although in its final form it offers more than many believed possible, many areas of the Protocol are weak and whole groups of GMOs have been excluded from risk assessment or advance notification. To this extent the industry's investment and efforts have paid off. But it was a victory for all those intent to ensure protection and sustainable use of biodiversity, that 'the Precautionary Approach (PA) became the guiding principle for the import of GMOs. The Protocol subjects imports to an Advance Informed Agreement (AIA) and secured its legal status in relation to the World Trade Organisation (WTO).'[28] Article 10.6 for Decision Procedure states:

> lack of scientific certainty due to insufficient relevant scientific information and knowledge shall not prevent [the importing country] from taking a decision, as appropriate, with regard to the import of that living modified organism ... in order to avoid or minimise such potential adverse effects.[29]

Though it appears straightforward, it is not easy to trigger the precautionary principle and prevent shipments of GMOs intended as food from entering a country. First, as explained by Dommelen,

> The PP [precautionary principle] may seem to imply that scientific knowledge is not required for its application, but this conclusion is misleading. In practice, the PP can only be triggered when sufficient reason exists to expect that some specific course of action will lead to 'a threat of significant reduction or loss of biological diversity'. Disagreement is likely to arise about what constitutes a sufficient reason for expecting such a threat. Policy makers will find that even scientific researchers are in disagreement about a qualified assessment of possible threats to biological diversity. This implies that a method must be found to make these scientific disputes productive for the purpose of applying the PP.[30]

Second, industry and US government representatives are known to pressurise any country trying to implement a moratorium on the import of GMOs (see chapters 7 and 8).

An example of appropriate use of the precautionary principle from 150 years ago

The precautionary principle made its first appearance more than 150 years ago in the context of urban public health. In 1854, a cholera epidemic in a specific neighbourhood in London led John Snow to suspect an association between the drinking water from a public water pump and the outbreak of cholera, although at this time no causal connection could be demonstrated. Nevertheless, he was able to convince the responsible assembly that the potential cost of closing the pump by removing its handle would be much smaller than the consequences of leaving [it] open, even if this decision might be wrong in the end. His theory of cholera as a waterborne disease proved correct and the plague ended. It was only 30 years later, however, that the bacterium *Vibrio cholerae* was discovered.[31]

The Cartagena Protocol also has provisions for the development of an international liability regime, the terms and extent of which are still being negotiated and need to be in place no later than four years after the Protocol has come into effect.

However, before they can ratify the agreement, many countries are obliged to frame national legislation to implement it, which in turn requires scientific, technical and legal capacity, for which they require funding, training and time. This provides plenty of opportunities for industry to intervene and undermine or take over the process. It also means the Protocol is delayed in coming into effect. Not all countries are in this position however: Bulgaria ratified early on because its laws only require a presidential signature; hence, although it has ratified, it has no law that complies with the Protocol.

Given that GM seeds imported for 'food, feed and processing' can be used for sowing, especially in times of shortages and crisis, it is a weakness of the Protocol that commodities are excluded from the strict AIA procedures and its risk assessments. Though the US, Canada and Argentine wanted commodities completely excluded from the Protocol, they are now covered by an extremely watered-down version of AIA, what some call 'AIA light'. Furthermore, the Miami Group refused to allow GM commodities to be labelled as such in shipments, which led to the current situation where they only need to be documented as 'may contain GMOs'. This, in effect, allows GM-exporting countries to avoid having to segregate GM from non-GM commodities, although public pressure may well force this anyway.

Though covered in the scope of the Protocol, two areas of GMOs were later excluded from regulation under it: GMOs intended for contained use and GMOs used for medical purposes. This is a serious shortcoming as these GMOs also have potential to cause harm to biodiversity and human health. This is especially true as 'contained use' under the Protocol is not defined in such a way as to exclude escapes of GMOs or leakages into the environment. It merely seeks to 'limit their contact with, and their impact on, the external environment'.[32] Many delegations were aware that 'contained use facilities' – such as fermentors, for example, or vials with bacterial or fungal cultures for the production of pharmaceuticals, additives or nutraceuticals – are indeed leaking or even actively discharging living organisms or their DNA into the environment. Yet delegations of the Miami Group and the European Union suppressed concerns.

In this case it became evident that the intense lobbying activity of the pharmaceutical industry in Europe, especially the UK, and North America had achieved these unfortunate exemptions. Some argue, however, that pharmaceuticals are actually covered unless they are, according to Article 4, 'addressed by other relevant international agreements or organisations'.

The Protocol clearly states that neither the WTO nor the Protocol take precedence. Although later agreements normally take precedence over earlier ones, it was actually perceived as a major victory to achieve equal status for the Protocol against major opposition from the Miami Group.

Attempts continue to be made by the US and industry to undermine, misrepresent and downgrade the Cartagena Protocol. There are also struggles over its implementation, as industry seeks to ensure that weak levels of protection are implemented and harmonised across entire regions with projects such as the Program for Biosafety Systems funded by USAID for $14.5 million.[33]

Notes

1 Geoffrey Lean, 'Plans to Promote GM Crops Defeated', *Independent*, 2 September 2002. http://news.independent.co.uk/world/environment/ story.jsp?story=329680

2 Industry data taken from the website publication of Fortune 500/Global 500. http://www.fortune.com/indexw.jhtml?channel=list.jhtml&list_frag=list_global50 0.jhtml&list=19)
   Data on the GNP of nation states is taken from the IMF/WEO website. http://www.imf.org/external/pubs/ft/weo/1999/01/data/ngdpd_a.csv

3 PANOS, 'More Power to the World Trade Organisation? The International Trade Controversy', PANOS Briefing, 37 (November 1999): 7.

4 *Guardian*, 17 November 1999.

5 The Edmonds Institute provides an excellent list of 'revolving' office holders, from which some of the above examples were taken. See 'The Revolving Door'. http://www.edmonds-institute.org/door.html

6 Website: <www.tabd.com> Information on the TABD can also be found in such Corporate Europe Observatory briefings as 'TABD: Putting the Business Horse before the Government Cart' (October 1999) and 'TABD: Doing Business in Berlin' (November 1999). http://www.xs4all.nl/~ceo/tabd/berlinbriefing.html

7 Corporate Europe Observatory: http://www.xs4all.nl/~ceo/observer2/tabd.html

8 TABD Newsletter 01/1, February/March 2001: http://www.tabd.com/about/ febmar.html

9 Corporate Europe Observatory.

10 *Ibid.*

11 Testimony of US co-chair Lodewijk J. R. de Vink, President and Chief Operating Officer, Warner–Lambert Company, on behalf of the Transatlantic Business Dialogue, before the House Ways and Means Committee, Subcommittee on Trade (23 July 1997).

12 TABD 1998 Mid-Year Scorecard Report.

13 Lodewijk J. R. de Vink and Jürgen Schrempp, message to US–EU Summit, May 1998.

14 Corporate Europe Observatory, 'TABD in Troubled Water', 3 October 2001. ceo@xs4all.nl

15 http://www.fao.org/es/ESD/at2015/toc-e.htm

16 Devinder Sharma, 'Rice Genome Mapping No Respite for the Hungry', *Deccan Herald* (n.d.).

17 Agence France-Presse, 'Going Organic Cannot Help World Hunger: FAO Chief Diouf', 17 February 2001.

18 P. Weber, 1992, 'A Place for Pesticides?' *World Watch* (May/June 1992): 18–25. Cited in 'Experience suggests countries can significantly reduce pesticide use', Ecological Agriculture Projects, 1997 http://www.eap.mcgill.ca/MagRack/ EC/ec1–4–1.htm

19 Final declaration from the World Food Summit, 'The International Alliance against Hunger', Rome, 2002. http://www.fao.org/DOCREP/MEETING/005/Y7106E/Y7106E09.htm

20 Codex website: www.codexalimentarius.net

21 *Ibid.*

22 Lisa Lefferts, 'Changing the Rules of the Codex Club', *Pesticides News*, 43 (March 1999): 6.

23 Corporate Watch USA website, http://www.corpwatch.org.

24 WBCSD website: http://www.wbcsd.ch/

25 Tewolde Berhan G. Egziabher, 'Biosafety Negotiations – Flashbacks', *Third World Resurgence*, 114/115 (2000): 24–6.

26 http://www.biodiv.org/biosafety/signinglist.asp

27 List of Participants, Conference of the Parties to the Convention on Biological Diversity (CBD), First Extraordinary Meeting (resumed session), 24–28 January 2000.

28 Hartmut Meyer, 'The Cartagena Protocol on Biosafety', *Biotechnology and Development Monitor*, 43 (2000): 2–7. http://www.biotech-monitor.nl/4302.htm

29 http://www.biodiv.org/biosafety/protocol.asp

30 A. van Dommelen, 'The Precautionary Principle: Dealing with Controversy', *Biotechnology and Development Monitor*, 43 (2000): 8–11. http://www.biotech-monitor.nl/4304.htm

31 'Working towards a Strong Protocol', Editorial, *Biotechnology and Development Monitor*, 43 (2000): 2–3. http://www.biotech-monitor.nl/4301.htm

32 Article 3 of the Cartagena Protocol on Biosafety defines 'contained use' as follows: '"Contained use" means any operation, undertaken within a facility, installation or other physical structure, which involves living modified organisms that are controlled by specific measures that effectively limit their contact with, and their impact on, the external environment.'

33 http://www.fas.usda.gov/icd/summit/2002/statearchive/USAIDbiotech.htm

7
Government Legislation and Corporate Influence

A well-informed and active public and a reasonably independent media are vital to balance the multifarious pressures exerted by the corporations, as the activities of the US, the EU and various governments in Eastern Europe and the former Soviet Union clearly reveal. In the US, the public has been relatively slow to respond to the issue of GM food and until 2000 there was little awareness or activity, so the companies have had a comparatively free hand. The US grew 66 per cent of the world's GM crops in 2002, and did not take action to segregate GM from non-GM crops. In Europe, on the other hand, resistance was quick to appear and has remained strong throughout most of the region. In the UK, where the government has allowed extensive field trials of GM crops, public opposition has been active and vocal. Experience in Eastern Europe demonstrates that where neither the government nor the people are aware or prepared to resist, the companies readily enter and do not set standards unless they are forced to do so. Thus Romania had 15,000 hectares of GM crops growing before any law was passed, and is now the source of much smuggled GM seed, while the countries of the former Soviet Union are the 'Wild East', where anything goes. Yugoslavia had some of the strongest laws in the region, but under cover of field trials the companies have got a foothold, as they have in the UK. In fact field trials are the Trojan horse of the industry, seen clearly as the precursor of commercialisation yet sometimes tolerated by a public that would not accept immediate commercialisation. They can be seen as part of a softening-up process: giving the impression that safety research is being carried out, getting people used to the idea of GM crops, and maintaining the idea that they can flourish alongside conventional and organic agriculture.

When Croatia decided to advertise itself as GM-free, it suddenly found itself the object of threats from the US administration (see below, pp. 178–9). Currently, the EU is faced with US action through the World Trade

Organisation, an unelected and unaccountable body with the power to overrule any national government.

Exerting influence worldwide

It seems that they are trying to buy influence with key individuals, stack committees with experts who support them, and subvert the scientific agenda around the world.

Sue Mayer, GeneWatch UK and member of the AEBC[1]

A confidential report was leaked to GeneWatch UK[2] at the end of 2000 which summarised the activities of Monsanto's Regulatory Affairs and Scientific Outreach teams for May and June 2000. It revealed the corporation's involvement in a global campaign to promote GM foods and crops by lobbying for certain experts to get on international scientific committees and by promoting biotechnology through supposedly independent scientists. It describes developments in the regulation of GM crops, and Monsanto's efforts to influence them via the FAO/WHO committees and in 20 countries, including Japan, Bulgaria, Thailand, Mexico, Brazil and Korea, as well as the US and the European Union.

Cases have been recorded around the globe of Monsanto or US representatives applying pressure to judicial or national decision-making processes. Threatening to use the WTO is a common threat, as shown in the cases of Sri Lanka and Croatia. In both Brazil and India, Monsanto has applied enormous pressure to gain approval for its crops, succeeding in India and failing in Brazil (see pp. 215-16).

Monsanto is just one of the many biotech companies eager to sell their products globally. It is the best-known, since currently it is the company with the largest share worldwide in GM crops. Others might at present be less visible in their efforts to influence legislation and regulators, but not necessarily less effective in doing so.

Threatening Sri Lanka with the WTO

Rather than simply introducing labelling laws, Sri Lanka tried to establish a ban on the import of GM foods in May 2001. This followed prolonged internal discussion, supported by the Sri Lankan NGO Environmental Foundation Ltd. The World Trade Organisation called for the ban to be postponed, initially for 60 days. The reason given was: to allow exporters in other countries time to adjust.[3]

The US then threatened to use the WTO to overturn the ban. Sign-on letters to US Trade Representative Robert Zoellick protesting the right of Sri Lanka to determine what food products it allowed to be imported were developed by concerned NGOs such as Pesticides Action Network Asia–Pacific and Friends of the Earth International in an international campaign.[4]

Sri Lanka gave up its attempt to ban the import of GM food, however, and, although the Environmental Foundation Ltd renewed its efforts in early 2002 by lobbying the new Minister of Health, the ban has not been imposed since.

Teamwork to put pressure on Ireland

In 1997 Novartis and Monsanto joined forces to apply pressure to the regulatory and judicial system of the Republic of Ireland over its reluctance to allow the growing of GM sugar beet in field trials. GM sugar beet was the first GM crop to be tested on Irish soil. On behalf of many citizens Claire Watson tried to secure a court ruling that would prevent Monsanto from sowing GM sugar beet. In this legal case – 'Watson vs Monsanto' – Steven Moll asserted, for Monsanto, that if Monsanto was not allowed to go ahead with the trials, Novartis would withdraw all non-GM beet seed from sale to Irish farmers. He further stated, 'Given the importance of Novartis on the Irish market, this would have serious implications for the Irish sugar beet industry.'

Pulling strings in Pakistan

Under current WTO regulations, the TRIPs agreement obliges countries to implement law to protect intellectual property rights. Currently a major struggle is over the fact that countries are allowed to make an exception for plants and animals, although micro-organisms are part of the regime. In Pakistan, an official with the Ministry of Food and Agriculture told IPS news service that Monsanto was lobbying the government aggressively to implement patenting law. He said that 'Monsanto is pulling powerful strings to influence the legislative process in its favour, sending letters to government officials, holding meetings with politicians.'[5]

Monsanto was concerned that the legislation could favour farmers' rights over those of TNCs. According to Dr Shahid Zia, an NGO representative and research fellow with the Sustainable Policy Development Unit (SDPI), 'The proposed law would allow farmers to save, retain and exchange seeds.... [It] requires a genetically modified or transgenic plant to clear tough environmental impact and biosafety assessments before being given protection.'[6] The law was unacceptable to Monsanto. In a letter to the government's Seed Certification Department, Monsanto's Managing Director in Pakistan went on the offensive:

> In the presence of this clause, anybody from the public can sue us and ask for compensation for hazards and damages which are kind of open-ended risks. Hence, take out this clause.... Again I repeat that this clause is not acceptable to any multinational company and it should not be different than any non-transgenic variety.[7]

Substantial equivalence downgraded

As a result of public pressure from concerned individuals, non-government organisations, scientists, and individual politicians, certain industry corner-stones have begun to crumble, for instance the concept of substantial equivalence.

First conceived by the OECD in 1993, the concept was later endorsed by the FAO and WHO in 1996. The adoption of the concept of 'substantial equivalence' as a criterion for the safety of GM foods assisted the biotech industry in its desire for minimal regulation and testing. By comparing major biochemical components, GM food crops could be called substantially equivalent as long as any conventional counterparts could be found with similar compositional values, even if data was derived from 60-year-old research using different methods of analysis.[8] Equally, GM squash was regarded as 'substantially equivalent' despite containing 64 times less pro-vitamin A (beta-carotene). Whilst, for example, the Food and Drug Administration (FDA) and the Environmental Protection Agency (EPA) in the US regarded substantial equivalence as a safety assessment in itself, scientists and public interest groups around the world insisted that it was ill-defined and pseudo-scientific and should be replaced with an analysis that included biological, toxicological and immunological tests.[9]

Although the phrase is still being used, the argument about substantial equivalence has largely been won. It is no longer seen as an end point of safety assessment but as a starting point. The Joint FAO/WHO Expert Consultation on Foods Derived from Biotechnology summed up the position in its report (June 2000):[10]

> The application of the concept [of substantial equivalence] is not a safety assess-ment in itself; it does not characterise the hazard, rather it is used to structure the safety assessment of a genetically modified food relative to its conventional counterpart. As a starting point, the genetically modified organism (plant, micro-organism or animal), and/or foods derived from it, is compared with its closest traditional counterpart in order to identify any intended and unintended differences which then become the focus of the safety assessment.

The term, however, is still open to misinterpretation and continues to be used by industry and proponents alike as a description of safety in public relations situations.

US legislation

The US was the first country to develop and release genetically engineered crops. Close relationships with the biotech corporations appear to have continued unabated through different US administrations, with key players revolving between government and corporate posts on a regular basis.[11] It is hardly surprising therefore that the US promotes biotechnology at home and abroad so enthusiastically. Introducing GM crops and food into the US without labelling or segregation and with a minimum of regulation gave corporations a massive advantage in their approach to the rest of the world. Furthermore, the US also, through many administrations, deliberately designed its internal policies so as to have plenty of cheap food produce available to donate or dump on foreign markets, including GM food (see Chapter 8).

Arguments that have been used in international negotiations in an attempt to persuade other countries to trust US regulators and US-approved GM crops and food include:

- GM crops and food have been rigorously tested for health and environmental safety and approved in the US, and are thus safe.

- The US public is happy to eat GM food, as it trusts the regulatory system.

- Americans have eaten GM food for years and nobody has fallen ill or died from it.

US citizens have begun to respond to the issue of GM foods, however, and industry and government departments, which previously had a free hand, are being forced to react.

During the 1970s genetic engineering for commercial purposes was first developed by small companies. When GM applications moved into agricultural crops, the US federal government took up industry's cause, so as to allow the US to maintain and expand its position as the world's agricultural leader. This view continued under Presidents Reagan and George Bush (senior), who did not want to stifle the development of biotechnology under 'regulatory excess', or send Wall Street the wrong message.

The Reagan administration decided in the mid-1980s under the 'coordinated framework' that no new regulations were needed to deal with this emerging technology, as genetic engineering was claimed to be just an extension of traditional plant and animal breeding without new risks. Instead, the technology would be covered under existing USDA, FDA and EPA regulations. Each of the various agencies had to develop proposals for how to do this. The EPA, for example, put out the Plant Pesticide Proposal in 1994. Thus a plant engineered with insect resistance (Bt toxins) is regulated as a pesticide. Yet field trials fall under USDA.

This piecemeal approach led to confusion over which department had jurisdiction over what. For example, genetically engineered micro-organisms that might be released into the environment ended up being regulated by the EPA under the Toxic Substance Control Act – which is not really appropriate because the kind of tests required for new chemicals are very different to those needed for novel organisms.

It remains unclear how GM animals are going to be regulated; at present there is no pre-market requirement for any new animal variety to be reviewed for safety or environmental impact before it is released. Engineered animals may be categorised as new drugs – but the FDA has not yet proposed any regulation.

United States Department of Agriculture (USDA)

In 1862, when President Abraham Lincoln founded the US Department of Agriculture, he called it the 'people's department'. Today it promotes US agriculture exports and its primary goal is the promotion of economic and trade opportunities. The emphasis on international trade is underlined by the comment in USDA's strategic plan that 96 per cent of American agriculture's potential customers reside outside US borders. Its designated responsibilities are the safety of meat, poultry and egg products, food and nutrition programmes in the US, forests, and research into 'new crop technologies', which included the regulation of GM field trials.[12]

After he left, former Secretary of Agriculture Dan Glickman described his Department's attitude to biotech:

> What I saw generically on the pro-biotech side was the attitude that the technology was good and that it was almost immoral to say that it wasn't good because it was going to solve the problems of the human race and feed the hungry and clothe the naked. And there was a lot of money that had been invested in this, and if you're against it, you're Luddites, you're stupid. There was rhetoric like that even here in this department. You felt like you were almost an alien, disloyal, by trying to present an open-minded view on some of the issues being raised. So I pretty much spouted the rhetoric that everybody else around here spouted; it was written into my speeches.[13]

The choice of Ann Veneman as Bush Junior's Secretary of Agriculture showed that this highly pro-GM attitude was set to continue.[14] She was actively involved in the negotiations for the Uruguay Round of GATT, NAFTA, and the US–Canada Free Trade Agreement. She served on the board of a Monsanto subsidiary, Calgene Inc., and is known to be a strong proponent of biotechnology. 'We are delighted with her selection,' BIO commented, 'it is hard to imagine a better choice.'

However, in its March 2002 report ('Environmental Effects of Transgenic Plants: the Scope and Adequacy of Regulation') on the USDA/APHIS[15] review process , the National Research Council (NRC, part of the National Academy of Sciences) strongly criticised USDA/APHIS testing for lack of rigour, inadequate ecological and non-target impact assessments, failure to demand the submission of full data on the gene sequences after insertion into the plant, and permitting companies to exploit commercial confidentiality to avoid disclosure.

This marks a change at the National Academy of Sciences, which has slowly been developing a more rigorous approach to the issue of GM. In 2000, for instance, it examined the EPA and pointed out that its regulations for plant pesticides were inadequate, and needed to be strengthened.

The Food and Drug Administration (FDA)

The FDA's mandate covers the regulation and safety of drugs, food (other than meat, poultry and egg products), cosmetics and electronic radiation. A major aim stated on the FDA's website is to 'Participate through appropriate processes with representatives of other countries to reduce the burden of regulation, harmonise regulatory requirements, and achieve appropriate reciprocal arrangements....'[16]

The FDA does not require human safety testing for GM plants; instead there are 'voluntary safety consultations'. FDA's biotech policy was announced on 28 May 1992 by US Vice-President Dan Quayle at the press conference of a biotech industry conference. It was introduced as a de-regulatory initiative and was based on the notion 'that the new techniques [such as genetic engineering] are extensions at the molecular level of traditional methods and will be used to achieve the same goals as pursued with traditional plant breeding' (57 FR 22991, 29 May 1992). Consequently it was concluded that they should be regulated in the same way.

The FDA could have regulated the new engineered traits as food additives. Instead – a crucial difference – it placed them under the GRAS – 'generally regarded as safe' – provisions of the Federal Food, Drug and Cosmetics Act. This is now causing problems, as under this provision the FDA cannot require safety testing. Companies themselves are allowed to declare a new substance 'GRAS'.

The voluntary notification system means that no one actually knows how many GM products are on the market in the US, since the corporations conduct their own safety tests and only notify the FDA if they suspect a problem. According to US law, such tests can be considered trade secrets. It would be naïve to consider the FDA ruling as simply an oversight. The interrelationship between industry and government, in particular the FDA and the EPA, is eye-opening:

- William D. Ruckelshaus is a former chief administrator of the EPA and, for more than a decade, a member of Monsanto's board of directors.

- Linda Fischer is a former assistant administrator of the EPA's Office of

Pollution Prevention, Pesticides and Toxic Substances and, more recently, vice-president of government and public affairs at Monsanto.

• Margaret Miller is a former chemical laboratory supervisor for Monsanto and now deputy director of human food safety and consultative services in the new animal drug evaluation office at the Center for Veterinary Medicine of the FDA.[17]

GM foods: not approval – just acknowledgement

Michael Hansen of Consumers Union US has pointed out:

> Lack of adequate safety testing can be seen in the letter FDA sends to the company after completion of a 'safety consultation'. For example, the letter sent to Monsanto on 25 September 1996 about its MON810 Bt maize states: 'Based on the safety and nutritional assessment you have conducted, *it is our understanding that Monsanto has concluded that corn grain and forage derived from the new variety are not materially different in composition, safety, or other relevant parameters from corn grain and forage currently on the market, and that they do not raise issues that would require premarket review or approval by FDA*' (italics added).[18]
>
> Note that the FDA does not state its own opinion about the safety of this crop; it only states what the company believes. The letters for all 52 'safety consultations' done since the Flavr Savr tomato contain basically the same language.

The FDA thus does not approve a novel GM food but only acknowledges that the company regards it as safe.

The after-glow of the Flavr Savr tomato

The Flavr Savr tomato was the first and only GM product the FDA looked at in some detail. Other GM products since have been released on to the market without any government testing or need for approval. Instead, the government chooses to conclude that the company has conducted the relevant tests (see Box above).

The Flavr Savr tomato was developed by the California-based biotech company Calgene – now owned by Monsanto. This tomato was genetically engineered to slow down the softening process during ripening, thus facilitating transport and increasing shelf life. Since the action of the inserted 'anti-sense' or reversed gene was to block the product of another gene, rather than producing its own, the only novel 'gene product' (protein) in the GM tomato came from the kanamycin antibiotic resistance marker gene. Calgene therefore put the marker gene – not the whole tomato – through the food additive petition process. Approved in 1994, it was put on the market in the same year with a big fanfare. Yet three years later the GM-tomato quietly disappeared from the shelves; Flavr Savr failed the market test. However, according to an FDA internal memo, Flavr Savr also failed to meet Agency safety standards. Robert J. Scheuplein, director of the Agency's Office of Special Research Skills, found problems with some of the testing data on the Flavr Savr.

As the investigative journalist Kristi Coale reported:[19]

Although he regarded the effect as small, Scheuplein did say: 'The data does not show the Calgene product to be unsafe but the data falls short of "a demonstration of safety" or "a demonstration of reasonable certainty of no harm" which is the standard we typically apply to food additives.' Concerning how the Agency was instructing its scientists to regard GM foods in testing, Scheuplein said, 'It has been made clear to us that this present submission [the Flavr Savr] is not a food additive petition and the safety standard is not the food additive standard. It is less than that, but I am not sure exactly how much less.'

A chilling implication is revealed by Scheuplein's memo: all GM crops approved since 1992 have undergone less stringent testing. In fact, testing is handled not by the Agency but through voluntary consultations between the companies and the FDA with company scientists running the tests.

Previously undisclosed papers such as these tell the story of how the FDA flouted its own laws and ignored the advice and warnings of its own scientists in the process of pushing through a food technology that seemed to have immediate benefit only for the producers – namely agrochemical companies including Monsanto, DuPont and Novartis.

Dr Belinda Martineau, the scientist who conducted the safety studies on the Flavr Savr tomato at Calgene, wrote a book about the whole approval process (*First Fruit: the Creation of the Flavr Savr Tomato and the Birth of Biotech Foods*). She argues:

Rather than personal opinion, the scientific community should give the public facts, hard facts; the results of studies that indicate these foods are safe to eat and that growing them on a large scale will not cause environmental damage. Scientists and regulators throughout the ag biotech industry agree that more public education about genetic engineering research is necessary, but, thus far, few have provided much information beyond how the technology works and the wondrous things that might be done with it.... *And simply proclaiming that 'these foods are safe and there is no scientific evidence to the contrary' is not the same as saying 'extensive tests have been conducted and here are the results'. In fact, without further elaboration, 'no scientific evidence to the contrary' could be construed as 'no scientific evidence, period'* (italics added).[20]

In May 1998 a lawsuit was filed against the FDA by a coalition of groups including the Center for Food Safety, the Alliance for Bio-Integrity and others. The suit alleged:

that current FDA policy, which permits such altered foods to be marketed without testing and labels, violates the agency's statutory mandate to protect public health and provide consumers with relevant information about the foods they eat. It also charges that the policy violates religious freedom.[21]

In particular, the plaintiffs alleged that because such foods have been implanted with foreign genes and the substances they produce, FDA policy violates those sections of the Food, Drug and Cosmetic Act which (a) require that substances added to food be labelled, (b) prohibit 'false or misleading' labelling, and (c) mandate disclosure of material facts. The suit also reflects a wide range of spiritual concerns, from the concerns of those who wish to avoid animal products, through to the opposition of those who object to procedures that they see as irresponsibly and arrogantly disrupting the integrity of God's creation.

At a public hearing on the FDA on 30 November 1999, papers that had come up during the course of the lawsuit revealed that FDA scientists themselves were warning about potential health hazards of GM foods. However, they were systematically being ignored by the politicians and policy makers at the FDA.

FDA microbiologist Louis Pribyl had stated, 'There is a profound difference between the types of unexpected effects from traditional breeding and genetic engineering.' Several aspects of gene splicing, he had added, 'may be more hazardous'.

Similarly, E. J. Matthews of the FDA's Toxicology Group had warned that 'genetically modified plants could … contain unexpected high concentrations of plant toxicants', and cautioned that some of these toxicants could be unexpected and could 'be uniquely different chemicals that are usually expressed in unrelated plants'.

Despite these warnings, the FDA's policy statement asserted that 'the Agency is not aware of any information showing that foods derived by these new methods differ from other foods in any meaningful or uniform way….'[22]

On 2 October 2000 the court decided that the FDA's decision not to regulate GM foods was technically legal. The coalition claimed that the decision was flawed.

However, the FDA was already beginning to change. It had held three public hearings (Washington, Chicago and Oakland) in 1999–2000, attracting responses from more than 35,000 people calling for strict mandatory safety testing. Partly as a result of this, in January 2001 the FDA proposed a plan to require data from companies on every aspect of a new GM product. They also acknowledged for the first time that there is a difference between genetic engineering and conventional breeding. These were tacit admissions that previous FDA policy had been inadequate.

European Union legislation

In the 15 member states of the European Union,[23] GMOs such as GM crops have had a very mixed reception. Equally, the democratically elected European Parliament has remained critical of GMOs, trying to establish safeguards. However, the European Commission, the most powerful and unelected decision-making body in the EU, has often encouraged pro-industry legislation (such as the European Directive on the Protection of Biotechnological Inventions, 1998). Furthermore, both Jacques Santer, former President of the European Union (1995–9) and his predecessor Jacques Delors (1985–95) had spoken out in favour of biotechnology as an area for potential economic growth and competitiveness in Europe, with potential for creating millions of new jobs.[24]

Funding was given to projects supporting crop biotechnology. For example, the European Commission contributed $1.6 million in 1996 towards an industry-led four-year project entitled Familiarisation with and Acceptance of Crops Incorporating Transgenic Technology in Modern Agriculture (FACTT). In spite of this broad title, FACTT actually focused on comparing yield performance of Plant Genetic Systems (PGS) transgenic hybrid oilseed rape and conventional varieties and hybrids. PGS and Hoechst (AgrEvo) (both now part of Bayer CropScience) were centrally involved. However, the results were unimpressive and PGS oilseed rape failed to outperform the best conventional and hybrid varieties tested.

In the spring of 1997 the European Commission decided to approve a variety of transgenic maize produced by Novartis (now Syngenta). This decision was challenged by 13 out of 15 member states, but to little avail because procedures demand a unanimous ruling to overturn a Commission decision. Meanwhile, the European Parliament voted resoundingly for a resolution condemning the Commission for 'a lack of responsibility' in approving the maize, which contains a functional antibiotic resistance gene.

The pro-biotechnology stance of the European Commission is partly due to the lobbying of EuropaBio, the self-styled 'voice of the European bio-technology sector' which has been remarkably successful in convincing the Commission of the desirability of supporting biotechnology (see pp. 59–60). Lobbyists from EuropaBio regularly meet with Commissioners and organise dinner debates for MEPs, civil servants and academics.[25] According to the PR firm Burson–Marsteller, a main adviser for EuropaBio's lobby strategy, EuropaBio has an 'indispensable direct role in the policy-making process'.[26]

If EuropaBio subtly influences the European Commission agenda, a more direct influence on the European Union came in 1997 at the nego-tiations on the European Directive on the Protection of Biotechnological Inventions – nicknamed, among other things, the Life Patent Directive. The

Genetic Interest Group, assisted by SmithKlineBeecham, encouraged wheel-chair users to demonstrate in favour of the directive by claiming that new drugs would not be developed unless patents were allowed on human genes.[27] The corporations used emotions aroused around human genetics to win the right to patent plants and plant genes. The Directive was accepted in July 1998, although the Dutch and other EU governments challenged this decision at the European Court of Justice. Their challenge was dismissed in late 2001, but by mid-2003 eight EU states had still not implemented the directive.

Tensions between Europe and the US

Tensions are high between the US and the EU with regard to US exports of GM crops and foods. There is a constant background menace of trade wars and sanctions if Europe fails to open up its markets. At times it appears that the US and its farming bodies realise that the EU block on GM food and increasing resistance to GM feed are not fuelled by economic protect-ionism but by consumer demands. The US government and biotech corpo-rations have been leaning hard on European governments and regulators to address the problem. As a result, in May 2000 then US President Bill Clinton and the European Commission President Romano Prodi agreed to establish a new transatlantic high-level EU–US Biotechnology Consultative Forum to 'review and assess the benefits and risks of biotechnology and prepare a report on these issues for the December US–European Union Summit'.[28] The group was made up of 20 experts, including Norman Borlaug (see pp. 72–3). Published on 18 December 2000, the report called, amongst other things, for the precautionary approach (not the precautionary principle) on biosafety and food safety. It also stated that 'There is a lack of substantial scientific data and evidence, often [presented] more as personal interpretations disguised as scientifically validated statements.'[29]

Dr Michael J. Phillips, executive director of BIO, said that his organisa-tion was 'heartened to see support for content-based labelling regulations, rather than process-based. These reflect the current regulations enforced by the US Food and Drug Administration.' He added that BIO was 'very opti-mistic that this report will be instrumental in ending the European mora-torium on approval of crops and foods enhanced through biotechnology'.[30]

Tensions have not subsided and in early 2003 the US threat of bringing trade sanctions against Europe through the WTO began to loom again, fuelled by the GM food aid issue. On 9 January US Trade Representative Robert Zoellick called the European view 'Luddite'. He said he found it immoral that Africans were not supplied with food because people had invented fears about biotechnology. In response, European Development

Commissioner Poul Nielson proposed a deal to the US: 'The deal would be this: if the Americans would stop lying about us, we would stop telling the truth about them. This is a proposal for normalising the discussion.'[31]

In May 2003 the US challenged the EU over GMOs at the WTO, citing the moratorium on approvals between 1998 and 2002. However, the US is equally opposed to the new legislation, especially that on traceability and labelling currently being developed within the EU and intended to end the moratorium.

EU public still against GM crops

Opposition to GM crops and foods in Europe has been strong ever since RoundUp Ready soy was first pushed on to the market in 1996. Opinion polls continue to show that the public objects to GM. At the end of 2001, the European Commission published the results of a Eurobarometer survey on 'Science and Society', including a section on GMOs. In the survey:

- 94.6 per cent say they have the right to choose about GM foods;

- 79.9 per cent don't want this type of food;

- 59.4 per cent say GMOs could have negative effects on the environment.

Furthermore, Eurobarometer says that – contrary to responses towards other areas of science – the knowledge/education factor does not make citizens more favourable towards GMOs.

> People interviewed could have a high level of knowledge and still believe that biotechnologies should be subject to more control and demand more safety studies, etc. In this case, information is not enough and could even be counter-productive.[32]

Central and Eastern Europe: a corporate paradise

Foxes guarding the henhouse

> *The situation in CEE–NIS [Central and Eastern Europe – Newly Independent States of the former Soviet Union] is very diverse between countries in the region, with Hungary having a relatively well-controlled and transparent regulatory system, while in some second-round EU accession countries, such as Bulgaria and Romania, there is no government control on releases of GMOs. Indeed, both countries are already growing GM crops commercially and becoming a source of GMO contamination of the entire region.*
>
> Iza Kruszewska, June 2001[33]

This region promises great profits for the corporations because agriculture is still a major part of the economy and there are millions of farmers.

However, there is still little public awareness of GM in Eastern Europe and the Newly Independent States (former USSR). Moreover, the public has very little access to information and there is little monitoring of GM food in the region. Corporate double standards reflect the differences between the EU countries and further east. While Tesco and Unilever are eager to reassure consumers in the EU about the absence of GM in their products, in South-east Europe (the Balkans) they have no such scruples because they have not experienced the necessary pressure, and evidently do not feel bound to act without it.

In the same way the corporations, notably Monsanto and Pioneer Hi-Bred International (now owned by DuPont) have exploited the lack of regulation and public awareness in Eastern Europe and the Newly Independent States (NIS) in order to promote the widespread use of genetically engineered crops.

EU accession is creating its own dynamics. The countries involved in the first round of accession (Poland, the Czech Republic, Slovakia, Hungary, Slovenia, Lithuania, Latvia, Estonia) are harmonising their legislations with EU directives. Several of them have superior requirements for public participation to most current EU members, because they are parties to the Århus Convention.

Newly independent states (NIS) of the former Soviet Union

The NIS is the 'Wild East' for biotech corporations. The lack of official and public awareness of the problems of GMOs means there is a policy vacuum and a complete absence of biosafety legislation in almost all the countries of the region. Although Russia does have some GMO provisions scattered among several regulations, they are piecemeal and the means and political will to enforce them are lacking. This creates a haven for biotech corporations.

THE UKRAINE

> *Foreign companies are exploiting the very poor economic situation and the absence of instruments of control in the Ukraine.*[34]

> Yuri Samoilenko, Ukrainian parliamentarian,
> Chairperson of the Environment Committee

In 1997 Monsanto first imported GM Bt potatoes to the Ukraine for trials at state breeding stations and collective farms. After two years of field trials, Monsanto and a Canadian company, Solanum PEI, held a press conference in Kiev to announce their intention to establish seed production, timed to coincide with the visit of the Canadian prime minister. This was Monsanto's way of putting pressure on the Ukrainian authorities to register their potatoes for commercialisation. However, the Ukrainian media had picked up on the controversy raging across Europe and the Minister of Health refused to certify transgenic potatoes for human consumption. Without this approval, they were advised to destroy the 1998 harvest of seed potatoes. Rather than being destroyed, however, they were crushed and covered in compost, so failing to comply with government rules. In March 2000 Monsanto once again tried to register their GM NewLeaf potatoes with the Ministry of Health – and once again they failed.

However, according to the Ukraine Green dossier, Monsanto's potatoes have continued to be grown across the country, without public awareness, labelling or government control.[35]

The Citizens' Network for Foreign Affairs (CNFA, see pp. 126–9) – which despite its name is a front for US agribusiness – works closely with the Ukrainian government. Their representative collaborated with the Ukrainian Ministry of the Environment in 1998 to prepare weak and belated legislation on GMOs and to define the responsibilities of different ministries, as well as co-organising a conference on regulating biotechnology with the Environment Ministry.

An extremely permissive draft biosafety law, lacking any rights to public information or participation in decision making on GMOs, was presented to Parliament in January 2001. NGOs managed to thwart the acceptance of this draft by preparing a petition addressed to Parliament. Several NGOs, including Eko-Pravo (Eco-Law) then drafted a new law but there was no time for it to go through Parliament. Another government draft almost identical to the one presented in 2001 was put forward in October 2002 and was adopted by the Ukrainian Parliament in November 2002.

In December 2002 it was announced that the US Large Scale Biology Corporation (LSBC) and the German company Icon Genetics would develop GM pharma-plants to express vaccines and therapeutic proteins in the Ukraine. It seems likely that the plants in question would be wheat and oilseed rape (canola). According to the press release from LSBC, Ukraine's government is undertaking this project to develop medicines for domestic use in order to avoid dependence on imports.[36] Experience in the US with ProdiGene's pharma-crops suggests that there is likely to be serious contamination through cross-pollination and lack of segregation of seed or grain in the future with unforeseeable consequences (see Chapter 4, especially pp. 95–6).

GEORGIA

Georgia has also experienced the Monsanto Bt potato. This time the US organisation involved was the Agricultural Cooperative Development International (ACDI/VOCA),[37] promoting US agricultural products and market opportunities for US agribusiness. It was financed in part by USAID. The seed potatoes came from the US and there was no monitoring of the impacts on pests. The crop basically failed through the potato not being adapted to local conditions, but no compensation was paid and farmers say they are still in debt.

RUSSIA

Like other countries in the region, Russia has had little public debate on the issues surrounding GM, although there were protests across the country in April 2002 according to the Socio-Ecologic Union.[38] Russia, which received the Colorado beetle via US food aid following the Second World War, could have Bt potatoes designed to combat it by mid-2005. Monsanto is working with the Center of Bioengineering at the Russian Academy of Sciences and providing funds to insert its technology into three Russian varieties of potato. At the press conference announcing these developments, the US Ambassador to Russia advised Russia not to regulate the technology 'to hinder the sector's development'.[39]

South-East Europe – the Balkans region[40]

The Balkans region includes Yugoslavia (Montenegro and Serbia), the former Yugoslavia (Slovenia, Croatia, Bosnia and Herzegovina, Macedonia), Bulgaria and Romania. Government policy on GMOs is extremely diverse in this region, with some countries having very restrictive GM policies (Slovenia and Croatia) and others (Romania and Bulgaria) already growing GM crops commercially.

BULGARIA

In 1999, Bulgarian farmers harvested the first crop of GM herbicide-tolerant maize. Most of this maize passed unlabelled into animal feed and thus into the food chain. Whilst the official line was that Bulgaria had only undertaken field trials in GM maize and wheat, the seed catalogues for the year 2000 from Pioneer and Monsanto were already advertising GM varieties of maize. Monsanto's GM maize was grown on 12,000 hectares and in 2000 Monsanto expected this area to increase to 25,000 hectares. In 2001, the same area was approved for growing GM maize, once again without any controls.

In 1996, Bulgaria became the first country in Eastern Europe to establish a regulation, based on a 1958 seed law (thus bypassing Parliament) allowing a Council for the Safe Use of GM Higher Plants to grant permits independently of the government for field trials, commercial cultivation, and import and export of GM plants, seeds and planting material. A register of releases is kept but this is not available to the general public, as it is considered an administrative secret.

On the Council are various government officials and scientists from research institutes. A key figure is Professor Atanas Atanassov, the Executive Secretary of the Council. He gives permits to companies, and his Institute for Genetic Engineering (recently renamed AgroBioInstitute) in Kostinbrod undertakes projects for Monsanto and Pioneer. During the mid-1990s, the Institute carried out extensive field trials of virus- and bacteria-resistant tobacco and transgenic alfalfa. It is not clear what has happened to these trials. This kind of conflict of interest is common across the region.

Bulgaria has an export market in maize derivatives and fodder. The lack of segregation and labelling poses a real threat to this export market as well as to internal consumer rights and the Bulgarian environment. In June 2000 Parliament withdrew all state financing of research and development of GM tobacco and vines, fearing for these export markets.[41]

Why was Bulgaria targeted by the corporations? Countries in the first round of EU accession, such as Poland and Hungary, were protected from the worst corporate excesses by the fact that they would be expected to harmonise their regulations with those of the EU. Bulgaria and Romania, by contrast, are unlikely to join the EU until 2007 at the earliest. While Bulgaria could boast of being the first country in Central and Eastern Europe to establish regulations for biosafety of GM higher plants,[42] this was probably exactly what biotech corporations needed. It gave them the legal basis for starting field trials of transgenic varieties of plants – the first step to commercialisation. As already noted, Bulgaria was also one of the first countries to ratify the Biosafety Protocol, which was easy because (according to its own laws) it merely required a presidential signature, whereas most countries have first to develop legislation to transfer the provisions to national level.

ROMANIA

Monsanto's commercial cultivation of RR soybeans in Romania already covered 15,000 hectares in 1999, some 20 per cent of the total area under soybeans.[43] In January 2000 Romania introduced a government ordinance on the development, testing, use and marketing of GMOs and their products, creating a National Biosafety Commission with the power to grant permits for the release of GMOs. This enabled Monsanto to legalise its operations and Monsanto was quoted as saying that 30,000 hectares – nearly half of all soybeans grown in Romania – were genetically engineered.[44] For

2002 the area was said to have expanded to 45,000 hectares, according to ISAAA's draft figures for that year.

Since 1997, US seed companies have tested and registered at least six GM corn and one GM soybean variety in Romania. Until the GMO law was introduced, testing was allowed using the provisions of the law for basic seeds.[45] Romania is alleged to be a major source of smuggled seed to the rest of the region.

CROATIA

Following a resolution by the Croatian Parliament in 1998, four government ministries agreed the text of a draft law in June 2001 to ban the import, production, marketing and use of GMOs in Croatia pending the implementation of legislation. Later in June, eight ministries decided that Croatia should advertise itself as GMO-free: welcoming billboards were placed at the border promising natural food and a healthy vacation, and a firm line through the letters 'GMO' drove the message home.

It was not long before this drew the attention of the US. A leaked memo of November 2001 from the US embassy in Croatia asked if Croatia had notified the WTO of its intended law, and warned that it must comply with WTO rules. US NGOs were alerted and protested jointly with Croatians. At a roundtable meeting in Zagreb in December 2001, government and NGO representatives voiced their support for the proposed ban and highlighted the potential advantages to Croatia of remaining GM-free and growing organic food. The Environment Minister said: 'Biodiversity makes Croatia unique in Europe, and this is our comparative advantage.'

A tour by North American farmers opposed to GM was organised for January 2002. The day before it began, the US embassy in Vienna held a press conference at which they reminded Croatia of its obligations under the WTO. They also stated that GM crops had been rigorously tested and that the US had experienced no problems over the seven years that GM products had been in its markets. GM crops were 'substantially equivalent' to their non-GM counterparts, so labelling was unnecessary. Finally, planting GM crops reduced chemical inputs and increased yields. Despite this pressure, however, a public opinion poll in January showed 80 per cent of Croatians in favour of the proposed ban.

Yet the proposed legislation to ban GMOs has since been dropped and new laws intended to harmonise with the EU directives are planned. Croatia remains vulnerable because it lacks biosafety provisions.

YUGOSLAVIA (MONTENEGRO AND SERBIA)

Yugoslavia has the most effective GMO legislation in its region, despite a decade involving three wars in the 1990s. Imports of whole GM grains were forbidden from January 2001 and a GMO law was passed in May 2001, which is backed up by three laboratories capable of testing material.

Vojvodina province, bordering Hungary, Croatia and Romania, is an important centre for seed breeding and production of soy, maize, sunflower and wheat. Seed is sent to Russia, Eastern Europe, India, Italy and France. The Institute for Food and Vegetable Crops (IFVC) is based in Novi Sad in the province.

Corporate influence is being felt in a number of ways. Monsanto and Pioneer are both doing field trials of herbicide-resistant maize (glyphosate and glufosinate respectively). They are working with centres where two of Yugoslavia's three testing laboratories are based, the IFVC and the Institute for Maize Research, which could lead to conflicts of interest. Monsanto has access to locally adapted varieties of maize in which to insert the RoundUp gene. The IFVC seems to be trying both to produce GM-free seed and soy products and to work with Monsanto and Pioneer on GM, with obvious implications for contamination, including cross-pollination, leading to multiple resistance. It is also a member of ASSINSEL, the International Association of Plant Breeders for the Protection of Plant Varieties, founded in 1938, which focuses on IPRs for plant varieties. Its members, apart from IFVC, are all developed-country institutions and include a number of the major corporations.

The two companies have also become involved in the biosafety process. When the GMO law was passed, a biosafety committee was established, composed entirely of scientists, mostly crop breeders, without a single geneticist. There are no members of the public or experts from other disciplines. It seems that most of these scientists were invited to the US to visit the laboratories of Pioneer and Monsanto. The president of the committee is from the IFVC, which is already cooperating with Monsanto and Pioneer.[46]

GM contamination has already been discovered in Vojvodina. In 1997, Sojaprotein, which exports soya derivatives to the EU for companies such as Nestlé and Coca-Cola, discovered contamination with RoundUp Ready genes, in spite of war and economic sanctions. Since then, small areas of cultivation with RoundUp Ready soybeans have been discovered every year somewhere in the province. The likely source of the illegal seed appears to be Romania. The Yugoslav authorities freely admit that they are unable to prevent crossborder smuggling.

Another source of contamination is GM food aid. Yugoslavia received 50,000 tonnes of soyameal in 2001, following a serious drought which caused a shortage of animal feed. Since then it has refused the offer of donations of GM maize. Kosovo, however, which has received a great deal of aid over the years, is another likely source of GM smuggling.

EU and Eastern Europe

The date of accession of 10 new member states[47] to the EU has now been set for May 2004. The EU may try to use the accession process for weakening policy on GMOs. For example, GMOs that have not been approved in the EU but are found in accession countries could receive *de facto* approval. The European Commission may attempt to weaken any provisions in the laws of the new members that go further than those in the EU. The worst possible outcome would be if the accession states provided an entry point into the EU as a whole for unlabelled GM soybeans and maize imported illegally across their vulnerable borders with non-EU countries.

At present, accession countries are making no effort to influence the EU legislative process on GMOs. The EU is currently preparing several pieces of GMO legislation, whose provisions the new member states will have to enforce from the day of accession. The legislation includes traceability/labelling and novel foods/feeds, while internal discussions continue on co-existence and liability.

All the accession countries now have GMO laws that require authorisation and labelling of GM foods. Indeed two countries, Slovenia and Slovakia, have already implemented the revised Directive 2001/18/EC on deliberate release, ahead of almost all existing member states except the UK and Denmark.

In several cases, provisions in the GMO laws are stronger than those in the EU, especially with regard to public access to information and participation in decision making on GMOs – an emphasis driven by those countries' ratification of the Århus Convention.[48] Almost all countries include representatives of environmental and consumer NGOs on their national biosafety commissions. Poland's GMO law, passed in the summer of 2001, has a provision on liability that in certain cases enables the Environment Ministry to demand some insurance – this could take the form of a deposit, a bank guarantee or an insurance policy – before granting a permit for releasing GMOs. However, civil society in most of these countries is not yet accustomed to active participation in legislative processes.

The biggest problem in accession countries is implementation. With the exception of Hungary and the Czech Republic, all the countries lack the institutional capacity – certified laboratories, for example – to enable the enforcement of the GMO authorisation and labelling requirements.

GM-FREE ORGANIC ZONE PLANNED

The three smallest states in the region, Croatia and the accession states

Slovakia and Slovenia, have attracted the least interest from the large companies. One of these states, Slovenia, is working with Carinthia (Austria), and Friuli–Venezia–Giulia (Italy) to establish a GM-free organic agriculture zone. They hope to support and develop the particular specialities of the region, ensuring livelihoods for local farmers, and encouraging eco-holiday-makers. Slovenia hopes to be fully integrated into the project once it accedes to the EU in 2004.[49]

Notes

1 The Agriculture and Environment Biotechnology Commission (AEBC) is appointed by the UK government to advise on genetic engineering issues.
2 Available from www.genewatch.org
3 Reuters, 'Sri Lanka's GM Food Ban Delayed Indefinitely', *Times of India*, 3 September 2001. <http://timesofindia.indiatimes.com/articleshow.asp?art_id=869444898>; Inter Press Service, 'Lobbying Puts Ban on GE Food at Risk', 24 August 2001.
4 Larry Bohlen, Friends of the Earth International, letter to support Sri Lanka's GE food ban. lsinger@foe.org; July 2001
5 Muddassir Rizvi, 'Monsanto Fiddles with Plant Protection Act', Inter Press Service, 31 August 1999. http://www.twnside.org.sg/title/fiddle-cn.htm
6 *Ibid.*
7 Letter from Dr A. Rehman Khan to Chief of the Seed Certification Department, 6 August 1999, quoted in *ibid.*
8 Hartmut Meyer, 'Precise Precaution versus Sloppy Science', *Bulletin of Science, Technology and Society* 19, 2 (1999): 91–5.
9 Responses included those by Eric Millstone, Eric Brunner and Sue Mayer; Ho and Steinbrecher.
10 http://www.worldfoodscience.org/vol1_2/FAO.pdf
11 John Vidal, 'GM Lobby Takes Root in Bush's Cabinet: Biotech Firms Could Have Undue Influence', *Guardian*, 1 February 2001.
12 www.usda.gov
13 'Outgoing Secretary Says Agency's Top Issue Is Genetically Modified Food', *St Louis Post–Dispatch*, 25 January 2001.
14 Ann Veneman, biographical sketch: www.usda.gov/agencies/gallery/veneman.htm
15 APHIS: Animal and Plant Health Inspection Service of USDA.
16 FDA website: <http://www.fda.gov>; mission statement: www.fda.gov/opacom/morechoices/mission.html
17 Uncovered by the Edmonds Institute, US. Longer list available.
18 www.cfsan.fda.gov/~acrobat2/bnfL034.pdf
19 Kristi Coale, 'Anti-GE Lawsuit against FDA Has Clinton Administration Worried', 12 January 2000. <http://www.salon.com/news/feature/2000/01/12/food> or <http://www.purefood.org/ge/antigesuit.cfm>. Kristi Coale is an associate with the San Francisco-based Center for Investigative Reporting. Her work for this story has been supported through the Center's Fund for Investigative Reporting on the Environment.

20 Belinda Martineau, *First Fruit: the Creation of the Flavr Savr Tomato and the Birth of Biotech Foods*, McGraw-Hill Professional, New York, 2001, pp. 231–2.

21 The Center for Food Safety, 'Landmark Law Suit Challenges', press release, 27 May 1998. http://www.centerforfoodsafety.org/li/GEpress1.html

22 'Statement of Policy: Foods Derived From New Plant Varieties', *Federal Register*, 57, 104 (29 May 1992): 22991, as quoted by Steven M. Druker, executive director of the Alliance for Bio-Integrity, in the presentation for the FDA public meeting, Washington, DC, 30 November 1999, by the Panel on Scientific, Safety, and Regulatory Issues. http://www.linkny.com/~civitas/page140.html.

23 The member states of the EU in 2002 were: Austria, Belgium, Denmark, Finland, France, Germany, Great Britain, Greece, Ireland, Italy, Luxembourg, Netherlands, Portugal, Spain, Sweden.

24 'Europe Inc.', a report by Corporate Europe Observatory, ceo@xs4all.nl, 1998.

25 *Ibid.*

26 Adam Ma'anit, 'Exposing the Biotech Lobby', *Link* (Friends of the Earth International magazine), 93 (April/June 2000). www.foei.org/publications/link/93/e93biotechlobby.html

27 George Monbiot, *Captive State: the Corporate Takeover of Britain*, London: Macmillan, 2000.

28 Environmental News Service, 'Europe, US Aim to Resolve Differences on Genetically Engineered Foods', 31 May 2000. http://ens.lycos.com/ens/may2000/2000L-05-31-02.html See also archive: http://www.gene.ch/

29 The full report is available at: http://europa.eu.int/comm/dgs/external_relations/index_en.htm Download report at: http://europa.eu.int/comm/external_relations/us/biotech/report.pdf

30 Julianne Johnston, 'US/EU Biotech Report Contains Positive Consensus', Agweb News, 19 December 2000. See archive: http://www.gene.ch/genet.html

31 Reuters, 'EU's Nielson Blasts US "Lies" in GM Food Row', 22 January 2003. Archive: http://www.gene.ch/genet.html

32 http://europa.eu.int/comm/research/press/2001/pr0612en.html

33 Iza Kruszewska, 'Corporate Influence in Central and Eastern Europe in the Field of Agricultural Biotechnology', report, June 2001.

34 Quoted in *ibid.*

35 Tanja Topchiy, 'Ukraine's Cabinet of Ministers Forms a Scientific Body to Support Biotechnology', Green Dossier, Ukraine, 25 December 2001.

36 Large Scale Biology Corporation, US ,'Ukraine to Develop Biopharmaceuticals in Living Plants for Regional Needs in Pact with USA's Large Scale Biology Corp. and Germany's Icon Genetics AG', press release, 3 December 2002. http://www.lsbc.com/wt/tert_middle.php?page_name=pr_1038873460&lm=1&sec_page=press_release_archive&tert_page=pr_1038873460&press=ln& level=3

37 ACDI combines the profits of US agribusiness and banks with a political agenda and aid. Its members include US agricultural banks and seed companies. ACDI describes itself as a 'private, non-profit international development organisation providing high-quality expertise at the request of agribusinesses, cooperatives and private and government agencies abroad'. See: www.acdivoca.org

38 SEU Campaign for Biosafety, 'Simultaneous Action Against GMOs Held Across

Russia', press release, 9 April 2002. seupress@seu.ru

39 Sarah Karush, 'Russian Scientists, US-based Monsanto Develop Beetle-resistant Potato Varieties', Associated Press, 4 June 2002.

40 Additional information on the whole region can be found in three Northern Alliance for Sustainability (ANPED) briefings prepared by Iza Kruszewska for ICCP-3 (3rd Meeting of the Intergovernmental Committee for the Cartagena Protocol on Biosafety) (The Hague, 22–26 April 2002): 'The Urgent Need for Biosafety Frameworks in South-East Europe: Bulgaria, Croatia and Yugoslavia'; 'Biosafety Policy and Practice in Yugoslavia'; 'Croatia's Attempts to Introduce a Moratorium on GMOs'.

41 Iza Kruszewska, 'Bulgaria: Torn between North American Seed Producers and EU Consumers', *Biotechnology and Development Monitor*, 44–45 (March 2001).

42 Atanas Atanassov (Institute of Genetic Engineering, Kostinbrod), 'Biosafety and Regulation of GMOs in Bulgaria', in Proceedings of the Fifth Central and Eastern European Conference for Regional and International Cooperation on Safety in Biotechnology, Sofia, 12–14 December 1999.

43 Holly Higgins (US Embassy), 'Romania – Planting Seeds: Romanian Legislation for GMO Seeds', Global Agriculture Information Network (GAIN) Report No. RO0005, US Department of Agriculture, Foreign Agricultural Service, 28 February 2000.
http://www.fas.usda.gov/scripts/gd.asp?ID=25667501)

44 Costin Motroasa, 'Watchdogs Monitor GMO', *Bucharest Business Week*, 4, 30 (4 September 2000).
http://www.bbw.ro/article.cfm?sec= headlines&art_id=619&vol=4&nr=30

45 *Ibid.*; Higgins, 'Romania – Planting Seeds'.

46 Interview with Professor Miodrag Dimitrijevic, Department of Genetics, Faculty of Agriculture, University of Novi Sad.

47 The 10 EU candidates are: Poland, Czech Republic, Slovakia, Hungary, Slovenia, Lithuania, Latvia, Estonia (from CEE), Cyprus and Malta.

48 United Nations Economic Commission for Europe (UNECE) Convention on Access to Information, Public Participation and Access to Justice in Environmental Matters, signed in Århus, Denmark, June 1998 and ratified in October 2001.

49 Elisabeth Steiner, 'GE-free Organic Zone', *Der Standard*, Austria, 25 October 2002. German text at http://derstandard.at/Textversion/Spezial/20021025_1/271.htm

8

Opening Up the South

The end is control. To properly understand the means one must first understand the end. A farmer who doesn't borrow money and plants his own seed is difficult to control because he can feed himself and his neighbours. He doesn't have to depend on a banker or a politician in a distant city. While farmers in America today are little more than tenants serving corporate and banking interests, the rural Third World farmer has remained relatively out of the loop – until now.[1]

As the tables which follow show clearly, most GM crops to date have been planted in the North, primarily the US. Argentina is the only country in the South that grows them on a large scale; GM soya has been grown there since 1996. China is growing Bt cotton commercially, and a comparatively small amount of tobacco. However, the push into the South is beginning to accelerate. As noted earlier, 60 per cent of Indian farmers, 80 per cent of farmers in the Philippines and 90 per cent of African farmers still save their own seed. In Africa, small farmers are fundamental to food security at household level, both saving and breeding their own seed. Most of the smallest farmers are women. The green revolution never really reached them and their use of inputs has remained small. Capturing new constituencies and markets is an essential part of corporate strategies. The millions of small subsistence farmers in the South who rely on farm-saved seed and do not use agrochemicals are seen as a largely untapped market with massive potential. Critics have often noted that GM agriculture does not address the real needs of the South and the companies recognise that they need to adapt their presentations accordingly, in order to find ways to reach this important constituency. Not surprisingly, considering that its traits are in 91 per cent of the GM crops planted worldwide, Monsanto is at the forefront of this search. Pioneer also features strongly, a reminder of the agreement in 2002 between Monsanto and DuPont, owner of Pioneer, to share their technologies for mutual benefit. With combined seed sales of

$3.5 billion out of total commercial seed sales of $30 billion for 2001 (see Chapter 4), they are also the biggest seed players.

In order to progress, the companies are looking for allies and networks they can use, such as the CNFA (see pp. 126–9). It is also important to influence the governments and institutions (such as universities and extension services) of countries in the global South, so that their funding and activities can support the priorities of the corporations. Syngenta has two foundations, the Syngenta Foundation and the Novartis Foundation, while Monsanto has the Monsanto Fund; these 'non-profit' arms can help to broker and fund projects with universities and research institutions in both North and South.

Farmers may have no money to purchase company products: micro-credit schemes can help here, by providing loans, collecting debts and helping to link the farmers into industrial agriculture networks. Moreover, credit schemes can be linked to the use of GM technology, so there is a potential captive market here. Monsanto's proposed partnership with the Grameen Bank may have been prevented, but the intention is clear. Extension services provide a ready-made network for promoting products packaged with shiny presentations.

As will be shown in this chapter, the corporations, in particular Monsanto, have made good use of existing institutions such as micro-credit agencies, rural extension networks and development aid to reach into this uncharted territory. Talking about Monsanto's strategy, the World Bank commented explicitly that 'many of these transactions were designed specifically to help the company move more rapidly into emerging markets'.[2] The overseas development agencies of the different Northern governments, especially the US government, provide plenty of support. The World Bank and the World Trade Organisation, backed by the US government in particular, are promoting the drive towards the harmoni-sation of laws that facilitate the activities of the corporations, such as intellectual property rights or investment and biosafety regimes. Disasters, meanwhile – whether floods, droughts or famines – provide an opportunity to unload subsidised US agricultural produce on stricken countries. This destroys local markets, weakening local economies and undermining self-reliance.

The importance of reaching women is a recurring theme. Monsanto, for example, promises that its technologies will benefit women in developing countries, because they will need to do less weeding and spraying. They can spend more time with their children, while girls will have more time for education. Increased productivity will provide women with surpluses to sell and improve their quality of life.[3] It is difficult for audiences in the developed world to respond critically to such persuasive arguments, especially if they lack experience of the lives of women in the Third World. Micro-credit schemes have also targeted women, who have been shown to be reliable payers of their debts, even though interest is often set at high levels.

The corporations wish to ensure they control the technologies they introduce, using 'growers' contracts' where appropriate patent legislation is not yet in place. Several corporations have been continuing with the development and introduction of technologies to control the germination of seeds or the expression of traits. These genetic use restriction technologies or GURTs, such as the Terminator and Traitor technologies, were first developed to increase company profits by preventing seed saving and restricting access to the genetically engineered characteristics, so as to gain more from emerging markets.

This chapter presents some particular cases, with a case study on Argentina, a section on GM aid in Africa, and a look at the underlying GM strategy for Africa, using Uganda as an example. There is also a section on conservation tillage, used to promote herbicides, plus two cases of resistance to Monsanto's attempts to force its products into the key countries, India and Brazil.

GM crops worldwide

The tables which follow show in which countries GM crops were planted in 2001 and 2002 and in what quantity; they also show which GM crops were grown and their share of the total hectares planted with that type of crop.

What shows up most clearly is that the vast majority (66 per cent in 2002) are planted in the USA and that GM soybeans formed by far the largest proportion of the GM crops planted. While looking at these figures, it helps to remember that Monsanto dominated massively, with 91 per cent of GM crops carrying its patented traits, representing 48 million out of a total of 52.4 million hectares in 2001.[4] In 2002, GM soybeans used mostly for animal feed constituted more than half the world total for the first time. GM corn remains a fairly small percentage of the global crop total and most of the increase for 2002 took place in the US.

Agricultural research and development

Agricultural R&D as it is known today has its roots in the public agricultural 'experiment stations' of the 1800s, set up by agricultural societies in various European countries to explore science-based solutions to agricultural problems. Over time such stations were spread through the South by the process of colonisation. Indeed they were an essential part of ensuring that

Table 8.1 • Countries planting GM crops in 2001 and 2002

Rank	Country	Million ha		% world GM crops		Annual growth rate	
		2001	2002	2001	2002	2001	2002
1	USA	35.7	39.0	68%	66%	18%	9%
2	Argentina	11.8	13.5	22%	23%	18%	14%
3	Canada	3.2	3.5	6%	6%	6%	9%
4	China	1.5	2.1	3%	4%	300%	40%
5	South Africa	0.2	0.3				50%
	TOTAL	52.4	58.4	99%	99%		

Source: Based on ISAAA figures.

Table 8.2 • GM crop areas and percentages (of total crop and of total GM planted globally) in 2001 and 2002

Crop	Land planted globally with crop (m ha)	Land planted with GM		GM as % of world crop		GM crop as % of total GM	
		2001	2002	2001	2002	2001	2002
Soy beans	72	33.3	36.5	46	51	63	62
Cotton	34	6.8	6.8	20	20	13	12
Canola	25	2.75	3.00	11	12	5	5
Corn	140	9.8	12.4	7	9	19	21
TOTAL	271	52.65	58.7	19	21.6	100	100

Source: Based on ISAAA figures.

Table 8.3 • Traits expressed by GM crops planted worldwide for 2001 and 2002, as areas and percentages

Trait	Percentage		Land use (million ha)	
	2001	2002	2001	2002
Herbicide tolerance	77	75	40.6	44.2
Bt toxin (insect resistance)	15	17	7.8	10.1
Stacked genes: herbicide tolerance & Bt toxin	8	8	4.2	4.4

the colonies developed food supplies (plus new consumer commodities such as coffee, tea, chocolate, sugar, etc.) for their colonising countries. However, countries that were the object of this process were not always receptive:

> To overcome the biases against the development and diffusion of agricultural technologies among developing countries, agricultural research that was internationally conceived and funded began in the mid-1940s. It expanded through the 1950s as the Ford and Rockefeller Foundations placed agricultural staff in less-developed countries to work alongside scientists in national research organizations on joint-venture research.[5]

The international agricultural research centres (IARCs, see Chapter 5) are part of this development and were central to spreading green revolution technologies and high-bred crop varieties in the South, thus eliminating local systems of farmer innovation, varieties, and knowledge in many regions.

Whilst the level of publicly funded agricultural R&D in the North was already at $7.1 billion in 1976, the South was at $4.7 billion and yet to increase its investment. As detailed in the International Food Policy Research Institute (IFPRI) report in 2001, between 1976 and 1995 global public expenditure on agricultural research and development nearly doubled from about $11.8 to $21.7 billion a year:[6] $10.2 billion of this was spent in the North and $11.5 billion in the South. However, during the 1990s, growth in global public expenditure slowed drastically to 2 per cent. By 1996 China still reported a growth of 5.5 per cent, yet Africa's budget was actually shrinking by 0.2 per cent annually and the North stagnated to near zero. In each region expenditure was dominated by a few countries: in the North, by the US, Japan, France and Germany, and in the South by China, India and Brazil.

The amount available to the Consultative Group for International Agricultural Research (CGIAR) system has also been on the decline, representing just 1.5 per cent of the 1995 global public-sector agricultural research spending.

By the mid-1990s, the private sector was spending about $11 billion on agricultural research and development, roughly equal to half the global public sector spending on agricultural R&D, and 94 per cent of the private sector budget was spent in the North. Private expenditure tends to be less farm-focused and more focused on machinery, post-harvest research, food and food processing. There is also a strong focus on chemicals, as most herbicides and insecticides have been developed by the private sector. During the 1990s, 40 per cent of private research expenditure in the UK and US has gone into chemicals, while in Germany it is up to 75 per cent. Plant breeding and veterinary and pharmaceutical research have become increasingly important as well. Private research outputs are generally more suited to capital-intensive, value-added farming. They are no substitute for publicly funded research.

Productive research tends to be cumulative, with people building on previous findings to create a growing stock of knowledge. In Africa, for example, wars have many times disrupted research and infrastructure profoundly. Now the rush for intellectual property is helping to interfere with the accumulation of knowledge by blocking the exchange of information. Complicated labyrinths of patent protection may have to be negotiated in order to access vital knowledge, for which licences may have to be obtained. 'Moreover, the needs of industry are yet to be properly reconciled with the rights of indigenous people and poor farmers who maintained many of the landraces on which today's improved varieties depend.'[7] Even though patents may not yet be obtainable in many countries, databases of knowledge may increasingly require fees for access. With current pressure to extend patenting regimes rapidly to the South, we may also be faced with a 'tragedy of the anti-commons', caused when too many individuals have rights of exclusion in a scarce resource.

It seems therefore that not only is public agricultural research in decline, but that agricultural research itself is becoming increasingly removed from and irrelevant to those closest to the soil, those who are still working as farmer breeders, continuing to innovate as they have always done, developing and maintaining living knowledge and seed stock on which we all depend and which we risk losing at our peril. Some would say, in fact, that the effect of agricultural R&D and its promotion has largely been to destroy the existing innovation systems and knowledge of farmers, making the latter dependent on outside actors.[8]

Much could be achieved through developing more publicly funded collaborative research led by farmers, something which has been called for constantly by critics of the CGIAR and by NGOs such as MASIPAG and SIBAT in the Philippines, which actually practise it.

Promoting technology to farmers

Rural extension work was developed as a service offered by governments on aspects of farming. Like agricultural research and development initiatives, its beginnings can be traced to colonialism and it was instrumental in the promotion and spread of the green revolution. All too often, rural extension work involved people from the North, trained in college rather than on the land, teaching farmers with far more experience than themselves. Increasingly around the world, corporate-funded foundations, NGOs and companies are privatising the formerly publicly funded rural extension networks. The public funding often came from Northern donors like the World Bank or USAID, who now encourage and support privatisation and collaboration with corporations – as in Uganda, for example.[9]

Privatisation of rural extension work systems provides companies with a perfect opportunity to promote their products to farmers, who thus become familiar with their brands and may begin to trust them. In this way a new cycle of dependency begins. It is difficult for farmers who have once adopted new seeds and inputs to return to their former methods, and farmer varieties quickly disappear if they are not maintained.

Trial seeds or pesticides may be issued free at first to attract farmers. Credit may be offered on condition that farmers use certain products. Companies may work with local credit facilities to tie in their packages with credit given (see below, pp. 196–9). Slick presentation by the companies of modern technologies in shiny packaging, promoted with videos, helps to convince farmers that the companies have superior knowledge, especially when the confidence of farmers in their own knowledge and calling has been undermined and they have been made to feel outdated and out of touch. Presenting the farmer with only herbicides at first (glyphosate or glufosinate, for example) lays the ground for introducing GM herbicide-resistant seed later. It has been alleged in India and Thailand that farmers have been given GM seed to try without being told what it is.

Monsanto's *Sustainability Report 1999–2000* shows how the corporations operate, revealing the links between the different players and the central involvement of the Sasakawa–Global 2000 Programme (SG 2000, see below, pp. 194–5):

> The primary classroom is the demonstration plot. Extension workers enlist farmers who agree to provide labour and a piece of their land for an 'experiment'. Farmers gain a realistic idea of what labour and costs the new technology entails. They almost invariably harvest two to three times the yield they formerly enjoyed at less cost and labour. Farm families in the area are invited to field days and the ideas and technology are taken up by more smallholders every year. Then SG 2000 moves on. During the last 14 years SG 2000 has helped national extension personnel and small-scale farmers to establish 600,000 demonstration plots in more than a dozen African countries.[10]

This section looks at some of the different entities involved, including company foundations, and one example of a government using taxpayers' money to assist a corporation.

Monsanto and PEACE

In June 1999 Monsanto announced that it would jointly develop rural initiatives with generic pesticide manufacturer Rallis, which operates local promotion agencies – the Pesticide Efficacy Advisory Centres (PEACE) – throughout India. According to Agrow, the agrochemical industry analysts, 'the company will provide technical inputs, farm management training and other services to improve farm productivity and incomes'.[11]

As noted above, this kind of practice provides a vehicle for the introduction of GM by promoting herbicides as precursors of herbicide-resistant seeds, which can be added later.

Zeneca

Zeneca (now Syngenta) has a similar programme to promote the use of pesticides widely.

> Zeneca's 'Farmer Education and Training Team' has developed cartoon comic papers for distribution in schools under the title of the 'Adventures of the Grow Safely Team'. Children learn to link pesticides and agriculture and are unlikely to receive balanced material on participatory-IPM [Integrated Pest Management], organic and other ecological approaches.[12]

Once again, this is a scenario which leads readily to the promotion of GM technology.

The Novartis Foundation for Sustainable Development (NFSD)

Before spinning off its agribusiness in November 2000, Novartis was keen to point out that it was 'more than a typical Life Science company'.[13] One of the ways it differentiates itself from the others is through the Novartis Foundation for Sustainable Development. 'Development cooperation is not a vehicle for public relations,' the website stresses, 'it is difficult work that demands long-term commitment.'

The NFSD is a development organisation funded entirely by Novartis which 'supports efforts made by poor people themselves to satisfy their basic needs'.[14] But critics say that the company has little interest in serious reform to meet the needs of poor people and that the new image has only been superimposed on existing activities. In such circumstances it is always important to ask who decides and who designs the projects. Are the local people in control of what happens? Do local people or the company benefit most from these activities?

One project organised by the NFSD is a centre for the training and education of small farmers in Negros, the Philippines. The project was initiated in 1995 by an organisation called Provincial Advocates for Sustainable Agricultural Development (PASAD) to assist farmers to break out of dependency on large landowners, food companies and chemical farming. Another is an agricultural extension service in Laos. The Novartis Foundation is at pains to point out that there is no commercial link between Novartis and the NFSD. Since October 2001 many of these agricultural projects have been moved to the Syngenta Foundation for Sustainable Agriculture (see below), including the goal to support poor people in their efforts to survive.

The executive director of the Foundation, Professor Klaus M. Leisinger, is one of Novartis's main spokespersons for biotechnology. He argues that sustainable agriculture is not possible without what he refers to as 'green biotechnology', and he accuses the movement against genetic engineering, which he refers to as 'bio-McCarthyism', of delaying nutritional improvements that could save thousands of lives.[15] Before joining the Foundation in 1990, Klaus M. Leisinger was the manager of Ciba Pharmaceuticals in East Africa and thereafter the head of the Department of Relations with Developing Countries at Ciba in Basel.[16]

The Syngenta Foundation for Sustainable Agriculture

The Syngenta Foundation was officially launched on 12 October 2001, with Klaus Leisinger as interim executive director in addition to his position at the Novartis Foundation. Its stated goals are very similar if not identical to the agricultural programme section of the Novartis Foundation for Sustainable Development. AgBioWorld reported:

> In his presentation at the founding ceremony, Dr David Evans, Head of Research & Technology at Syngenta, underscored the role of modern technology in agriculture: 'With sustainable agriculture as the framework, research and development can help developing countries control pests and fight plant diseases while increasing yields and improving crops. In addition to selling its products, Syngenta is making available at no cost a number of innovative technologies to subsistence farmers.[17]

The foundation has three African projects: insect-resistant maize in Kenya; millet and sorghum improvement in Mali; and land and resource management in Eritrea.

SYNGENTA AND IRMA: BT MAIZE FOR AFRICA

The Kenya project, Insect-Resistant Maize for Africa (IRMA), involves working on maize genetically engineered to resist the attacks of the corn borer by expressing a version of bacterial Bt toxin. It brings together CIMMYT (the International Maize and Wheat Improvement Centre, with headquarters in Mexico and 17 branches in developing countries, including Kenya), KARI (the Kenyan Agricultural Research Institute) and the Syngenta Foundation, which is providing the financial support for the project. CIMMYT is providing expertise and training to KARI in genetic engineering technology. The project aims to introduce insect-resistant maize and avoid the problem of rapid development of resistance to Bt toxin among maize pests by designing appropriate refuges (places where non-Bt maize is planted). Intercropping with other useful non-GM plants which also are host to or attract maize pests is regarded as the most acceptable form of refuge for small farmers. There are, however, non-GM methods of combating the corn-borer which Syngenta does not fund. These include growing napier grass around the field to attract the pest away from the crop, and intercropping *Desmodium* with the maize to repel it. *Desmodium* is a nitrogen fixer and suppresses the parasitic witchweed, while all the plants are good fodder.

SYNGENTA FOUNDATION AND PUBLIC–PRIVATE PARTNERSHIPS

The Foundation's Mali project provides further evidence of how its activity benefits Syngenta agribusiness. The United Nation's International Fund for Agricultural Development (IFAD) sees poverty eradication as linked to economic growth. It provides loans to more than 100 governments for projects providing 'economic opportunities for rural dwellers' and sees its role as promoting equitable partnerships between smallholders and agribusiness.

According to Nikolaus Schultze – coordinator of private sector and capital markets operations at IFAD – Mali presented a case where small farmers lacked access to adapted seeds and seed treatment packages. As stated on their website, the Syngenta Foundation helped to:

> convince the Syngenta-agribusiness to participate in our programme. This led us to engage in a public–private partnership that has proved fruitful for all partners and stakeholders involved: Syngenta-agribusiness, the Syngenta Foundation for Sustainable Agriculture, IFAD, and ultimately the smallholders the Fund supports through its projects.

From this one can see how the Syngenta Foundation works with Syngenta's agribusiness operation and how all the players are facilitating access to poor farmers for agribusiness, providing new markets for the latter which it would be difficult to reach without considerable expense.

BORROWING THE POINTS MADE BY THE OPPOSITION

Klaus Leisinger is at pains to state that biotechnology cannot solve problems without social and political reform but he sees it as an important tool and wants it to reach the poorest. Certainly, judging from this website, the initial, almost evangelical fervour in promoting GM crops has been moderated and some of the points put forward by development organisations and others sceptical of the benefits of GM have been adopted and incorporated into the language. All the information above was publicly available on the Foundation's website in June 2002.[18]

Monsanto Fund

'We must be the change we wish to see in the world' – Gandhi.

Monsanto Fund website[19]

Founded in 1964, the Fund has four main areas of activity, which it calls: Agricultural Abundance, the Environment, Science Education and Our Communities. Its operating principles include the phrase 'Be humbled by and appreciative of our responsibility.'

Through the Agricultural Abundance programme, Monsanto aims to increase yields and nutritional values through improved technologies. It also aims to create partnerships among the private, public and academic sectors and it focuses on extension work and training.

Under the heading 'One of the projects that makes us proud' it gives a brief description of the Buhle Farmers' Academy, Delmas, South Africa, and says that small farmers are trained there in commercial and technical farming skills. In addition the Fund focuses on environmental and science education for young people in the US.

Sasakawa–Global 2000 Programme (SG 2000)

In 1985, the late Japanese philanthropist and billionaire Rioichi Sasakawa sponsored a workshop in Geneva to assess the possibilities of introducing the green revolution into Africa. The Sasakawa Africa Association (SAA) was registered as a non-profit, tax-exempt organisation in Geneva in 1986. At about the same time, former US president Jimmy Carter offered to engage national leaders in discussion of critical economic and agricultural policy issues. Subsequently SAA and Global 2000, a programme of the Carter Center in Atlanta, combined forces to form a partnership called Sasakawa– Global (SG) 2000. Since 1986 the Sasakawa Africa Association (SAA) has supported agricultural extension work, while Global 2000 provides infor- mation about the latest technologies and methods. Monsanto has cooperated with SG 2000 since the early 1990s, and in 2000 actively supported pro- grammes in Ghana, Ethiopia, Tanzania, Malawi and Mozambique.[20]

SG 2000 works mainly with and through ministries of agriculture in Southern countries, primarily with national extension services, but also with national agricultural research systems (NARSs) and IARCs. Its main means of communication with farmers is through field demonstration programmes for small-scale farmers to introduce new food crop production and post- harvest technology.

According to the website in 2001, Ghana, the Sudan and Ethiopia have adopted the Global 2000 approach. There are now projects in Benin, Nigeria, Tanzania and Togo. Most recently, SG 2000 has been invited to begin work in Burkina Faso, Eritrea, Guinea, Mali, Mozambique and Uganda.[21]

The SG 2000 programme is funded by the Sasakawa and Nippon Foundations (the latter also founded by Ryoichi Sasakawa). The Nippon Foundation is proud to announce that it gets its revenues from the profits of legalised gambling on motorboat racing.[22]

Norman Borlaug is senior consultant for SG 2000 (see pp. 72–3).

SG 2000 Agribusiness Forum

SG 2000 has established relations with a number of major transnational agri-businesses to encourage increased investments in project countries. Beyond assisting at the policy level, they also collaborate at the grassroots level in various enterprise development activities. As seen in Table 8.4, all collaborating corporations focus on 'input dealer development'.

Table 8.4 • SG 2000 collaborators

Corporation	SG 2000 development activity
Monsanto	Conservation tillage
Novartis	Crop protection
Norsk Hydro	Fertiliser
Cargill	Field crop seeds, agro-processing
Seminis	Vegetable seeds, market development
Pioneer Hi-Bred International	Field crop seeds

Winrock International

In 1985 the Winrock International Livestock Research and Training Center, founded by Arkansas governor Winthrop Rockefeller, merged with the Agricultural Development Council, founded by John D. Rockefeller and the International Agricultural Development Service, to form the Winrock International Institute for Agricultural Development.

Winrock International is a 'private non-profit' organisation which works in over 40 Southern countries with farmers, local organisations, research and educational institutions, and policy makers to 'improve agricultural product-ivity, sustainability, and income in developing countries'.[23] Its stated focus is to promote new farm technologies and improved seed varieties, and to create market-driven agriculture, especially post-harvesting processing, to add value and create public–private partnerships.

Monsanto is working as a partner with Winrock International in small-holder projects that promote the use of conservation tillage practices in

Senegal, Mali, Ivory Coast and Indonesia. These partnerships include co-operation by Monsanto in Winrock's On-Farm Agricultural Resources Management (ONFARM) programme to help move selected parts of Africa and Indonesia from subsistence to market-driven agriculture. In 1998 Monsanto gave $225,000 for a four-year project promoting conservation tillage using glyphosate-based herbicide (see pp. 217–20) in West Africa and $300,000 to promoting conservation tillage in Indonesia.[24]

Winrock International board members include corporate stalwarts like Whitney MacMillan, former chief executive and chairperson of Cargill Inc.

Canadian Development Aid to Monsanto in China

In 1998 the Canadian government approved more than $280,000 to promote GM crops directly to farmers in China. Over objections from some government officials, including Canada's embassy in Beijing, the Canadian International Development Agency (CIDA) is funding rural extension work to encourage farmers to grow Monsanto's GM cotton and corn.[25] The Canadian government is thus actually funding a corporate rural extension programme that will help Monsanto reach new constituencies and gain profits. The *Toronto Star* reported in February 2001:

> 'The goal of the project is to be able to conclusively demonstrate to the govern-ment of China the production benefits derived by applying Bt cotton and weed control technologies, in combination with other management technologies,' states CIDA's project management report.
>
> 'The company (Monsanto) put $280,000 in goods and services into the project and was expected to invest another $20 million in a campaign to promote its biotechnology in China if the project proves successful,' another CIDA document states.[26]

The project is continuing under the sponsorship of Monsanto and IMC Global, an international mining, fertiliser and animal feed producer that operates potash mines in Saskatchewan, Canada, through a subsidiary, IMC Kalium.

Micro-credit agencies

> *Monsanto sees micro-credit ... as a way to develop new markets by helping the people in those markets participate in economic development.*
>
> Monsanto, *Sustainability Report 1997*[27]

Micro-credit is commonly defined as the extension of small loans to entrepreneurs, especially women, too poor to qualify for traditional bank loans. Rather than being based on collateral, it is based on mutual trust that these loans will be repaid. Muhammad Yunus, who founded the Grameen Bank in Bangladesh in the mid-1970s, pioneered this idea of micro-credit.[28] The Grameen Foundation website states:

> The Grameen Bank was started in Bangladesh in 1976 as an action-research project that attempted to provide tiny loans to very poor people to allow them to start 'micro-businesses'. Twenty-five years later, Grameen Bank has 2.4 million borrowers, 94 per cent of whom are women, and has loaned more than $3.7 billion in amounts averaging less than $200.[29]

At the Micro-credit Summit held in February 1997 in Washington and opened by Hillary Clinton, a campaign was launched to globalise the micro-credit movement. More than 2,900 people from 137 countries met to found this nine-year campaign to provide small loans to 100 million of the world's poorest families by the year 2005. According to interim reports, 13.8 million 'poor clients' had already been served by the year 2000. Monsanto's website carried the following message about the Micro-credit Summit campaign in December 2002:

> The people of Monsanto are proud to participate in the Micro-credit Summit Campaign, a nine-year effort to reach 100 million of the world's poorest families, especially the women of those families, with credit for self-employment and other financial and business services, by the year 2005.... The solutions developed and offered to smallholder farmers are often a package of existing commercial technologies, including improved seeds, biotechnology traits where approved and applicable, conservation tillage practices, crop protection products and other inputs, as well as training and technical assistance.[30]

Monsanto's collaboration with micro-credit agencies is part of a deliberate plan announced in its 1997 *Sustainability Report* which stated that it would have micro-credit operations in all the world's regions by the end of 1998. Monsanto has been for some years chair of the Council of Corporations for the Micro-credit Summit Campaign. The Grameen Bank and Muhammad Yunus are also involved in this project.

Whilst the schemes are praised by the North as the way forward to alleviate poverty, those affected by micro-credits do not always agree. Farida Akhter of UBINIG (Policy Research for Development Alternatives, Bangladesh) called it the 'women's indebtedness programme' and stated in a speech in Jakarta in 2000:

> The major development support that the poor people, mainly the poor women can receive today is Micro-Credit. It is seen as *the solution* for poverty. It has a magic capacity that the poor can be indebted and then they can overcome poverty. The impression that is given is that there is no need to develop the health sector, education facilities, or any other social support system for the poor;

micro-credit alone can solve all the problems. While, since the 1970s, the Third World governments are failing to pay back the loans and increasingly becoming defaulters, the poor were lauded for their disciplined submission to the rule of credit money, that is the financial capital mediated through development agencies and the banks 'for the poor' like Grameen. Money circulated through the poor communities self-expanded often to 130 per cent, appropriating the remaining resources of poor in the form of interest. Indebting poor has become the new game of development and swept the development discourse and the practice.[31]

Monsanto and the Grameen Bank in Bangladesh

In June 1998, the Grameen Bank and Monsanto announced an unlikely alliance. Monsanto was offering US$150,000 to help set up the Grameen Monsanto Centre for Environmentally Friendly Technologies. This was intended to offer Bangladeshi farmers soft loans to buy hybrid seeds (including hybrid rice and cotton, both important crops for Bangladesh) and agrochemicals including Monsanto's own proprietary herbicides and. Other projects were to include demonstration farms and conservation techniques. Monsanto noted at the time that Bangladesh lacked the regulatory procedures adequate for the introduction of GM seeds.[32]

Grameen's alliance with Monsanto triggered an international wave of protest, initiated by women in the South. For example Vandana Shiva of the Research Foundation for Science, Technology and Ecology, India, stated in an open letter to Mohammad Yunus, President of the Grameen Bank:

> The micro-credit scheme linked to the Grameen Monsanto centre will create markets for Monsanto's products, not the products based on the creativity of Bangladesh peasants. They will not build on the skills and knowledge and resources which women of Bangladesh have; they will wipe out their knowledge and resources and destroy their livelihoods and food security.
>
> Monsanto's skills in agriculture are in the field of genetically engineered crops. These crops are designed to use more agrichemicals like Round-up which is a broad spectrum herbicide that kills anything green. Your micro-credit venture with Monsanto will directly finance the destruction of the green vegetables that women collect from the fields. Round-up also has negative impacts on fish which provide 80 per cent of the animal protein in Bangladesh.[33]

After worldwide protest, Grameen withdrew from the project.

Micro-credit and the enforced introduction of new technologies

The introduction of (F1) hybrid seed into Bangladesh is intimately connected to micro-credit. After the 1998 floods, private companies were for the first time allowed to import rice seed as part of the government's post-flood rehabilitation programme. Advance Chemical Industries Ltd (ACI) took the opportunity and imported Indian hybrid rice (Aalok 6201) from Hybrid Rice International, a subsidiary of Proagro owned by Aventis (now Bayer). Without informing farmers that they could not save seeds, ACI together with the Bangladesh Rural Advancement Committee (BRAC) – a large micro-credit agency – put the seeds on the market. Farhad Mazhar of UBINIG commented:

> Micro-credit is the only way that hybrid seed can be sold in countries like Bangladesh .... Immediately after the flood, BRAC aggressively promoted Aalok 6201 .... Farmers had to accept credit and pay very high interest, but at the same time had to accept the proprietary technology of ACI.[34]

Binding the farmer to the corporation

Growers' contracts

There are also more direct means of securing farmer dependence. Patent laws and contractual agreements can be marshalled to dictate practice to farmers, above all to prevent them from saving seed. In the US, Canada and, more recently, South Africa, Monsanto uses growers' contracts with its RoundUp Ready seeds. These agreements stipulate that farmers who save and re-use the harvested seed the following season will face potentially unlimited costs and fines. Farmers also agree to Monsanto sampling their crop to ensure that they are not violating the contract or the patent. Furthermore, the company may dictate most steps in the farming process and even control where the farmer sells the crop. The farmer generally has to pay a technology fee on top of the seed price.

By 1999 Monsanto had already accused 600 farmers in the US and Canada of violating its patents, even stating in advertisements that it was investigating farmers for saving seeds. It has since brought a number of cases against farmers, the most famous being that against Percy Schmeiser. However, the companies still have to maintain vigilance in order to prevent 'illegal' seed saving. Monsanto even hired detectives from the Pinkerton Agency to help with the task. In the South, where the biotech companies are now establishing themselves, surveillance would be far more difficult, due to poor communications, greater resistance and the sheer size of the problem: 1.4 billion people in the South depend on saved seed for their food.

Moreover, many developing countries do not yet have patent laws in place that allow the companies to punish seed saving. Faced by this diffi- culty, they may use growers' agreements, or (see Argentina case study below, pp. 203–6), they may be content to charge a technology fee, but still allow farmers to use, save and re-use GM seed, since this introduces the farmers to the company, ensures widespread use of the technology, promotes use of products such as herbicides, and begins to establish dependency – especially since farmers' own varieties and independence are rapidly lost once they begin to use the company's products. However, the corporations are developing another means of protecting their property – a technology built into the seed itself to prevent seed saving.

Terminator technology – technology protection system

The goal of the Terminator technology is 'to increase the value of proprietary seed owned by US seed companies and to open up new markets in Second and Third World countries'.

Willard Phelps, USDA spokesperson

My main interest is the protection of American technology. Our mission is to protect US agriculture, and to make us competitive in the face of foreign competition. Without this [patent] there is no way of protecting the technology.

M. J. Oliver, USDA, primary inventor of the Terminator technology

To deal with the threat of seed saving to company profits, the US Department of Agriculture (USDA) and the US seed company Delta and Pine Land developed and patented a technology protection system (US patent 5723765, 3 March 1998). It is designed so that if the farmer replants harvested seed, the seed will not germinate. This technology was rapidly nicknamed Terminator technology and the seeds 'suicide seeds' because they effectively commit suicide by producing a toxin when the germination process begins.[35] The Vice-President, Technology Transfer, Delta and Pine Land Company stated:

Benefits include protecting the environment from gene escapes into other plant species; maintaining the integrity of refugia acres by eliminating the planting of saved seed and protecting the technology provider's investment against free use of technology. Protection systems help insure that individuals and companies developing new traits and technologies for commercial varieties have the ability to earn a fair return on their investment.[36]

There was a tremendous public outcry all around the world against the technology, so Monsanto and (Astra)Zeneca (holding Terminator patents WO9403619 and AU 687008) publicly vowed in 1999 not to commercialise Terminator seeds, and Monsanto still maintains this is its pledge (see Monsanto website). Governments and civil society organisations were thus lulled into thinking that the crisis had passed, but companies see the potential benefits for industry as too valuable to let go. So companies have continued to acquire Terminator patents. Syngenta holds eight patents, two of which were acquired by Novartis and five by Zeneca, the latest dated 26 March 2002.

Delta and Pine Land gained two in 1999, after its initial patent in 1998. DuPont owns two terminator patents and BASF and Monsanto hold one each.[37] As Harry Collins of Delta and Pine Land said in January 2000,

> We've continued right on with work on the Technology Protection System [Terminator]. We never really slowed down. We're on target, moving ahead to commercialise it. We never really backed off.[38]

COULD TERMINATOR SEED SOON BE ON THE MARKET?

In August 2001 USDA announced that it had licensed Terminator technology to Delta and Pine Land after working with the company to develop the subject of its licence. USDA experienced internal opposition to issuing the licence, yet persisted. It claimed that use with heritage flower and vegetable seeds will be forbidden and that no plant on the market before 2003 would be engineered with the technology.[39]

Its attempt to justify the use of the technology includes the claim that it will prevent gene flow from GM plants. This line was also used by Delta and Pine Land (see quote above) and in the UK by the Royal Society and the Advisory Committee on Releases to the Environment (ACRE). However, scientists question whether Terminator technology will necessarily eliminate gene flow, especially as this would demand 100 per cent effectiveness and gene stability. Even if this could be achieved, it would not counterbalance all the potential threats to agricultural biodiversity and the broader environment, human health and food security. The consequences simply cannot be predicted from the current knowledge base.

Traitor technology

This is a variation on Terminator, designed to produce seeds that require the application of proprietary chemicals to 'switch on' desirable characteristics such as drought tolerance, salt tolerance, toxin production for pest resistance, and production of pharmaceuticals, or to 'switch off' undesirable ones, such as the production of allergens. The official name for this technology is 'genetic use restriction technologies' or GURTs. Chemical switches proposed and tested to date have included the plant hormone and gas ethylene (C_2H_4) and the antibiotic tetracycline. Parts of a Traitor switching mechanism have been tested in the UK at Zeneca's Jealotts Hill Centre. 'Desirable characteristics' may prove more difficult to develop than the switches, and switch mechanisms may prove to be unreliable and unstable.

However, genetically engineered 'Traitor coffee', designed to make all the berries on the bush ripen simultaneously with the spraying of ethylene, to enable the mechanical harvesting of all the coffee beans at one time, is already being developed. Production costs would fall, leading to even lower market prices and potentially out-competing those who could not afford the technology. It would inevitably encourage large-scale monocultures of open field varieties as opposed to shade varieties grown under trees in mixed plots, which is the pattern more often followed by the smaller farmer. If allowed to continue, this could effectively mean the final destruction of the small coffee producer in Africa, Asia and South America, already suffering from the collapsing world price of coffee, and would put even more control into the hands of the large coffee companies.[40]

Perhaps most threatening are the patents on Traitor technology which relate to plants with compromised immune systems, said to be developed for research purposes, to examine the effects of pathogens. The spread of such traits to staple crops could cause a major disaster. Syngenta (Novartis) holds three such patents, DuPont one.

Lack of choice for farmers

> We have always been under the gun of the multinational corporation. We are forced to get seeds from the two biggest seed companies .... Any arrangement where the farmer is not given a choice is bound to fail.
>
> Philippine Agriculture Secretary, Salvador Escudero, 1996[41]

Consolidation of the seed industry ultimately means lack of choice for the farmer. As seed companies phase out certain varieties, farmers who rely on purchasing seed could eventually find themselves with no choice but to buy hybrids or patented GM varieties.

Corn in South-east Asia

After rice, corn is South-east Asia's most important crop. For 12 million Filipinos, corn is a staple food, and in Indonesia more than 80 per cent of the crop goes to feed the country's people. Yet corn is increasingly being reduced to an animal feed crop which is either exported to the North or used to respond to the increase in meat and dairy product consumption and the globalisation of Asian diets. Only a handful of companies control almost 70 per cent of the hybrid corn seed market in South-east Asia. With the acquisition of Cargill Seeds International (excluding its US division) and DeKalb by Monsanto, only two companies – Monsanto and Pioneer – are, in effect, in control.[42]

GM corn will boost this process of corporate takeover. Corn is the subject of more biotech R&D and patent applications than any other crop.

> The majority of patents on transgenic corn are held by a handful of major US companies. Half of the 333 biotechnology patents granted or applied for on corn

worldwide can be traced to only six of the world's agrochemical giants. Not surprisingly, the top three (DuPont–Pioneer, Monsanto and Novartis) are also the top three companies controlling the seed trade worldwide. Some of the patent claims are very broad and sweeping and have been the subject of legal disputes.[43]

By 2002, genetically engineered Bt corn as well as herbicide-tolerant corn were already at various stages of testing in Indonesia, the Philippines and Thailand. Companies are determined to reach full market deployment of GM corn in South-east Asia as soon as possible, thereby securing an important market for their genetically modified products at a time when there is opposition to these in Europe. In December 2002 Monsanto's GM YieldGard 'Corn Borer' corn was approved for planting in the Philippines.[44]

Argentina: the cost of complying with US pressure

> Soya is not bringing wealth to Argentina. 'We are being occupied by the seed multinationals that have patented life and are forcing us to pay tribute to them,' says Jorge Eduardo Rulli, one of Argentina's leading agronomists. 'The more we produce the poorer we become.'[45]

Argentina was long held up as a model of compliance with IMF and World Bank regimes – until its economy went into meltdown, resulting in a popular revolt at the end of 2001. Argentina also showed itself a model of compliance with US policy on genetically engineered crops and has been for some time the second largest GM crop producer in the world, after the US (see Table 8.1, p. 187). Argentina was encouraged to focus on large-scale export agriculture to boost its economy and service its debt.

GM comes to Argentina

In the 1980s, demand for grains and oil seeds rose while the profit from raising cattle declined, which led Argentine farmers to abandon their mixed farming in favour of permanent crop cultivation systems.

> This was more lucrative since the production of soybean in rotation with wheat, maize or sunflower allowed three harvests every two years. Fences were removed and facilities for cattle dismantled to allow larger areas to be cultivated.[46]

A familiar pattern asserted itself, with farms growing larger and the smaller farmers abandoning or leasing out their land to contractors. 'In the heart of the soybean production area, north-west of Buenos Aires, half of the cultivated area is already managed by contractor holdings.'[47] It is estimated that some 7,000 farming families left the land each year. Millions of acres of land were put up for auction by the banks.[48]

Soil fertility soon began to decline and no-till farming was introduced (see ConTill, pp. 217–20). This involved the use of glyphosate to clear weeds instead of ploughing. It was but a short step from this to glyphosate-tolerant crops such as Monsanto's RoundUp Ready soya, introduced in 1996. The contractors found these methods suited their large-scale operations. In 1995, Monsanto's application for a patent on the RoundUp gene had been rejected by the Argentine national patent office. Plants cannot be patented under Argentine law. This means that Monsanto cannot protect its property with contracts, fines and court cases as in the USA. Furthermore, it had to cut the price of its seed in Argentina, which aroused some resentment among farmers in the USA, fearful of competition from Argentinian soybeans.[49] However, the factors protested by US farmers helped to get the crop massively established in Argentina, and Monsanto also benefited from the increased sales of glyphosate (up 250 per cent in two years – from 28 million litres in 1997/8 to 58 million litres in 1998/9 and 70 million in 1999/2000, much of it sprayed from the air).

By 2000, roughly 90 per cent of the soybeans (some 20 million acres) grown in Argentina were genetically engineered. Most of this soy was destined for export. GM maize (corn) and Bt cotton were also increasing, while RoundUp Ready cotton was expected soon. Official statistics reveal that some 12,000 acres of GM trials were held in 1999, including vegetables, cereals and fibres.[50] Nearly all (90 per cent) of the GM trials and all of the GM crops were introduced from outside Argentina. The country was used from early on as an off-season site for testing GM crops. Recently, the number of authorisations fell, perhaps in response to news of resistance to GM crops elsewhere.[51]

As GM crops took hold, smaller farmers found themselves caught in further traps. The price of soy began to fall on international markets, yet the price of loans increased. Once in financial difficulties, farmers could not recover, because the financial margins were too tight. On the way to the bottom, some farmers resorted to taking credit from agricultural input companies, to which packages of GM seed and inputs were often tied.

Furthermore, yields were not as good as had been promised. At the International Forum on Globalisation and Family Farmers and the Third Assembly of the RIAD (Red Interamericana de Democracia/Interamerican Network on Democracy) in Rio Grande do Sul, Brazil (4–10 July 2000), a representative from Argentina said there were growing rumours that GE soya yields were 10–15 per cent lower than the conventional yields and that the use of glyphosate was already having to be intensified, with stronger formulations also being required. This has since been confirmed by reports, one of which cites the rise of herbicide-resistant weeds as the cause.[52] It has also been confirmed by comparative experiments in the US that there is a yield drag of 5–10 per cent between RoundUp Ready soybeans and conventional cultivars.[53]

No public participation in decision making

The situation for obtaining consents for field testing or marketing of GM crops in Argentina resembles that in some East European countries. There are no civil society organisations represented on the GM commission. The commission consists largely of scientists, most of whom also work for the companies. Approvals have been granted on the basis of substantial equivalence (see p. 164). There has been no attempt to inform consumers or to have a national debate on the issue of GM and its impacts on human health, the environment and society.

Desperate times in Argentina

In December 2001 (around the same time as the popular revolt in Argentina) it was reported that the country was joining the US in bullying other countries to drop plans for moratoria, strict labelling and other measures to delay or prevent the introduction of GE crops. Bolivia had been planning a moratorium but dropped the idea in October, allegedly under pressure from Argentina.[54] Perhaps desperate Argentina had been bullied in its turn.

One result of the collapse of the economy was that Argentina's farmers planted more and more soy, because the tremendous squeeze on credit meant that they needed to find a crop with lower production costs. Conservation tillage methods mean that one farmer could farm a larger area alone, hence saving labour costs, but also depriving people of jobs. Production of sunflower and corn have fallen while soy, of which 90 per cent is said to be GM, covered 43 per cent of Argentina's farmland in 2002.[55] Lower yields and falling market returns have caused the area of cultivation to be extended, at the expense of indigenous forest – the mountain rainforest region of the Yungas in the north of Argentina – echoing developments in Brazil, where the fragile Cerrado forest is also being destroyed, often for soya, although not of the GM variety.[56]

Argentina's over-reliance on a single crop leaves it with little flexibility in its time of crisis and undermines food security in the country. Food prices have risen steeply, and deaths from hunger were reported in November 2002 among children in the north of the country. Lack of other food supplies, fear of food riots and difficulties with exporting GM soya led the government to devise programmes (such as 'Soya Solidarity') to feed its people soya, most of which is GM, originally destined for export as animal feed. Since it is not a food Argentinians normally eat, they had to be given directions as to how to use it and had no choice over whether to eat GM food. This is the first time soybeans have been consumed directly by human beings in such large quantities. Normally soya is fed to animals, or else, as in China, fermented or precipitated before consumption. Argentinians, it seems, are being subjected to a massive food experiment.

Rebuilding self-reliance

The wide adoption of GM soya has therefore accelerated the loss of food sovereignty, and of food and livelihood security, so increasing dependency. However, there is some cause for optimism in Argentina. People have started to create their own food gardens, most recently in the centre of Buenos Aires itself. By mid-2002, there were said to be some 450,000 of these *huertas* or gardens in the country, providing some food for about 2.5 million people, and the number is growing. These projects are mostly urban, however, and it is essential to get small farmers back on to the land, producing a diversity of food crops, and setting up seed banks, for the sake of future food security. As the gardens have spread, so the movement has become more political and is now strongly allied with Kick Them Out, which played a major part in the events of December 2001. With high unemployment, rocketing food prices and economic turbulence, some are looking to their own skills, energy and capacity to negotiate a way forward.

> Both the neighbourhood assemblies and the unemployed groups put a strong emphasis on the autonomy that the *huertas* allow them to achieve from the government. They also emphasise the *huertas*' cooperative, self-managed nature. The most radicalised participants go one step further. They see the vegetable gardens as an embryonic form of organisation for a new society based on the principles of self-sufficiency and community-based direct democracy.[57]

Preparing the ground for GM

Flood, famine, collapsing economies and wars all offer corporations opportunities to introduce their seeds, agrochemicals and other products to countries in the South, both directly and through NGOs or UN bodies such as the World Food Programme. Such assistance may sometimes be given free, but often has to be paid for, either directly or indirectly.

Economic crisis in Indonesia

In Indonesia, Monsanto's subsidiary PT Monagro Kimia used the economic crisis and crop failures to introduce its products to farmers. At a September

1998 ceremony to inaugurate its upgraded factory, Monagro donated 20 tons of Polaris herbicide (glyphosate) and $20,000 cash to the Minister of Agriculture to distribute to farmers.[58] In July 1999 it donated five tons of its C-5 hybrid maize seeds (not GM) and one ton of Polaris to Indonesian rice farmers who had lost crops to pest outbreaks. The July donation was followed by an announcement in August that the company was installing a factory for hybrid maize seed that would be capable of producing 3,000 tons of seed per year.[59]

This is an example of how companies use a disaster or crisis to gain entry and also how they give their products away at first to encourage farmers to begin using them. The hybrid seed and glyphosate formed part of a typical intensive agriculture package. From there it is a short step to the introduction of GM seed resistant to glyphosate, as has been noted previously.

Flooding in Bangladesh

This is another example of companies being swift to exploit opportunities to introduce their products. In 1998, Bangladesh was hit by floods lasting two months, which affected over 20 million people. Farmers lost whole paddy crops and were unable to save seeds for the following year. The government was slow to react and no comprehensive assessment was made of the immediate needs of the affected farmers. TNCs and foreign aid agencies, on the other hand, quickly seized the opportunity to determine the 'needs' of the farmers. Novartis issued special bulletins outlining the need for imported (HRV) seeds and pesticides; it even distributed hybrid tomato seeds and other vegetable seeds to farmers.

Novartis's efforts paid off. The flood opened the Bangladesh seed market to imported hybrid seeds, which previously had been prohibited. The media and the government's Agriculture Extension Department were persuaded to promote the expanded use of pesticides. The Extension Department set up a post-flood agriculture programme, which included seeds and cash credit to buy pesticides. The media played its part by releasing several articles about how farmers were in need of nothing but pesticides. The headline of one article in a national daily said, 'We do not want relief. We want pesticides.'[60]

GM as emergency and development aid

The Food for Progress program is authorized under Section 1110 of the Food Security Act of 1985. The authority provides for a responsive food aid mechanism to encourage and support the expansion of private enterprise in recipient countries and is meant to help countries seeking to implement democratic and market reforms. Section 416(b) of the Agricultural Act of 1949 provides for overseas donations of surplus commodities to developing countries and friendly countries.

US government[61]

Aid is the last unregulated export market open to US farmers and grain and commodity traders as consumers around the world shun GM foodstuffs and their respective governments begin to introduce strict import and labelling rules.[62] In effect, the US government is subsidising the biotech industry through allowing unlabelled, unsegregated GM crops to be used as emergency and development aid.

The issue of GM aid has become increasingly prominent over the last few years. According to Declan Walsh of the *Independent*, in 1999

> the US donated 500,000 tons of maize and maize products worth $111 million (£70 million) to international relief programmes. It is 'safe to assume' that 30 per cent of this aid was genetically modified, according to USAID, the US government's aid wing. Lucrative maize contracts were awarded to giant GM grain merchants such as Archer Daniels Midland (ADM) and Cargill .... The UN's World Food Programme (WFP) received just under half of the US maize donations.[63]

The WFP does not know how much food aid is GM nor does it have a policy on it. 'We have many issues to face and GM is way down the list,' said a WFP spokeswoman in Nairobi. It is likely that UN policy was influenced by its dependence on the US: during 1999 the US contributed $711 million to the WFP, almost half its global budget. The WFP food aid is distributed mainly by charities working in the region, such as Save the Children, CARE, and Action against Hunger. In 1999, the WFP's executive director was Catherine Bertini, a former US Department of Agriculture official from the Illinois cornbelt region.[64]

Rafael Mariano, chairperson of the Filipino peasant farmers' movement KMP, condemned these deals: 'The agricultural monopolies are very cruel, knowing that starving people have little choice but to accept the food and be grateful even if our biological future is being slowly corrupted with dangerous technologies.'[65] But the WFP information officer, Brenda Barton, took a pragmatic position, 'It would be pretentious to say that GM food matters to these people,' she said. 'When people are dying they don't question where the food is coming from.'[66]

Recipients do not necessarily hold the same opinion. In January 2001, the US withdrew a $4 million donation of GM corn grown originally for animal feed after Bosnian officials hesitated to approve it over fears of health risks to humans. In a statement the US embassy said it was 'disappointed' that governments of both entities – the Serbs' Republika Srpska and the

Muslim–Croat federation – 'could not decide in a timely fashion to accept its donation of 40,000 metric tons of corn for animal feed'. The US embassy statement stressed that 'The inclusion of the genetically modified corn is not unusual,' adding that 'such corn was routinely exported all over the world for human and animal consumption'.[67]

Similarly, in September 2000 the director of the Africa regional office of the International Organisation for Consumers wrote to President Clinton informing him about the dispatch of unlabelled GM maize by two American companies, Archer Daniels Midland and Cargill. The Association of Burundi Consumers (ABUCO) addressed a similar letter to the US ambassador to Burundi, asking him to convey its concerns to President Clinton. ABUCO asked Clinton to launch an investigation into 'the countries to where the aid is sent, and to ensure that all food aid to Africa is clearly labelled to allow the consumer to enjoy his right for information and choice'.[68]

More recently, Africa has been at the centre of further disputes over GM food aid (see below, pp. 210–13).

Not all aid is a gift

As well as emergency programmes, aid is directed at particular sectors such as women and children, through, for example, school feeding programmes. This kind of aid is generally not a donation, but linked to credit with long payback periods.

The Report from the Latin American Meeting on Food Aid (2001) in Ecuador points out that food aid, using excess production supported by subsidies, is at least in part designed to open up markets for US products and provide employment for US firms. Heavily subsidised food and crops are purchased in the US by organisations such as the Commodity Credit Corporation. The US government's PL480 emergency and development food aid programme provides food and also sets up credit lines so that countries can buy food. Food may be sold on the markets of recipient countries, with the proviso that the proceeds shall be used for specific development programmes. Because the price and transport of the food aid are subsidised, basically by the US consumers' taxes, its sale frequently undercuts local producers, who may then go out of business.

In this way, food aid can undermine the internal markets of recipient countries for local farmers and food processors; create dependency on food imports; provide a means of dumping products past their sell-by date and GMOs rejected by the EU and Japan, and generate good business for US transportation companies.[69] The impacts of such dumping are stark. The food sovereignty of countries like Bolivia, Ecuador and Colombia has been compromised by these programmes. The undercutting of local producers destroys livelihoods and disrupts agricultural traditions which may date back thousands of years, and which are adapted to local conditions and needs. The countries may then become dependent on imported food.

The dumping of GM food and feed compounds the problem further. Since GM is rejected by many Northern countries, the incentive to dump it on the South becomes even greater. It is almost as if aid were being used as an alternative form of subsidy for US farmers who are finding it difficult to sell their GM products legitimately. There are also consequences linked to the technology itself. For instance, some food aid which arrives in the form of seed is bound to be used for planting by hungry people to secure food for the next year, leading inevitably to GM contamination of local crop varieties. This could be seen as a strategy to contaminate the world so widely with GM crops and food that resistance will seem pointless.

The struggle for Africa's agriculture

'Food is power. We use it to change behaviour. Some may call that bribery. We do not apologise,' exclaimed Catherine Bertini, Executive Director of the World Food Programme, at the Beijing Woman's Conference (September 1995).[70]

The issue of GM food aid to Africa generated headlines in 2002, when it appeared that famine threatened, first in southern Africa (Zimbabwe, Zambia, Malawi, Mozambique, Swaziland and Lesotho) and then in Ethiopia. Western press reports tended to reproduce the old picture of Africa, the helpless and hopeless, needing to be fed once more because its governments were corrupt and modern farming had never been able to establish itself, except where white farmers had taken control – as in Zimbabwe, where now they were being pushed out and their land given to people who did not know how to cultivate it. In May 2002 Zimbabwe refused US food aid, on the grounds that it did not want GM food, and the US (apparently with no sense of irony) warned the Zimbabwean government not to play politics with food aid.[71] US food aid is known to contain many varieties of GM corn because the US does not segregate GM from non-GM. In July 2002 Zambia followed suit, also refusing food aid because it consisted of US corn. The US then accused Europe of causing starvation in Africa by refusing to accept GM out of hysteria or protectionism. The argument is that African countries may not accept GM crops or food aid out of fear they could lose exports to Europe because of concern over possible GM contamination. In September 2002 a delegation of Zambian scientists visited the US, the UK and South Africa on a fact-finding mission, after which Zambia announced that it would not change its position.

In August 2002 the head of the WFP announced: 'There is no way that the World Food Programme can provide the resources to feed these starving people without using food that has some biotech content.'[72] Later the WFP stated that countries had the right to choose; then it announced that it would try to find supplies of wheat instead of maize for Zambia, which had begun to call for funds to buy food instead of food donations. The EU responded to African appeals with some funding and NGOs pointed out that there was plenty of non-GM food to be purchased, for example from India.

Analysis of the realities underlying the emergency reveal another struggle for control. In many of the countries threatened with famine there were similar issues to be addressed, that if tackled properly could contribute to helping African countries build up their food security or sovereignty in the long term, instead of being forced into dependence. For example, in both Ethiopia and Zambia, while there were food shortages in some regions, there were food surpluses in others. What was lacking was money to purchase that food, the infrastructure to move it and storage facilities to keep it until it was distributed. Bringing in food from outside might be a short-term solution, but what was really needed was money to buy and transport the food produced in these other parts of the country, which would help to boost local and regional markets. Investigation showed that distortions caused by subsidy meant that it was actually cheaper to bring in US-produced food from outside, including subsidised international transport for it, than to move food within Africa. Once again, a controversy over GM has helped to reveal underlying issues. What African countries need is long-term sovereign solutions arrived at through a bottom-up process, with donors responding rather than imposing their own priorities.

Africa – a new frontier for US business

The GM food aid issue served as a timely reminder of other US activities in Africa. USAID's Agricultural Initiative to Cut Hunger in Africa (AICHA)[73] aims to accelerate smallholder-based agricultural growth in Africa. The initiative is supported by IFPRI, which points out that smallholder agriculture is the 'predominant source of livelihoods in Africa', and that smallholders are as efficient as larger farmers when they 'have received similar support services and inputs (seeds, fertiliser and credit)'.[74] IFPRI notes that women form 70 per cent of the labour in African agriculture and says that a smallholder-led agricultural transformation of Africa is feasible.

In its publicity on AICHA, USAID is at pains to point out that

US exports to Africa are already substantial, totaling $6.1 billion in 1996 alone and creating an estimated 100,000 American jobs, but an expanding African agricultural sector and greater African economic growth means expanding markets for US exports and even more American jobs.[75]

At the World Food Summit – Five Years Later (June 2002), USAID announced the Collaborative Agricultural Biotechnology Initiative (CABIO), designed to help countries access biotechnology and develop 'local private sectors to help integrate biotech into local food systems'. The press release goes on to say: '"Biofortified Crops to Combat Micronutrient Deficiency" is an international collaboration focused on raising Vitamin A, iron and zinc content in crops.'[76] The CGIAR is involved in the initiative through a 'challenge programme' of the same name, revealing the linkages between the organisations.

The USAID report 'Assessment of Biotechnology in Uganda',[77] reveals cooperation between governments, government agencies, publicly financed institutions and private corporations even more clearly. It shows how USAID is working with Monsanto plus a number of other players (including Makerere University, the National Agricultural Research Organisation, the Rockefeller Foundation, CIMMYT, and CABI-Biosciences, based in the UK and funded by the Monsanto Fund) to facilitate the development of biotechnology in that country. It notes that 'While Monsanto has an interest in the development of the company's own transgenic crops, the other crops of importance to Uganda do not provide sufficient commercial benefit for a multinational company to develop on its own.' The transgenic crop of interest to Monsanto which is nearest to commercial production in Uganda is Bt cotton. While USAID sees Africa as an important target for US exports, the organisation Investment in Developing Export Agriculture (IDEA), when discussing the African Growth and Opportunity Act (AGOA) suggests that Uganda should focus *its* food exports on markets in Europe.[78]

When one sees these developments in the context of the World Bank's Initiative on Seed Supply in Sub-Saharan Africa (ISSSSA – see pp. 104–6) and of efforts to promote the development of IPR and biosafety law as quickly as possible through interplay between research projects and building institutional capacity (see pp. 124–9), the breadth of the US initiative becomes apparent.

The AGOA[79] adds to the richness of the mixture. Signed into law by President Clinton on 18 May 2000 as Title 1 of the Trade and Development Act of 2000, the Act purports to offer trade advantages to eligible African countries provided they can demonstrate that they are making progress towards establishing

market-based economies; the rule of law and political pluralism; elimination of barriers to US trade and investment; protection of intellectual property; efforts to combat corruption; policies to reduce poverty, increasing availability of health care and educational opportunities; protection of human rights and worker rights; and elimination of certain child labor practices.

This is a familiar mixture of measures required to create a good working context for corporations and standard Western democracy. Under AGOA by the end of 2002, 80 per cent of African exports to the US were crude oil, and only 1 per cent agriculture products:

> To date 38 countries have been declared eligible for Agoa benefits, but only 22 had exported something under the programme by mid-2002. Five countries account for 95 per cent of Agoa exports and most of that is oil.... In the first half of last year, more than 80 per cent of Agoa exports to the US were made up of oil-related products. Textiles and apparel made up 10 per cent and transportation equipment 6 per cent. Agricultural exports were a mere 1 per cent of the total imports under Agoa. The primary benefit to the US economy as a result of Agoa is that oil from eligible countries is landed at lower cost to refiners.[80]

Moreover, according to a letter from US Trade Representative Robert Zoellick to Senator Byrd in November 2002, commented on by Larry Goodwin of the Africa Faith and Justice Network, 'the [US] President intends to initiate negotiations for a free trade agreement (FTA) with the five member countries of the Southern African Customs Union (Botswana, Lesotho, Namibia, South Africa and Swaziland, hereinafter SACU)'. As Larry Goodwin comments, this has implications for the whole of Africa. On IPRs, the letter proposes that the US should 'seek to establish standards that reflect a standard of [patent] protection similar to that found in US law'.

It is therefore evident that the US intends to ensure harmonised regimes in Africa that suit the biotech industry and facilitate the profitable 'modernisation' of African agriculture by and for US interests. There is a lot to play for. Most African farmers use saved seed for planting, and small farmers are the main seed breeders too, with a great wealth of knowledge and locally adapted varieties, which companies could use for developing GM or for other breeding programmes. The green revolution largely failed in Africa, and the use there of inputs has remained low. Many farmers are *de facto* organic. There are massive opportunities for expansion. Africa represents a new frontier for the US and its industries.

Meanwhile, Europe and the US continue to snipe at each other over Africa.

> International environment and development groups accuse the US of manipulating the crisis to benefit the biotech corporations, and of using the UN to distribute domestic food surpluses which cannot find a market. America responds that hysteria stoked by Europeans is endangering starving people.[81]

Resistance in the South

Monsanto has expended great efforts in recent years to try and gain approval for GM (Bt) cotton in India and GM soya in Brazil. Just before each planting season the pressure reaches its height in each country. In Brazil, resistance has been spearheaded by NGOs and farmer organisations working with the judiciary, together with a handful of states in resistance to the federal government. In India, NGOs have exposed corruption and incompetence among the government committees responsible for the issue. In Thailand, Monsanto has been accused of releasing Bt cotton illegally. More recently the ISAAA has set up there, following clear actions to resist GM by government and people.

Resistance to Bt cotton in India is finally overwhelmed

In June 2001 Monsanto just failed to gain approval for large-scale planting of Bt cotton in India.[82] Shortly before the planting season, even though all the tests called for had not been completed, the Maharashtra Hybrid Seed Company (Mahyco) in India, in which Monsanto had a controlling interest, tried to rush through approval for planting in the July 2001 season. There were complaints of unprecedented pressure being applied to scientists and bureaucrats – it was said that not even the battle over whether patents should cover living organisms had been so intense.[83]

Trials of Monsanto's Bt cotton had been carried out in India, but had persistently been planted too late in the season to properly test the crop for its resistance to its main problem, the American bollworm. The committees involved in monitoring the trials were denounced for corruption and incompetence. The Genetic Engineering Approval Committee (GEAC) called for another year of trials,[84] but a source in the Indian Department of Plant Biotechnology said this would not be enough to examine the implications of gene flow, the impact on bees, and whether the antibiotic resistance gene used in the crop could cause resistance to streptomycin, commonly used in the treatment of TB.[85]

The Forum For Biotechnology and Food Security, New Delhi, called for a major investigation into the conduct of all the government departments and committees involved, and for Mahyco to be blacklisted for misrepresentation of the facts. It also called for two further years of trials in view of the defective nature of data gathered so far.[86]

In March 2002 the GEAC gave approval for the commercial production in some parts of India of Bt cotton varieties BT MECH 12, BT MECH 162 and BT MECH 184, all containing the Bt toxin CRY 1 Ac. Mahyco, which Monsanto calls its 'seed partner', was the company authorised. The approval was given provided that certain conditions were met, such as the establishment of refugia (places where non-Bt cotton would be planted) so as to discourage the appearance of resistance among the target pests. However, reports suggest that farmers have not been informed of these conditions, while many of them do not have enough land to implement them. Rumours about the capacity of the new product have led to seed being smuggled to areas for which it was not authorised and to which it was not adapted and fake GM seed has been sold to farmers. Problems have been compounded by monsoon failures and have led to assertions of disaster for small farmers. Meanwhile the Indian government is still working towards the production of its own Bt varieties, which it claims will be better than Mahyco's and will provide choice on the market. With farmers so ill-informed, and so vulnerable to rumours, it is hard to see how they can either benefit or make a balanced choice.

Resistance to RoundUp Ready soybeans in Brazil is successful

The release of GM crops in Brazil was halted by the courts of the country. After Monsanto received approval for its RoundUp Ready soybeans from Brazil's National Technical Biosafety Commission (CTNBio), a class action suit was filed in 1998 by the Brazilian Consumer Defence Institute (IDEC) and Greenpeace. They got an injunction in 1999 on GM releases, pending proper labelling and an environmental impact assessment, which is required under the Brazilian constitution. Following a challenge, the injunction was upheld and extended in a judgement issued by federal judge Antonio Prudente (aptly named for a judge endorsing the precautionary principle) in June 2000: it ordered the government to carry out more complete environmental and health impact studies before approving any commercial GMO releases.[87]

Weak rules on labelling for packaged GM products were rushed through in July 2001. However, the country's agriculture minister failed (August 2001) in a bid to gain consent for Monsanto to plant RoundUp Ready soybeans commercially just before the new growing season, and was accused of trying to sidestep the court rulings on the matter. Prior to this setback Monsanto's shares were rising, but they fell sharply on this news.[88] In February 2002 all field trials of 'biopesticide' plants were suspended pending the enforcement of Brazil's agro-toxin legislation. All this adds up to a kind of judicial moratorium on commercial releases of GM crops and most field trials, including those of herbicide-tolerant crops.[89]

The state of Rio Grande do Sul in the south of the country was the first to act decisively against the introduction of GMOs, with crops on some illegal trial sites being impounded or burned. It was prevented by the federal government from passing a state law to ban GM crops, but has prevented most of the field trials authorised by the federal government from taking place. However, it has also been the worst victim of RR soya seed smuggled across the border from Argentina, and is reported to have levels of up to 70 per cent GM soya.[90] Three other Brazilian states (Santa Catarina in southern Brazil, Mato Grosso do Sul in the west – said now to have a contamination level of 30 per cent GM soya[91] – and Pará in the Amazon region) all resisted strong pressure from the federal government to accept GM crops in 2001–2. These states have now set up their own biosafety commissions, with strong participation from farmers and consumers, that give their governments decision-making powers over all aspects of GM crops in order to be able to resist any federal decision to allow them in the future. A project to decontaminate the south of the country and further promote small-scale ecological and organic agriculture is just beginning.[92]

Government aid for RoundUp factory in Brazil

In December 1999 Monsanto was granted about US$150 million (R285.9 million, at the time) in low-interest, long-term credit from the federal development agency FINOR to help build a factory in the state of Bahia's Camaçari petrochemical complex, just outside Salvador. This was about half of FINOR's total annual budget for promoting industrial development in north-eastern Brazil. The purpose was the manufacture of several chemical precursors to glyphosate, currently imported by Brazil. It was expected to create 319 new jobs when completed.

This investment was made, of course, on the assumption that RoundUp Ready soybeans would soon be released in Brazil and the market for RoundUp would explode. Meanwhile, the government's 2001 budget for fighting the worst drought in the impoverished north-east of the country in 70 years was about a quarter (R77 million) of what Monsanto was granted, even before the falling value of the Real was taken into account.[93] The factory opened in December 2001 and in January 2003 was reported to be making good profits by producing the components for RoundUp for sale in Brazil and for export to Argentina and Belgium.[94] However, as reported in August 2002 by the *Guardian,* Monsanto appears to have accepted that it will make little headway in Brazil until 2005.[95] Meanwhile, the country is consolidating its position as an exporter of GM-free soya, much of it to Europe, and commercial interests are pointing out to the government that its GM-free status is likely to become increasingly valuable. Late in 2002, the famous Worker's Party stalwart Luiz Inacio Lula da Silva, known as Lula, became President of Brazil. The party called for a moratorium on GM several years ago. However, the Minister of Agriculture represents agribusiness interests and is in favour of GMOs. The struggle continues, but extreme pressure from the federal government and Monsanto to commercialise GMOs has so far met with even stronger resistance.

Illegal cotton planting in Thailand

In September 1999 BIOTHAI – an NGO based in Bangkok, Thailand – sent out an open letter accusing Monsanto of illegally releasing GM cotton for cultivation in Thailand.[96] During August and September 1999 farmers' groups monitoring cotton crops in provinces in the central and north-east regions of Thailand sent samples of cotton from fields recently leased by a local company. Tests confirmed that the cotton was a Bt transgenic variety. Bt cotton was on Thailand's quarantine list and, under the provisions of the Plant Quarantine Law of 1964 (amended 1994), it had to go through biosafety testing before it could be released to farmers' fields.

While Monsanto denied involvement in the illegal plantings, BIOTHAI argued that 'the evidence clearly points to the company's contempt for Thai laws and sovereignty'. BIOTHAI also claimed that Monsanto had been promoting GM crops in the Thai press:

> Meanwhile, Monsanto has poured a huge amount of money into public relations by running a series of full-page advertisements or special sections in Thai newspapers about the 'miracle of GM crops'. These advertisements, disguised as newspaper articles, appear as a 'special issue' of the newspapers claiming that GM crops and technology would help alleviate the economic crisis in Thailand. The advertisements selectively quote leading Thai scientists as stating that GMs are necessary to increase food yields and decrease pesticide use. However, they do not mention the various harmful effects associated with GM crops.[97]

Following a ban on field trials (April 2001) and imports of genetically engineered crops (January 2002) in Thailand, the ISAAA (see pp. 124–6) set up an office in Bangkok in April 2002 and began to try to counter NGO opposition to GM crops, which it says is unfounded.[98] At the same time, the Thai senate set up a special committee to investigate Thai NGOs to find out whether 'they had been hired by foreign organisations opposed to the development of Thailand'.[99]

ConTill: Monsanto's brand of sustainable development

Soil erosion and degradation, often associated with green revolution farming methods, pose a massive threat to agricultural production worldwide, especially in the South, where soils are often more fragile and much poorer in nutrients, water retention, structure and micro-organisms (see Box, p. 10: 'Living soil'). As there are many factors involved in the loss of fertile soil, so there are many suggestions about how to overcome the problem. Soil scientists differ about the most sustainable ways of farming and, specifically, about how to increase organic matter (carbon, for example) in soil. For various reasons, ploughing – or tilling – has gone out of favour in large-scale and open-field farming, as explained by Bob Evans, a UK soil scientist:

> The *no-till*, or *non-inversion tillage* technique (i.e., the plough is not used to turn over the soil) was introduced in the USA as a way to save time, energy and money for the farmer when drilling his crop. In the UK in the 1970s and early 1980s it was a way of cultivating only the top 5–10cm or so of the soil, incorporating the crop residue, drilling into this layer and then rolling it and compacting it so that the seed had good contact with the soil. All this could be done with one pass, i.e., one big tractor with behind it a tine, chisel or disc cultivator, a drill and a roller. This is direct drilling. If it is done in two stages, i.e., shallow cultivation and then drilling, that is minimal or reduced cultivation, nowadays also called *lo-till*.
>
> It was realised in the USA that if crop residues were incorporated into the soil and especially if 30 per cent or more of the residue was left on the surface the soil was protected from water and wind erosion. This technique became known as *conservation tillage*. In the last two decades or so, and especially in the last few years, this technique has been hard pushed in the USA, Canada, Australia, Chile, Brazil and Argentina. The technique is now being promoted enthusiastically worldwide. In other countries, as in the UK, weeds and slugs can be a problem.[100]

The answer is glyphosate and slug pellets, and if bigger slug infestations occur, a tempting answer is 'more slug pellets'.

Although it was not developed for use with pesticides, agrochemical producers are very interested in no-till farming because they see a large market in the need to control weeds. For example, in its 1997 *Sustainability Report* Monsanto explains that:

> *No-till* farming eliminates plowing to prepare land for planting seeds and for weed control. Instead crop residue is left on fields and seeds and nutrients are placed in narrow rows or in drilled holes. Weed control is accomplished with herbicides such as Monsanto's RoundUp. No-till has been shown to decrease erosion rates by 90 per cent and nutrient and pesticide run-off by 70 per cent over conventional tillage.

Whilst scientists argue over the various figures produced in corporate reports regarding erosion or carbon sequestration, they seem to accept that no-till and conservation tillage, by incorporating crop residues into the cultivated layer, can contribute to the reduction of soil erosion and soil degradation in intensive farming systems.

In its 1998 annual report, Monsanto explains that conservation tillage – which it calls ConTill – is 'the practice of substituting the judicious use of herbicides for mechanical tillage', and that its widespread adoption has added to the increased global usage of Monsanto's top-selling pesticide, RoundUp (active ingredient, glyphosate).[101] Glyphosate has impacts on soil and water and is found in water courses at levels above those set by law.[102] Its increasing use for lo-till, as propagated for instance in the UK, could cause problems for the water industry in supplying potable water. Evidence is emerging that glyphosate use may be linked with the global increase in attacks from fusarium fungal diseases.

Conservation tillage has thus become strongly associated with high chemical inputs such as inorganic fertilisers, herbicides and slug poisons, and increasingly with herbicide-resistant GM crops. Many soil scientists favour more benign ways to improve soil structure and increase organic carbon content, for example by adding farmyard manure or compost to the land, or incorporating cover crops or grass into the crop rotation so that these can be ploughed in.

Non-inversion tillage can have a useful role, for instance on small tropical plots where weeds and crop residues are constantly incorporated into the topsoil. Here herbicide is replaced by manual labour.

Conservation tillage can (within limits) contribute to less carbon being released from soil or more carbon being incorporated. Monsanto is using the fact to hail their herbicide-resistant crops as a saviour in times of climate change. Monsanto lobbied to this effect at the UN Convention on Climate Change talks in the Hague (November 2000). In the Kyoto Protocol climate negotiations, the US government has consistently argued that 'carbon sinks' should be included in the climate convention. They say that trees (forests) and agricultural land which are said to absorb CO_2 emissions should be accepted as carbon sinks and should therefore be used to offset a country's CO_2 emissions. This position is fully supported by the agrochemical and biotech industry.

Conservation tillage has been promoted globally and successfully since the early 1990s. It has expanded massively, for example in southern Brazil and Argentina, but it is difficult to ascertain how much is treated with herbicide and how much is not.[103]

In Africa, ConTill is promoted through two NGOs, Sasakawa Global 2000 (SG 2000) and Winrock International (see above, pp. 189–96). In partnership with these groups, in 1992, Monsanto began to facilitate the transfer of Monsanto's ConTill technology to small-scale rice and maize farmers.

ConTill in Costa Rica

In Costa Rica, Monsanto is allied with Conservation International, a 'non-profit group dedicated to protecting the earth's biologically richest ecosystems', to promote ConTill in the 1.1 million hectare nature reserve called La Amistad, on the Panama border. The project aims to protect the biodiversity of La Amistad by preventing neighbouring hillside farmers from encroaching on the reserve. Monsanto does not mention that surface run-off of herbicides, which will increase through ConTill farming, is particularly dangerous in areas such as tropical regions where rainfall is intense.

Monsanto is one of Conservation International's 34 corporate sponsors, which include Chiquita Brands International, Citibank, Walt Disney, Mobil and Exxon.

Having opened doors to the richly biodiverse La Amistad through their ConTill project, Conservation International and Monsanto are also collaborating on a bioprospecting project with the University of Panama. This will allow them to search for plants, fungi, and insects that can be patented and turned into pharmaceutical and food products. Such bioprospecting or biopiracy is a major problem for Southern governments and communities. It means the privatisation of their biodiversity for the profit of the TNCs rather than the good of all.[104]

Monsanto urges FAO to create 'RoundUp Ready Organisation'

An international organization that champions the benefits of conservation agriculture is critically necessary to grow conservation agricultural practices around the world.

> Hugh Grant, chief operating officer of Monsanto, at an FAO-sponsored international conference on conservation agriculture, 3 October 2001

It is not surprising that Monsanto is trying to hitch a ride on yet another 'movement'. As lo-till agriculture spreads rapidly across South Asia, to convince farmers to use RoundUp would prove most profitable, especially if the FAO were providing the public relations cover.

'Conservation agriculture brings many benefits to the growers and the environment, yet there is still so much potential for growth of this farming practice,' Grant said. He estimated a current total of approximately 220 million hectares globally under conservation tillage – and the potential to extend this to 600 million hectares.

Notes

1 'New Technology "Terminates" Food Independence', World Internet News Distribution Source (WINDS), April 1998.
http://thewinds.arcsnet.net/archive/newworld/terminator_seeds04-98.html

2 *Impact*, in-house magazine of the International Finance Corporation of the World Bank, Spring 1998.
http://www.ifc.org/publications/pubs/impact/s8clientssp98/s8clientssp98.html

3 'Biotechnology a Tool to Help Improve the Quality of Life for Women, Monsanto Executive Says: Speech at International Business Conference Highlights Benefits of Plant Biotechnology for Women in the Developed and Developing World'.
http://www.monsanto.com/monsanto/layout/media/02/10-23-02.asp

4 'New Approvals and Increased Acreage of Monsanto Traits in 2001 Demonstrate Growing Acceptance of Biotech: Pre-commercial Field Trials Taking Place in 25 Countries', Monsanto press release, St Louis, 11 February 2002.

5 P. G. Pardey and N. M. Beintema, 'Slow Magic: Agricultural R&D a Century after Mendel', a report by the International Food Policy Research Institute (IFPRI), Washington, DC, 2001. http://www.ifpri.org/pubs/pubs.htm#fpr

6 Adjusted to 1993 international dollars.

7 Pardey and Beintema, 'Slow Magic'.

8 More details on agricultural R&D can be found in *ibid*.

9 www.usaid.or.ug/SO7%20annexes/ Uganda%20Assessment%20Report.doc

10 Monsanto, *Sustainability Report 1999–2000*.

11 Agrow Reports, No. 331 (6/99).

12 Barbara Dinham, 'Zeneca: the Impact of Pesticides on Food Security', in John Madeley (ed.), *Hungry for Power: The Impact of Transnational Corporations on Food Security*, UK Food Group, 2000.

13 Novartis Foundation for Sustainable Development website:
www.foundation.novartis.com

14 *Ibid*.

15 Klaus Leisinger, 'The Socio-Political Impact of Biotechnology in Developing Countries', <www.foundation.novartis.com/biotechnology_developing_countries.htm>; Colin MacIlwain, 'Developing Countries Look for Guidance in GM Crops Debate', *Nature*, 401 (1999): 831–2.

16 http://www.foundation.novartis.com/organization.htm

17 'Syngenta Launches Foundation for Sustainable Agriculture', www.agbioworld.org, quoted on Iowa Grain Quality Initiative, <http://www.extension.iastate.edu>, 12 October 2001.

18 http://www.syngentafoundation.com

19 Monsanto Fund, http://www.monsantofund.org/

20 Monsanto, *Sustainability Report 1999–2000*.

21 Sasakawa Africa Association, http://www.casin.org/sasakawa.htm#Origins

22 http://www.nippon-foundation.or.jp/eng/e_photo/2002218/20022181.html

23 Winrock International, annual report, 1999. See www.winrock.org.

24 *Ibid*.

25 Peter Gorrie, 'Taxpayers Fund Biotech Food Giant', *Toronto Star*, 11 February 2001.

26 *Ibid*.

27 Monsanto, *Sustainability Report 1997*.

28 See Grameen Bank website: www.grameen-info.org

29 Grameen Foundation website, January 2003, http://www.gfusa.org/

30 Monsanto write-up on the Micro-credit Summit Campaign, December 2002. http://www.monsanto.com/monsanto/layout/our_commitments/micro.asp

31 Farida Akhter, 'Micro-Credit: the Development Devastation for the Poor', speech for UBINIG (Policy Research for Development Alternatives), Bangladesh, at the Second Annual APRN (Asia–Pacific Research Network) Conference, Jakarta, Indonesia, 21–23 August 2000. http://www.aprnet.org/farida.htm

32 'Grameen, Monsanto Sowing the Seeds of Ruin', InterPress Service, 17 July 1998.

33 http://www.greens.org/s-r/17/17-15.html

34 Farhad Mazhar, 'Destructive Consequences of "Controlling Plant Gene Expression" or "Terminator Technology" for Food Security and Biodiversity', paper presented at the Pre-SBSST-4 Consultative Workshop, Bangladesh, 25 May 1999.

35 See also RAFI website; R. A. Steinbrecher and P. R. Mooney, 'Terminator Technology', *Ecologist*, September/October 1998; 'Patents on Life', Econexus website: www.econexus.info.

36 Harry B. Collins (Vice-President, Technology Transfer, Delta and Pine Land Company), 'New Technology and Modernizing World Agriculture', paper presented at 5th Extraordinary Session of FAO Commission on Genetic Resources for Food and Adgriculture, 1998.

37 '2001: a Seed Odyssey', RAFI communique, January–February 2001, <www.etc group.org>. See also 'The Terminator Gene List', <terminatorseedwatch@yahoo groups.com>.

38 Harry B. Collins, Delta and Pine Land Company, quoted in RAFI communique, 'Terminator 2 Years Later: Suicide Seeds on the Fast Track', February–March 2000.

39 'USDA Says Yes to Terminator', RAFI news release, 3 August 2001.

40 'Robbing Coffee's Cradle – GM Coffee and Its Threat to Poor Farmers', briefing by ActionAid, UK, May 2001.

41 Quoted by Luz Rimban, 'Multinational Firms Dictating RP Farming Processes', *Philippine Daily Inquirer*, 26 December 1996, cited in CGIAR, 'Agricultural Research for Whom?', *Ecologist*, 26, 6 (November–December 1996).

42 BIOTHAI, GRAIN, MASIPAG and PAN Indonesia, 'The Corporate Takeover Of Corn in South-east Asia: Whose Agenda?', August 1999. http://www.grain.org/publications/reports/takeover.htm

43 *Ibid*.

44 'Monsanto's Insect-Protected Corn Approved for Planting in the Philippines', Monsanto, press release, 5 December 2002. http://www.monsanto.com/monsanto/layout/media/02/12-05-02.asp

45 Sue Branford, 'Why Argentina Can't Feed Itself – How GM Soya Is Destroying Livelihoods and the Environment in Argentina', *Ecologist*, 32, 8 (October 2002).

46 'Latin American Meeting on Food Aid and GMOs, Quito, Ecuador, 6–9 August 2001', report by Red por Latina America Libre de Transgenicos. http://www.biodiversidadla.org/

47 *Ibid*.

48 *Ibid*.

49 Anthony de Palmer and Simon Romero, 'Super Seeds Sweeping Major Markets, and Brazil May Be Next, *New York Times*, 16 May 2000.

http://www.nytimes.com/library/national/science/051600sci-gm-seed.html#rice

50 'Latin American Meeting'.

51 Moisés Burachik and Patricia L. Traynor, 'Analysis of a National Biosafety System: Regulatory Policies and Procedures in Argentina', International Service for National Agricultural Research (ISNAR) (part of CGIAR) Country Report 63.

52 Branford, 'Why Argentina Can't Feed Itself'.

53 R. W. Elmore *et al.*, 'Glyphosate-Resistant Soybean Cultivar Yields Compared with Sister Lines', *Agronomy Journal*, 93 (May 2001): 408–12.
http://screc.unl.edu/Research/Glyphosate/glyphosateyield.html

54 'US, Argentina Bullying Other Countries', United Press International, 18 December 2001.

55 Damian Wroclavsky, 'Rise of Soy Makes Argentina a Mainly One-crop Country', Reuters, 18 October 2002.

56 'Record Harvest – Record Hunger: Starving in GE Argentina', report by Greenpeace, Rome and Buenos Aires, June 2002. See www.greenpeace.org/%7Egeneng/reports/food/record_harvest.pdf

57 'Grow Your Own Democracy', *Ecologist*, 32, 8 (October 2002).

58 *Jakarta Post*, 16 September 1998.

59 For more information see 'Turning the Paddy Field Gold: Corn in South-east Asia', *Seedling*, September 1999. http://www.grain.org/publications/set99/set992.htm

60 *Ibid.*

61 http://www.fas.usda.gov/excredits/pl480/progress.html

62 'Worldwide Initiatives against GMOs', Third World Network (TWN) report, 16 May 2000. www.twnside.org.sg

63 Declan Walsh, 'America Finds Ready Market for GM Food – the Hungry', *Independent*, 30 March 2000.

64 *Ibid.*

65 KMP rejoinder to Norman Borlaug's response in 'Letters to the Editor', *Independent*, to Walsh, 'America Finds Ready Market', April 2000; and 'Farmers Decry dumping of Hazardous GMOs from Relief Agencies, Biogen Firms', KMP press release, 14 April 2000.

66 Walsh, 'America Finds Ready Market'.

67 'US Withdraws Genetically Engineered Corn – Animal Feed Donation After Bosnia's Hesitation', Agence France-Press, Sarajevo, 30 January 2001.

68 'Burundi: Genetically Modified US Food Aid Suspect', Burundi news agency Net Press, 5 September 2000.

69 Report from Latin American Meeting on Food Aid and GMOs, Quito, Ecuador, 6–9 August 2001. The meeting brought together the Network for a GMO-free Latin America and representatives from Africa, Asia and Eastern Europe, and was organised by the Ecuadorian group Acción Ecológica.

70 Bertini is quoted in 'New Technology "Terminates" Food Independence', World Internet News Distribution Source (WINDS), April 1998.
http://thewinds.arcsnet.net/archive/newworld/terminator_seeds04-98.html

71 Loughty Dube, 'Government Rejects US Maize', *Zimbabwe Independent*, 31 May 2002. http://www.theindependent.co.zw/news/2002/May/Friday31/633.html

72 'WFP: Zambia Must Accept Biotech Food', Associated Press, edited and sent by Agnet, Canada, 26 August 2002.

73 USAID, Agricultural Initiative to Cut Hunger in Africa (AICHA).

http://www.afr-sd.org/Agriculture/AgInitiative.htm

74 'Ending Hunger in Africa: Only the Small Farmer Can Do It', International Food Policy Research Institute (IFPRI): Brief in Support of AICHA (see note 73), 2002. www.ifpri.org/themes/aicha/htm

75 USAID, Agricultural Initiative to Cut Hunger in Africa (AICHA). http://www.afr-sd.org/Agriculture/AgInitiative.htm

76 'USAID Announces International Biotech Collaboration: Says Program Will Help Poor Countries Reduce Hunger', USAID press release, June 2002. http://usinfo.state.gov/topical/global/biotech/02061202.htm

77 www.usaid.or.ug/SO7%20annexes/ Uganda%20Assessment%20Report.doc

78 IDEA, 'Agoa's Tricky Side', *New Vision*, Kampala, 7 November 2002.

79 http://www.agoa.gov/About_AGOA/about_agoa.html

80 Jonathan Katzenellenbogen, 'A Narrow Niche for African Exports', *Business Day*, Johannesburg, 14 January 2003. http://allafrica.com/stories/200301140198.html

81 Rory Carroll: 'Zambians Starve as Food Aid Lies Rejected: Despite a Terrible Drought, the African State Says It Is Right to Refuse GM Maize from the US', *Guardian*, 17 October 2002.
http://www.guardian.co.uk/gmdebate/Story/0,2763,813220,00.html

82 'Transgenic Cotton Fails To Get Environmental Nod', *Economic Times*, India, 21 June 2001.

83 Devinder Sharma, 'International Appeal for Support to Help Halt GM Authorisation in India', email, Forum for Biotechnology and Food Security, New Delhi, 17 June 2001

84 'Genetic Engineering Approval Committee (GEAC) Seeks Comprehensive Data after Fresh Large-Scale Field Trials of Bt Cotton', GEAC press note, 20 June 2001.

85 'Monsanto Setback as India Refuses to Grow GE Cotton', Greenpeace International, the Netherlands, 21 June 2001. http://www.greenpeace.com

86 'Call for Enquiry into the Department of Biotechnology's Promotion of Genetically Modified Seed MNCs', press release, Forum For Biotechnology and Food Security, New Delhi, 20 June 2001.

87 'Federal Court to Decide Today on Fate of GMOs in Brazil', Campaign for a GMO-Free Brazil, 25 February 2002.
www.gefoodalert.org/News/news.cfm?News_ID=3199

88 Todd Benson, 'Courts Force Brazil Government to Retreat on Monsanto GMO Soy', Dow Jones Commodities Service, 17 August 2001.

89 'Federal Court to Decide Today'.

90 'Soja Transgenica se Espalha Pelo Brasil', *Folha de Sao Paulo*, 14 May 2002.

91 *Ibid.*

92 'Estruturação da Cadeia de Produtos Orgânicos: Proposta de Inspeção e Descontaminação Dos Cultivos De Soja No Sul Do Brasil', Ecovida, January 2003. http://www.ecovida.org.br/

93 Personal communication from David Hathaway, economist, adviser to AS-PTA (Consultants in Alternative Agriculture Projects) and other Brazilian environmental NGOs.

94 Reese Ewing, 'New Chemical Plant Boosts Monsanto Brazil Exports', Reuters, 22 January 2003. http://biz.yahoo.com/rm/030122/markets_brazil_monsanto_1.html

95 David Teather, *Guardian*, 20 August 2002.
http://www.guardian.co.uk/gmdebate/Story/0,2763,777538,00.html

96 BIOTHAI, Alernative Agriculture Network, Foundation for Consumers, Greennet, Foundation for Thai Holistic Health, 'Monsanto's Bt Cotton Violates Thai Plant Quarantine Laws and Farmers' Rights', press release, 26 September 1999 www.gene.ch/genet/1999/ Oct/msg/00019.html

97 *Ibid.*

98 Kultida Samabuddhi, 'US-based Group to Counter "NGO Bias": Critics Say It Is a Tool of Biotech Industry', *Bangkok Post*, Thailand, 6 April 2002. http://scoop.bangkokpost.co.th/bkkpost/2002/apr2002/bp20020406/news/06apr 2002_news24.html

99 'Senate to Probe NGOs', *Nation*, Thailand, 6 April 2002.

100 Robert Evans, Department of Geography, Anglia Polytechnic University, personal communication, February 2003.

101 Quoted in PAN–AP, 'Monsanto, IRRI Push Pesticides on Thai Farmers through Thai Development NGO', press release, 6 April 1999.

102 *Design of a Tax or Charge Scheme for Pesticides 1999*, Department of Environment, Transport and the Regions, United Kingdom, Table 1.

103 For examples of projects defined as sustainable agriculture, see: Jules Pretty and Rachel Hine, *Reducing Food Poverty with Sustainable Agriculture: a Summary of New Evidence*, Centre for Environment and Society, University of Essex, SAFE-World Research Project, February 2001, Executive Summary. http://www2.essex.ac.uk/ces/ResearchProgrammes/safewexecsummfinalreport.htm http://www2.essex.ac.uk/ces/ResearchProgrammes/SAFEW47casessusag.htm

104 See also briefing on 'Patents on Life', http://www.wen.org.uk/genetics/genefiles/

9

Conclusion:

Summing Up and Moving On

Those who do not remember the past are doomed to repeat it.

George Santayana (1863–1952)

Throughout this book we have looked at different ways in which the source of the food stream, basic to human life, is being diverted through the advocacy of genetic engineering and the patenting of living organisms to serve the priorities of the transnational corporations. As we have seen, many of those corporations are larger in economic terms than countries, yet they are private bodies whose recent evolution into global giants has been extremely rapid. We take them for granted, yet we often forget that they have not always been there. The biotech companies are not among the largest in the world, but their ability to change our lives arguably places them among the most powerful, since their work involves bypassing the process of evolution and changing genomes irrevocably. We have given examples of the many levels on which they have been working and of how they are infiltrating and subverting a wide range of institutions in their efforts to promote genetically engineered crops.

The colonisation of indigenous agriculture through the green revolution has destroyed farming systems and eliminated locally adapted varieties and knowledge, undermining the agricultural diversity that has been nurtured over millennia. Each farmer variety that is lost means the loss of germplasm and knowledge painstakingly selected, built up, exchanged and passed on down the generations. Such wealth is irreplaceable. These systems are being replaced by crops that depend on inputs and farming systems that depend on agribusiness, while farmers are being displaced to expanding cities. All this has intensified cycles of dependence and struck at the roots of self-reliance. A system of commerce based on perpetual growth requires an unquestioning mass consumer culture in order to thrive. This provides the perfect context for the operations of the large corporations. Genetic engineering will intensify this process and GM contamination has already penetrated Mexico, the centre of origin for maize, transformed by farmers over thousands of years from a plant of little food value to a world staple.

The emergence of the biotechnology corporations in their present form would have been impossible without a number of facilitating factors, some old and some new. The gradual development of the charitable corporation into a for-profit entity with little liability, almost complete freedom to operate and only one main obligation – to maximise profit for shareholders – has played a major role. That corporations have also acquired many of the same rights as human beings without any of the limitations of being human adds to the danger.

Financial markets have been liberated over the last 20 years, enabling corporations to move their capital freely and change their focus at will. This has greatly facilitated the growth of corporate power. The World Trade Organisation's agreements are designed to give corporations freedom to operate wherever profits can be maximised. Many countries in the South lack national rules on monopolies, and there is currently no way to tackle global monopolies. Governments with the largest number of corporations – in the US, Europe and Japan – have become increasingly complicit in corporate interests. Politicians and corporate executives regularly swap places in a flurry of revolving doors, especially in the US. All this is facilitating the entry of private corporations into areas of public interest which were formerly the preserve of local communities or governments.

The extension of patents to cover living organisms from 1980 was vital to the biotechnology industry, enabling it to raise capital on the markets and to construct systems of exclusive monopoly control. It is not surprising that the corporations have invested so much energy in securing intellectual property rights legislation such as TRIPs and the European Directive on the Protection of Biotechnological Inventions. Now they seek a harmonised global patent regime. The effort to develop a genetic engineering tech- nology to prevent the germination of seed and to control the expression of traits (Terminator and Traitor technologies) was initially a collaboration between the US government and a US company. It aimed to increase profits and create an incentive for corporations by preventing farmers from freely saving and breeding seed, forcing them to purchase it anew each year. The level of control delivered by the technology is formidable, since it covers both the product and the intellectual property invested in the product. Nowhere else has the naked intent of the biotech industry been so clearly revealed.

Research is being profoundly affected by a creeping corporate takeover. The obsession with obtaining patents is restricting the free exchange of information and limiting access to information and technology. The quest for rapid returns on investment is distorting the sciences; the hunt for profitable applications risks turning the pursuit of knowledge into a race for technological fixes. Increasingly, technology is driving social development and this is particularly true of biotechnology, where technological optimism is endangering the principle of scientific scepticism. Governments have been complicit here too, hoping for technological solutions to problems that require political commitment. Vitamin A deficiency is one example of this, but the desire to avoid genuine political action permeates the agricultural debate, since, for example, democratic land redistribution is one thing that most governments quietly agree they would prefer to avoid. Instead, the tendency, assisted by new technologies, has been for further consolidation of land, in the name of efficiency.

But genetic engineering as presented by the industry has a deep psychological appeal. People have always longed for miracles. Genetic engineering technologies feed this longing very aptly and the industry has not held back, ably assisted by a burgeoning and rapidly consolidating public relations industry that is full of clever ideas about how to present GM biotechnology as benign. Since so much of the current excitement rests on projections of future possibilities, the painting of dream pictures is made even easier.

The consequences of all this are far-reaching. GM biotechnology is a microcosm for industrial development in general. The increased vertical and horizontal integration of the biotech industry means that ten companies control almost 33 per cent of the commercial seed market; five control 75 per cent of the vegetable seed market, while four control almost 100 per cent of the GM seed market. Two companies control 34 per cent of the global agrochemical market and ten control 85 per cent. Currently, Monsanto traits can be found in 91 per cent of GM crops grown worldwide. Recent mergers and acquisitions (such as the creation of Bayer CropScience and Syngenta) have been approved without building in any capacity for addressing the issue of global monopolies. Meanwhile, public interest research is being increasingly hijacked by corporate priorities and corporations are gaining access to public funding and publicly funded institutions such as universities and agricultural research centres.

So where is all this leading? History may provide us with clues. The British East India Company began as a group of traders and ended up ruling India:

> Yet an empire of trade unexpectedly became an empire of conquest. From 1740, interventions in local politics and the deployment of increasingly effective armed forces gave company employees the confidence and capacity to impose their will on annexed territories in northern India.
>
> The transformation from trader to sovereign was swift, brutal and decisive. By the 1770s, a company state had been created in Bengal, and further expansion was

sustained by the formation of a large army of Indian sepoys financed through the collection of land revenues. As the mathematician William Playfair pointed out, 'From a limited body of merchants, the India Company have become the Arbiters of the East.'[1]

Today, we run the serious risk of finding ourselves ruled by corporations far more completely and powerfully than the East India Company ever ruled India. They are busy recolonising every space that has experienced colonisation before, and a multitude of new spaces that could not previously be colonised either because the technology or the legal rights were not available – our bodies, our brains, the products of collective and traditional human experience and creativity. We therefore need to question not just the technology of genetic engineering itself, but the bid for power that it represents. Even if that bid for power is not always conscious amongst the human heads of the businesses, it is an inevitable outcome of the many freedoms we have given the corporations and the structures that they have developed and exploited, notably legal and financial.

A major consequence of the increasing domination of research by the corporations is that there is less funding and less intellectual energy available for looking at methodologies, innovations or regenerated old practices, such as the use of raised fields in South America, that cannot be patented or otherwise controlled to ensure private profit. The corporate mindset means that knowledge and practice accumulated all over the world, together with farmer varieties/germplasm, are seen simply as raw material for the development of privately owned technologies. If they can't use it, they see no point in promoting or protecting it.

GM biotechnology is increasing the tendency towards genetic uniformity in crops and cultivation of monocultures. Past experience suggests this will accelerate the development of new pest and disease attacks. Already some of the current generation of GM crops are beginning to show signs of failure. Evidence shows that yields are not as good as promised. Pests and weeds are developing resistance to pesticides and herbicides. It is often the case that new technologies reveal only their positive side at first. This may be explained by the suppression of less positive test results, the absence of tests, the fact that no-one was looking for problems, or simply the fact that those problems could not be predicted readily at the time of the introduction of the technology. However, this was certainly not the case with genetically engineered crops, where critics were long ago predicting the problems that have emerged to date, such as the build-up of resistance, contamination and gene flow.

Yet, the corporations may not perceive failures among the current generation of GM crops as a major threat. 'Miracle' high-response varieties of the green revolution often only lasted a few years before they were overwhelmed by pests and diseases, involving breeders in a constant race to find new varieties, while agrochemical companies sought new (patentable) chemicals to subdue the pests. Whatever the impact on the farmer, it was all good business for the companies. Moreover, chronically dependent customers, whoever they may be, are ideal fodder for generating profits. If those customers are tied up by debt and vanishing profit margins, all the better. The corporations are already promising new generations of GM crops designed to tolerate salt and drought.

They do not mention that there are already farmer varieties of crops worldwide that are able to do the same thing. They do not publicise the fact that all over the world people are maintaining, rebuilding and creating ways of producing food that thrives on diversity instead of monoculture, and that work *with* soil, climate, ecology and other species, instead of treating them as obstacles. In Cuba, where the collapse of the former Soviet Union left the country short of inputs and petroleum, they are developing organic food gardens; in Argentina, following the collapse of the economy, people are turning to their own resources to do the same thing. In Africa, where most farmers still save and breed their own seed, many are *de facto* organic or use very low levels of inputs. In a report produced in February 2001, Jules Pretty and Rachel Hine present 47 case studies and conclusions.[2] In a report for Greenpeace, Nicholas Parrott and Terry Marsden give more examples of alternatives to the chemical model of farming.[3]

For example, raised beds or *chinampas* have been developed in waterlogged regions of the world including China, Kashmir, the Andes of South America, Guyana and Mexico, where they have been in continuous use for over 2,000 years. They produce good yields. In China:

> Narrow beds are used for sugar cane and vegetables, while systems for longer duration crops, such as banana, citrus and lychee have wider beds and ditches. In the ditches rice, fish and edible snails are cultivated and mud is excavated to put on the beds. These high-bed, low-ditch systems have helped to lower water tables, reduce soil erosion and nutrient loss, preserve organic matter in ditches and increase the internal cycling of nutrients.[4]

All over the world, there are organisations and initiatives working at grassroots level, often focusing on women, who have been neglected until recently by the proponents of industrial agriculture. Just three examples are:

- UBINIG, in Bangladesh, worked with village women and farmers to set up Naya Krishi Andolan (New Agriculture Movement), which focuses on diversity cropping and maintains 'community seed wealth centres'. It involves 100,000 farming families.

- Deccan Development Society works with the poorest women in about 75 villages in Andhra Pradesh, India, based on the principles of access, control and autonomy. They have set up systems to protect and retrieve farmer varieties, uncultivated foods and medicinal plant resources, and established women's media.

• The Green Belt Movement began in Kenya in 1977. Its focus is tree planting, involving 5,000 nurseries and some 20 million trees to date. It has helped to increase the income and status in their own communities of some 80,000 women and there are now related projects in 30 African countries.

The message that comes from these initiatives is increasingly clear. We have to choose which path to take, as Brewster Kneen observes when writing about the Deccan Development Society:

> The choices facing the people of Andhra Pradesh (and the rest of us) are stark: the preservation or reconstruction of autonomous local food systems and biodiversity, or dependence of the wealthy on the monoculture of a single globalized, TNC-controlled industrial food system, while the poor are left to beg on the streets.[5]

The choices *are* stark, but people in the colonised North are gradually beginning to wake up to them. The companies have not succeeded in quietly integrating GM crops into the food chain, unannounced and unnoticed, as they had hoped. Concern about the imposition of genetic engineering has provoked great unease among the urban populations of the North – in the UK, for example – where the industrialisation and consolidation of the food chain is intense. The issue has become a core around which unease about food and power, government, technology and corporations has crystallised. More and more people want to take some responsibility for how their food is produced, even to produce it themselves. They feel that current applications of genetic engineering threaten to merely reinforce current power structures, in spite of the siren song of the PR specialists, and they want something different. Change is hard work. It means rejecting systems based on perpetuating old values and old power structures. It means deciding if we want corporations to continue in their present form, or whether we want to rethink and reshape them completely. The simplest way of overcoming existing power structures is to create our own, which requires commitment and effort from each of us. Above all it demands that we cancel the agreement to delegate responsibility for the state of society, so that we can get on with our private concerns. We have to assume responsibility ourselves, individually and collectively. We all have to choose, on an individual, family, community and societal level.

Only by assuming such responsibility can we bring about real change and offer real support to those, mostly in the South, who are already practising appropriate methods of food production. They have a great deal to teach us.

Notes

1 Huw Bowen, 'Imperial Adventurers', *Guardian*, 12 January 2002.
2 Jules Pretty and Rachel Hine, 'Reducing Food Poverty with Sustainable Agriculture: a Summary of New Evidence'.
http://www2.essex.ac.uk/ces/ResearchProgrammes/safewexecsummfinalreport.htm
http://www2.essex.ac.uk/ces/ResearchProgrammes/SAFEW47casessusag.htm
3 Nicholas Parrott and Terry Marsden, *The Real Green Revolution: Organic and Agro-ecological Farming in the South*, Department of City and Regional Planning, Cardiff University, for the Greenpeace Environmental Trust, February 2002.
4 Jules Pretty, *Regenerating Agriculture: Policies and Practice for Sustainability and Self-Reliance*, London: Earthscan, 1995, p. 127, quoting S. M. Luo and R. J. Lin, 'High Bed–Low Ditch System in the Pearl River Delta, South China', *Agricultural Ecosystems and Environments,* 36 (1991): 101–9; C. S. Zhu and S. M. Luo, 'Red Deserts Turn to Green Oceans', *ILEIA Newsletter*, 8 (4) (1992): 25–26.
5 Brewster Kneen, 'A Global Village', *Ram's Horn*, 207 (December 2002).
http://www.ramshorn.bc.ca/

Index

Abacha, General Sani 57
Action against Hunger 208
Advance Chemical Industries Ltd. (ACI) 199
Advanta 86, 89; *see also* AstraZeneca
Africa 3, 24, 34-5, 59-61, 90, 104-6, 111-13,
    123, 125-30, 138, 155, 173, 184, 188-90, 192,
    194-6, 201, 209-13, 230; East 113, 192;
    southern 127, 128-9, 210; West 196
AfricaBio 59-61
African Seed Network 105
African Seed Trade Organisation 105
AgBio Foundation 55, 67, 70-2, 192
Agent Orange 48-9
Agfa 48
Agracetus 31
AgrEvo 83-4, 88, 116, 125, 127, 134, 141, 171; *see*
    also Bayer, Hoechst
agriculture, biodiversity in 3-4, 6-9, 78, 86-7, 89,
    93, 104-5, 107, 117-18, 201, 220, 226, 229-
    31; cash-crop export production 16-17, 127,
    212-13; conservation tillage 186, 195-7, 204-
    5, 217-20; and dependence/independence
    184-5, 190, 200, 202, 206, 209-13, 226, 230-
    1; and food aid imports 209-10; and global
    commodity markets 80; growers' contracts in
    186, 199-200; indigenous 5-6, 24, 226; local
    knowledge/farmer seed varieties in 3, 6, 14,
    103, 106, 108, 114, 117-19, 136, 188-90, 198,
    200, 210, 213, 226, 229-30; monoculture 3,
    8-9, 107, 118, 125-6, 202, 229-31; organic 46,
    63, 65-9, 71, 73, 216, 230; rural extension
    work 189-96, 207; small-scale 3, 5-6, 24, 114,
    127, 128-9, 151, 184, 190-4, 202, 211, 213,
    216; subsidies 17, 106-7; subsistence 5-6, 124,
    184; sustainable 3, 14, 192, 195, 217-18;
    TNCs in 17; variety mix farming 103-4;
    women in 6, 184-5, 196-8, 211, 230-1; *see*
    also fertiliser, food, green revolution,
    herbicides, irrigation, pesticides, etc.
Agriculture and Food Research Council (AFRC)
    133
AgroBioInstitute 177

Air Lloyd 106
Akhter, Farida 197-8
All India Biotech Association (AIBA) 61
Alliance for Bio-Integrity 169
American Council on Science and Health (ACSH)
    67, 72
American Enterprise Institute 63-4
American Home Products Corporation 84, 127
Amgen 53
Andes region 230
Andhra Pradesh 7, 230-1
Application of Sanitary and Phytosanitary Measures
    (SPS) Agreement 153
Archer Daniels Midland (ADM) 64, 127, 208-9
Argentina 57, 61, 90, 125, 155, 158, 184, 186-7,
    199, 203-6, 216, 218-19, 230
Århus Convention 174, 180
Asgrow 88; *see also* Seminis
Asia 12, 24, 85, 89, 112-13, 119-20, 122, 125,
    129, 201; South 111, 220; South-east 138,
    202-3
Asia Pacific Seed Association (APSA) 120
Asia–Pacific Economic Cooperation (APEC)
    Forum 152
Asian Development Bank (ADB) 120
Association of Biotechnology Companies *see*
    Biotechnology Industry Organisation (BIO)
Association of Burundi Consumers (ABUCO) 209
Association of South-East Asian Nations (ASEAN)
    24
AstraZeneca *see* Zeneca
Atanassov, Atanas 177
AusBiotech Ltd 61; *see also* Australian
    Biotechnology Association
Auschwitz 48
Australia 32, 59, 61, 91, 102, 110, 113, 117, 130,
    140, 155, 218
Australian Biotechnology Association 59; *see also*
    AusBiotech Ltd
Australian National Insect Collection 141
Australian National University 141
Austria 97, 181

Avcare 153
Aventis 18, 38, 49, 53, 62, 73, 80, 83-4, 86, 89,
    107-8, 122, 125, 133-4, 137, 141, 199;
    StarLink contamination 78, 83, 92; see also
    AgrEvo, Bayer CropScience, Rhone–Poulenc
Avery, Alex 68
Avery, Dennis 64, 66, 68, 69, 73-4

Bangladesh 13-14, 121, 129, 138, 196-8, 207, 230
Bangladesh Rural Advancement Committee
    (BRAC) 199
Barton, Brenda 208
BASF 48-50, 62, 83, 106, 108, 201
Bate, Roger 63, 65-6
Bayer 13, 48-9, 58, 83, 86, 92, 106, 108, 122, 131,
    199
Bayer CropScience 38, 83, 92, 171, 228; see also
    AgrEvo, Aventis, Hoechst
Belarus 127, 128
Belgium 97
Bellon, Mauricio 93
Benin 194
Bernays, Edward 45
Bertini, Catherine 208, 210
Beyer, Peter 136
Bhopal tragedy 49, 57, 79
BIO 2001 59
BioDiscovery 141
biodiversity, and agriculture 3-4, 6-9, 78, 86-7,
    89, 93, 104-5, 107, 117-18, 201, 220, 226,
    229-31; biotechnology effects on 78, 87-9,
    93-4, 101, 104-5, 107, 117-18, 128-9, 158,
    190-1, 201, 229; as insurance for the future
    93; pathogens and pests controlled by 8, 10;
    see also Convention on Biological Diversity
    (CBD)
Biogemma 141
Biogen 53
BioIndustry Association (BIA) 61
bioprospecting/biopiracy 37, 113, 220
Biosafety Protocol see Cartagena Biosafety Protocol
BIOTECanada 61
biotech industry, and agriculture 87-9, 93-4,
    101, 104-5, 107, 117-18, 128-9, 158, 178,
    190-1, 201, 229; at Cartagena Biosafety
    Protocol negotiations 156; consolidation of
    78-98, 202; and contamination debate 88-98;
    development of 24-8; and food aid 207-13;
    government backing for 101-2; ISAAA and
    127; 'life sciences' concept in 78-82, 191;
    patent power of 3, 18, 24-5, 28-38, 79, 82,
    86, 88, 90, 106, 108, 111, 113-14, 117, 120-3,
    132, 134-5, 186, 189, 199-204, 213, 220,
    226-7, 230; public relations by 2-3, 45-74, 79,
    127, 135-7, 217, 228, 230; Rockefeller Foun-
    dation and 123, 127, 129; sanctions on 102;
    strategies for introduction of GM worldwide
    161-221; and TRIPS agreement 34; and
    universities 130-1; World Bank subsidises 106-
    7; World Food Summit (2002) favours 2
Biotechnology and Biological Science Research
    Centre (BBSRC) 125, 131, 133-4

Biotechnology Consultative Forum 172
Biotechnology Industry Organisation (BIO) 56,
    58-9, 96, 172
Biotechnology Institute 53-4, 62
BIOTHAI 136, 217
Bivings Group 93
Blueridge Institute 137
Blundell, John 65
Bolivia 209
Borlaug, Norman E. 67, 72-3, 125, 172, 195
Bosnia and Herzegovina 176, 208
Botswana 213
Boyer, Herbert 37
BP 154
Brazil 36, 51, 82, 90, 104, 125, 154, 162, 186,
    188, 214-16, 218-19; Brazilian Consumer
    Defence Institute (IDEC) 215; National
    Technical Biosafety Commission (CTNBio)
    215
Bristol Myers Squibb 34
British Biotech 26-7
Brookings Institute 63
Brundtland Commission 154
BSE crisis 57, 97
Bt crops 82, 86, 88-9, 91-2, 116, 121-2, 165, 168,
    174-6, 184, 187, 192-3, 196, 203-4, 212, 214-
    15, 217
Buhle Farmer's Academy 194
Bulgaria 91, 157-8, 162, 173, 176-7
Burkina Faso 195
Burns, Arthur F. 64
Burrill and Co. 37
Burson–Marsteller 46-7, 55-8, 171
Burundi 209
Bush, George (Snr) 165-6
Bush, George W. 64
Business Council for Sustainable Development
    (BCSD) 154
Butz, Earl 1
Byrd, Senator 213

CABI-Biosciences 212
Calgene 37, 166, 168-9
Canada 24, 31, 61-2, 81, 89-91, 102, 110, 130,
    137, 147, 155-6, 158, 166, 174, 187, 196,
    199, 218
Canadian International Development Agency
    (CIDA) 196
CARE 208
Cargill 26, 64, 86-7, 106-8, 113, 125, 127-8, 153,
    195-6, 208-9
Caribbean 24
Carinthia 181
Carlisle, John 68
Cartagena Protocol on Biosafety 2, 69-70, 127,
    140, 147-8, 150, 153, 155-7, 177, 180; see also
    precautionary principle
Carter, Jimmy 194
Cato Institute 63-4, 69
Celera Genomics 41
Center for Food Safety 169
Center for Global Food Issues 68

Center for Plant Biotechnology Research 70
Center for the Biology of Natural Systems 41
Center of Bioengineering 176
Central America 24
Central Rice Research Institute (CRRI) 7
Centre for Economic and Policy Research (CEPR) 104
Centre for Tropical Agriculture (CIAT) 110
Chao, Elaine 64
Chapela, Ignacio 92-3
Cheney, Vice-President Dick 64
Chiapas 5
Chile 13, 36, 155, 218
China 12, 24, 32, 39, 91, 119-20, 184, 187-8, 196, 230
Chiquita Brands International 220
Christopher, Warren 112
Ciba 50, 192; *see also* Ciba–Geigy
Ciba–Geigy 48, 50-2, 82; *see also* Novartis
CIMMYT *see* International Maize and Wheat Improvement Centre
Citibank 220
Citizens for the Integrity of Science 68
Citizens' Network Agribusiness Alliance (CNAA) 127, 129
Citizens' Network for Foreign Affairs (CNFA) 47, 127-9, 175; Agribusiness Partnerships Program 128; Rural Agricultural Input Supply Extension (RAISE) 128-9
civil society 108, 127, 180, 200
Clinton, Bill 149, 172, 209, 212
Clinton, Hillary 197
Coale, Kristi 169
Coca-Cola 153, 179
Code of Conduct on the Right to Food 2
Codex Alimentarius 152-3
Codex Committee on Pesticide Residues (CCPR) 153
coffee 15-16, 18, 188, 200-2
Cold War 15, 23
Colombia 110, 209
Commodity Credit Corporation 209
Commonwealth Scientific and Industrial Research Organisation (CSIRO) 140-1
Competitive Enterprise Institute (CEI) 67-9, 71
Conko, Gregory 68-9, 71
Conservation International 220
Consultative Group for International Agricultural Research (CGIAR) 2, 33, 83, 85, 107-22, 124-5, 152, 188-9, 212; Change Design and Management Team (CDMT) 111; Private Sector Committee 114, 116; Technical Advisory Committee (TAC) 111
Consumer Alert 56, 67-9
Convention on Biological Diversity (CBD) 35, 147, 154-8
Convention on Climate Change 62, 154, 219
Conway, Gordon 123, 136
corn *see* maize
Cornell University 88, 125
corporations, consolidation of agbiotech sector 78-98; and environmental damage 154; and

and financial markets 23-8; free trade 17-18, 23-4; government backing for 101-2; green revolution and 5-6, 12; growers' contracts with 186, 199-200; history of 21-4; individual status and rights of 22-3; patent control by 3, 18, 24-5, 28-38, 79, 82, 86, 88, 90, 106, 108, 111, 113-14, 117, 120-3, 132, 134-5, 186, 189, 199-204, 213, 220, 226-7, 230; public relations by 2-3, 45-74, 79, 127, 135-7, 217, 228, 230; recolonisation of the world 229; regulation of 161; rhetoric of 4; sanctions on 102; and structural adjustment programmes (SAPs) 16-17; and subsidiary companies 23; transnational (TNCs) 17-18, 23, 34, 87, 101, 105, 116, 124, 128, 131, 141, 147-8, 150, 154, 163, 207, 220, 226-7, 231; and universities 130-1; World Bank subsidises 106-7; and the World Trade Organisation 147
Costa Rica 125, 220
Costello, John H. 128
Cosun 86
cotton 16, 18, 31, 51, 59, 78, 82-3, 91, 140-1, 184, 187, 196, 198, 204, 212, 214-17
Cotton Seed Distributors (CSD) 140-1
Council for Biotechnology Information (CBI) 53, 61
credit 5, 185-6, 190, 196-9, 204-5, 207, 209, 211; micro-credit schemes 185-6, 190, 196-9
Croatia 161, 176, 178-9, 181
Cuba 230
Cyanamid 83-4, 106, 127-8, 130
Czech Republic 174, 180

Da Silva, Luiz Inacio Lula (Lula) 216
Davidson, Jeff 53-4
DDT 48, 51, 63, 67-8, 106
debt, national 3, 16; farmers 103, 186, 230
Deccan Development Society 230-1
Degesch 48
Dekalb Genetics 127, 202
Delors, Jacques 171
Delta and Pine Land 86, 200-1
Denmark 97, 180
Developed Technology Resource Inc. 128
Diouf, Jacques 151-2
Direct Impact Company 55, 57-8
Diversa 82
Dow 37-8, 47, 49, 58, 62, 73, 83-6, 107-8, 125, 127, 130, 149, 153
drought 7, 10, 80
DuPont 18, 34, 38, 47-8, 56, 58, 62, 72, 82, 84-6, 88, 108, 127, 134, 137, 148, 154, 169, 174, 184, 201-3; *see also* Pioneer
Durkin, Martin 65

Earth Summit *see* United Nations Conference on Environment and Development
East India Company (British) 21-2, 228-9
Ecuador 209
Edison, Thomas 29
education 15-16, 52-4, 62, 104, 131, 134, 191, 194-5, 213

Egypt 51, 125
Eko-Pravo (Eco-Law) 175
Emergent Genetics 108
environmental damage 3, 9, 16, 24, 154
Environmental Foundation Ltd 162-3
Eritrea 192, 195
Escudero, Salvador 202
Estonia 174
ETC Group 84-7, 113, 137
Ethiopia 17, 148, 194, 210-11
EuropaBio 57, 59-60, 171
Europe 15, 30, 36, 64, 82, 106; Central 173-4; Eastern 161, 173-9, 205; South-east 174-7
European Directive on the Protection of Biotechnological Inventions (1998) 171-2, 227
European Science and Environment Forum (ESEF) 55, 64-6
European Union (EU) agricultural subsidies in 17; biotech corporations in 59, 227; Biotech Programme 136; and the Cartagena Biosafety Protocol 155, 158; environmental regulations in 65, 70; Familiarisation with and Acceptance of Crops Incorporating Transgenic Technology in Modern Agriculture (FACTT) 171; and food aid 211; GM contamination in 89, 96-8, 180; GM crops opposed in 80, 82, 96-8, 161-2, 171-3, 209-10, 216; GM entry into 180; and Golden Rice project 136; patents in 113; 'protectionism' of 69; regulatory regime in 161-2, 171-3, 180; and the Transatlantic Business Dialogue (TABD) 149-51; and the US 149-51, 161, 172-3, 210, 213; vitamin producers fined for price fixing by 50
Exxon 57, 220
Exxon Valdez oil spill 57

famine 17, 210-11
Farmland Industries 127
fertiliser 3, 5-6, 8-13, 72, 103, 118, 128, 196, 211, 219
Fischer, Linda 167-8
Fisher, Sir Anthony 64
FMC Corporation 84, 106
Food and Agriculture Organisation (FAO) 2-6, 39, 105, 108-10, 113-14, 120, 138, 151-2, 162, 164, 220; Global Perspective Studies Unit 151; *see also* Treaty on Plant Genetic Resources
food, dependence/self-sufficiency 1, 2, 35, 202, 206, 209-11, 230-1; distribution 14; dumping of 153, 165, 209-10; Food and Drug Administration (US) 55, 63, 67, 164-70; germplasm as ultimate source of 108-9, 112; global trade in 16-17; GM contamination of 4, 9, 31, 78, 80-2, 88-98, 101, 177, 179-80, 210, 216, 227, 229; malnutrition 1; as political tool 1; security 1, 3, 14, 17, 39, 89, 92, 106, 108-11, 117, 124, 127, 198, 201, 205-8, 210-11, 214; standards 152-3; TNCs 17; Vitamin A deficiency projects 138-9, 228
food aid 91, 95, 102, 165, 176, 179, 186, 207-13
Food Pro 128

Ford Foundation 5, 109, 119, 122, 188
Ford Motor Company 5
Foro Argentino de Biotecnología 61
Forum For Biotechnology and Food Security 214
Foundation for Clean Air Progress 58
France 23, 83, 86, 89, 97, 103, 106, 179, 188
Free Market Foundation (South Africa) 56
free trade 17-18, 23-4, 104
Free Trade Area of the Americas (FTAA) 24
Free Trade Institute (Peru) 56
Friends of the Earth 117, 162
Friuli–Venezia–Giulia 181
Furchgott-Roth, Diana 64

G8 Summit (2000) 151
Gandhi, Mahatma 194
Gatsby Charitable Foundation 109, 125, 134
Geigy 50; *see also* Ciba–Geigy
Genentech 37, 41
General Agreement on Tariffs and Trade (GATT) 23-4, 34, 101, 147, 149, 166; Uruguay Round 24, 34, 147, 149, 166
General Agreement on Trade in Services 130
General Motors 34, 148, 154
GENET 136
Genetic Interest Group 172
Genetic Resources Action International (GRAIN) 105-7, 112-13, 137
genetic use restriction technologies (GURTs) 4, 56, 106, 113, 122, 186, 200-2, 227
genetically modified (GM) food/seeds, African market penetration by 59-61, 104-6, 125-9; animals 166; biodiversity loss from 87-9, 93, 101, 104-5, 107, 117-18, 158, 201, 229; contamination factor 4, 9, 31, 78, 80-2, 88-98, 101, 177, 179-80, 210, 216, 227, 229; corporate strategies for introduction worldwide 161-221; debate over 3-5; FAO and 151-2; and food aid 207-13; global picture (tables) 187; Golden Rice as public relations saviour of 135; green revolution continuity with 13-15, 103; growth of biotech industry 24-36; high-response/high-yielding seed varieties 3, 5-9, 13-14, 72, 103, 119; and hunger 1-18, 106, 151-2; hybrid seeds and 29-30, 85, 88, 91, 171; John Innes Centre champions 134; monopoly control of 18, 32; and patents 28-38, 79, 82, 86, 88, 90, 108, 111, 117, 121-3, 134-7, 186, 189, 199-204, 213, 226-7; poor lose access to seed 12; proportional share of world seed market 83-5; public relations campaigns to promote 54-5, 58, 63-4, 67, 69-74, 79, 135, 217, 228; regulation of 2, 69-70, 126, 140, 147-8, 150, 153, 155-7, 161-81, 198; rice varieties 121-2; smuggling of seeds 90-1, 161, 178-9, 215-16; and substantial equivalence concept 164, 178, 205; testing for safety of 161, 164-70; vulnerability to pests and disease 8-10; in World Bank's Action Plan for Africa 104-6
Genetix plc 133
GeneWatch UK 162

genome studies 25, 28, 37-41, 87, 111, 115, 121, 131, 151; human genome 25, 28, 38, 40-1
Genzyme 53
George C. Marshall Institute 67
Georgia 175
Germany 13, 23, 83, 86, 103, 106, 124, 135, 175, 188
germplasm conservation 108-9, 112-14, 116-19; privatisation of 113-14, 116-18
Ghana 194, 219
Giddings, Val 56
GlaxoSmithKline 109, 133; see also SmithKlineBeecham
Glickman, Dan 166
Global Agricultural Management Enterprises 128
Global Conservation Trust 109
Global Crop Protection Federation 153
Global Environment Facility 110
Global Forum on Agricultural Research (GFAR) 111
globalisation, 15-18, 80
Grameen Bank 185, 197-8
Grameen Foundation 197
grassroots 47 53, 55, 57-8
Greece 97
Green Belt Movement 231
green revolution in Africa 129-30, 184, 194, 213; and agricultural biodiversity 6-9, 103, 117; alternatives to 103; in China 12; claims disputed 5-12, 103; and corporations 5-6, 12; and dependency 103; father of (Norman E. Borlaug) 72; and food security 1; GM seeds a continuation of 13-15, 103, 135; high-response/high-yielding seed varieties 3-4, 5-9, 13-14, 72, 103, 106; international agricultural research centres and 188; ISAAA and 125; land degraded by 6, 9-11, 103, 217; large-scale farmers benefited most by 103; as narrow view of farming 14, 135; plant breeding regimes for 85; and power structures 12; Rockefeller Foundation and 123; rural extension work and 189; small farmers and 103, 151; technical not socio-political solution 135; war industry links 13; water consumption/pollution by 9-10; World Bank major promoter of 103
greenhouse effect 62, 79, 154
Greenovation 135
Greenpeace 51, 135, 215
Groupe Limagrain 86
Grupo Pulsar see Seminis
Guinea 195
Guyana 230

Hale, Marcia 149
Hansen, Michael 168
Haryana 9
health 3, 9, 11, 15-16, 28, 35, 57, 135-8, 150, 155, 158, 201, 213-15
Heavily Indebted Poor Countries (HIPC) Initiative 16
herbicides 10, 13, 31, 49, 73, 79, 82-3, 89, 103, 176, 179, 186-8, 190, 198, 200, 203-4, 207,

215, 218-20, 229
Heritage Foundation 63-4
Hill and Knowlton 46
Hitachi Foundation 125, 144n
Hoechst 48, 83, 106, 131, 171; see also AgrEvo, Bayer
Hoffman–La Roche 37
Hoover Institution 67, 69
Hudson Institute 66, 68, 73-4
huertas 206
Humphrey, Hubert 1
Hungary 173-4, 177, 179-80
hunger, biotech agriculture as 'solution' to 1-18, 106, 151-2; different approaches to 3; famine 17, 210-11; food (in)security 1, 3, 14, 17, 39, 89, 92, 106, 108-11, 117, 124, 127, 198, 201, 205-8, 210-11, 214; hidden 138, 140; malnutrition 1; and revolution 5; structural causes of 3-4
Hybrid Rice International 199
hybrid seeds 29-30, 85, 88, 91, 103, 106, 113, 118-22, 136, 140, 171, 198-9, 202, 207

IG Farben 48
ICI 66
Icon Genetics 175
IMC Global 196
IMC Kalium 196
India 22, 39, 49, 51, 57, 61, 80, 82, 85, 91, 110, 119, 121, 162, 179, 184, 186, 188, 190-1, 211, 214-15, 228, 230-1; Genetic Engineering Approval Committee 214
indigenous people 5-6, 114, 119, 154, 189, 226
Indira Gandhi Agricultural University (IGAU) 7
Indonesia 57, 107, 119, 125, 152, 196, 202-3, 206-7
Industrial Biotechnology Association see Biotechnology Industry Organisation (BIO)
Initiative on Seed Supply in Sub-Saharan Africa (ISSSSA) 104-6, 212
Institute for Food and Vegetable Crops (IFVC, Yugoslavia) 179
Institute for International Economics 64
Institute for Maize Research (Yugoslavia) 179
Institute of Arable Crop Research 133
Institute of Economic Affairs (IEA) 55, 64-6
Institute of Food Research 133
integrated pest management (IPM) 124, 191
intellectual property rights (IPRs) 25, 30, 32, 105, 107-8, 111, 113-17, 120-3, 125, 126, 134-7, 141, 163, 179, 185-6, 189, 212, 227; see also patents, TRIPs
intercropping 103-4
Intermediate Technology Development Group (ITDG) 2
international agricultural research centres (IARCs) 4, 110-12, 115-17, 188, 194
International Association of Plant Breeders for the Protection of Plant Varieties (ASSINSEL) 179
International Atomic Energy Authority 134
International Centre for Agricultural Research in Dry Areas (ICARDA) 110, 116

International Centre of Insect Physiology (ICIPE) 124

International Consumers for a Civil Society 67

International Crops Research Institute for Semi-Arid Tropics (ICRISAT) 110, 113, 115, 140

International Food Policy Research Institute (IFPRI) 110, 112, 188, 211

International Fund for Agricultural Development (IFAD) 193

International Livestock Research Institute (ILRI) 115

International Maize and Wheat Improvement Centre (CIMMYT) 5, 72, 93, 110, 112-13, 115-16, 125, 192-3, 212

International Monetary Fund (IMF) 16, 23, 101-4, 203

International Organisation for Consumers 209

International Policy Council on Agriculture, Food and Trade 74

International Policy Network 63

International Potato Centre (CIP) 110, 116, 125

International Rice Genome Sequencing Project 39, 121, 131, 151

International Rice Research Institute (IRRI) 4, 8, 12, 72, 85, 110, 116, 118-21, 125, 136, 140

International Rice Sequencing Group (IRGSP) 39

International Seed Treaty 2

International Service for the Acquisition of Agri-Biotech Applications (ISAAA) 73, 108, 123-7, 136-7, 178, 214, 217

Interpublic 46

Investment in Developing Export Agriculture (IDEA) 212

Iowa Export–Import 127

Iowa State University 54, 131

Iran 5

Ireland 17, 163

irrigation 3, 5-7, 9-10, 12

Israel 61

Israel Biotechnology Organization 61

Italy 89, 179, 181

Ivory Coast 196

J. Walter Thompson Group 46

Japan 13, 15, 24, 39, 50, 61, 86, 92, 103, 106, 125, 147, 151, 162, 188, 194, 209, 227

Japan Bioindustry Association 61

John Innes Centre 125, 134

Johnson, Ian 110

Kantor, Micky 149

Kashmir 230

Kenya 5, 107, 115, 124-5, 126, 192, 231

Kenyan Agricultural Research Institute (KARI) 126, 192-3

Kilusang Magbubukid ng Pilipinas (KMP) 135-6, 208

Kirk, William F. 56

Kissinger, Henry 127

Kosovo 179

Kraft 64, 127

Krattiger, Anatole 125

KWS AG 86

Kyiv-Atlantic 128

Kyoto Protocol/Treaty 67-8, 219

La Amistad nature reserve 220

labelling (of GM products) 63, 67, 69, 96-7

Lamy, Pascal 149

land, access to 3, 12, 230-1; concentration 5-7, 228; degradation 6, 9-11; distribution of 12; exodus/removals 6-7; reform 5, 12, 228; removals 6

Laos 191

Large Scale Biology Corporation (LSBC) 175

Latin America 112, 125

Latin American Meeting on Food Aid 209

Latvia 174

Leisinger, Klaus M. 192-3

Lesotho 210, 213

Liberty Link System 86

Like-Minded Group 155

Lindsey, Lawrence 64

Lithuania 174

local knowledge/farmer seed varieties 3, 6, 14, 103, 106, 108, 114, 117-19, 136, 188-90, 198, 200, 210, 213, 226, 229-30; see also traditional knowledge

Luxembourg 97

MacArthur Foundation 122

Macedonia 176

MacMillan, Whitney 196

Madhya Pradesh Rice Research Institute (MPRRI) 7

Maharashtra Hybrid Seed Company (Mahyco) 108, 214-15

maize 4-6, 18, 30, 38, 59, 72, 82, 85, 88, 92-5, 111-13, 141, 168, 171, 176-80, 186-7, 192-3, 202-4, 207-8, 211, 219, 227

Makerere University 212

Makhteshim–Agan 84

Malawi 17, 60, 104, 129, 194, 210

Malaysia 7, 125

Mali 192-3, 195-6

Marcos, President Ferdinand 119

Mariano, Rafael 1, 208

market forces 3, 5, 15-17, 23-8, 63, 111, 195-6, 212

Martineau, Belinda 169

MASIPAG (Farmer–Scientist Partnership for Development, Philippines) 121, 136, 189

Massachusetts General Hospital 131

Massachusetts Institute of Technology 132

Matthews, E. J. 170

Mauritius 60

Max Planck Institute 131

Mazhar, Farhad 199

McNamara, Robert S. 5

media 2, 58-63, 71, 73, 83, 91, 94, 136, 169, 175, 178, 207, 217, 231

Merck 53

Merial Ltd 108

Mexico 5, 24, 72, 82, 87, 92-5, 104, 107, 111-13,

125, 126, 162, 192, 227, 230
Miami Group 140, 155, 158
Michigan State University 73
MicroFlo 83
Millar, Andrew 26-7
Miller, Henry I. 67, 69
Miller, Margaret 168
Milloy, Steven J. 68-9
Mobil 220
Moldova 127, 128
Moll, Steven 163
Monsanto 2-3, 18, 31-2, 34, 37-8, 40, 48, 53-8,
    62, 72-3, 78-9, 82-8, 90-1, 93, 108, 116, 121-
    2, 124-7, 130-2, 134, 137, 148-9, 153-4, 156,
    162-3, 166-9, 174-7, 179, 184-6, 195-206,
    212, 214-20, 228
Monsanto Fund 185, 194, 212
Morris, Julian 55, 65-6
Mozambique 60, 104, 127, 194-5, 210
Multilateral Agreement on Investment (MAI) 24
Mulvany, Patrick 2
Murdoch, Rupert 65
Myanmar 121
Mycogen Corporation 37, 149
Myriad Genetics 39

Namibia 60, 213
National Agricultural Research Organisation
    (Uganda) 212
national agricultural research systems (NARSs) 194
National Center for Public Policy Research 68
National Consumer Coalition 67
Nature 93-4
Naya Krishi Andolan (New Agriculture
    Movement) 230
Nazi legacy 48-9
Nestec 153
Nestlé 64, 133, 153, 179
Netherlands 23, 86, 107, 172
New Zealand 32, 61, 89
New Zealand Biotechnology Association 61
Nielson, Poul 173
Nigeria 57, 66, 106, 113, 194
Nippon Foundation 195
non-governmental organisations (NGOs), in
    Argentina's GM debate 205; as biotech
    industry conduits to the South 206; in
    Brazilian resistance to GM crops 214; in/and
    CGIAR 109-12, 117, 189; and collaborative
    research 189; in Croatian stand against GMOs
    178; at the Earth Summit (1992) 154; and
    food aid 208, 211; in Indian resistance to GM
    crops 214; and IRRI 119; on national
    biosafety commissions 180; and plant patenting
    125; as public relations targets 47, 54, 69; and
    Rockefeller Foundation 123; and rural
    extension networks 189; and Sri Lankan stand
    on GM 162-3; and Thailand's illegal GM
    cotton 217; and Ukrainian GM legislation
    175; and World Bank's African seed initiative
    105; at World Food Summits (1996, 2002) 2;
    at World Summit for Sustainable Development

(2002) 155
Norfolk Genetic Information Network 66
Norsk Hydro 195
North, Richard 65
North American Free Trade Agreement (NAFTA)
    24, 149, 152, 166
Novartis 4, 50-4, 58, 62, 73, 80, 82, 84, 93, 116,
    122, 125, 127, 132, 134, 137, 153-4, 163,
    169, 171, 185, 191-2, 195-6, 200, 202-3, 207;
    see also Ciba–Geigy, Sandoz, Syngenta
Novartis Foundation for Sustainable Development
    (NFSD) 110, 116, 185, 191-2

Ogoniland 66
oil 15-16
Omnicom 46
O'Neill, Paul H. 64
Open University 131
Organisation for Economic Cooperation and
    Development (OECD) 109, 131
Organisation of Petroleum Exporting Countries
    (OPEC) 15-16
Orynova BV 122
Oxfam 117

Pakistan 91, 107, 163
Panama 220
Patent Cooperation Treaty (PCT) 36
Patent Law Treaty 36
patents 3, 18, 24-5, 29-38, 59-60, 79, 82, 86; 88,
    90, 108, 111, 113-14, 117, 120-3, 132, 134-7,
    154, 186, 189, 199-204, 213, 220, 226-7, 230
PCBs 48
Peasant Movement of the Philippines *see* Kilusang
    Magbubukid ng Pilipinas (KMP)
Pennsylvania Biotechnology Association 53
Pepsi Cola 153
Peru 110
Pesticide Action Network 93, 106, 163
Pesticide Action Network Asia–Pacific (PAN–AP)
    163
Pesticide Action Network North America
    (PANNA) 93
Pesticide Efficacy Advisory Centres (PEACE) 191
pesticides 3, 5-6, 8-10, 12-13, 38, 48-51, 63, 72,
    79-80, 83, 86-7, 90-1, 103, 106, 118, 124,
    128, 141, 152-3, 165, 167, 188, 190-1, 207,
    215, 229
Pfizer 34, 53
PGS (biotech company) 31
pharmaceutical industry 34, 37-8, 40-1, 50, 59, 66,
    69, 79-81, 89, 95, 141, 158, 175, 188, 220;
    'biopharm' products 79-81, 95-6, 175
Pharmacia 82, 84, 132
Philip Morris 69
Philippines 4-5, 8, 12, 72, 82, 85, 107, 119, 121-2,
    125, 135-6, 184, 189, 191, 202-3, 208
Phillips, Michael J. 172
Pioneer Hi-Bred International 30, 82, 84-6, 113,
    125-7, 131, 174, 176-7, 179, 184, 192, 202-3;
    see also DuPont
Plant Biosciences Limited 134

plant breeding (history of) 85-6, 92
Plant Genetics Systems (PGS) 122, 171
Poland 174, 177, 180
Portugal 23
Potrykus, Ingo 135-7
poverty 3, 5, 101, 107, 213, 231
Pragnell, Michael 81
Prakash, Professor Channapatna 54-5, 67, 70-2
precautionary principle 2, 69-70, 89, 102, 150,
    155-7, 172, 215; see also Cartagena Protocol
Pribyl, Louis 170
privatisation 38, 87, 104, 113-14, 116-18, 220,
    227, 229; of biodiversity 220; of germplasm
    conservation 113-14, 116-18; of knowledge
    heritage 38, 87, 113-14, 189-90, 229
Proagro 199
ProBiotech 68
Prodi, Romano 172
ProdiGene Inc. 95-6, 175
Progressive Genetics 128
Prohuerta 206
Promar International 88
protectionism 64, 69, 150, 172
Provincial Advocates for Sustainable Development
    (PASAD) 191-2
Prudente, Antonio 215
PT Monagro Kimia 206-7
public relations (PR) 2-3, 45-74, 79, 127, 135-7,
    217, 228, 230
Punjab 9
Pure Sunshine 128

Quist, David 93

rainforest 65, 68
Rallis 190-1
Rand Corporation 64
Reagan, Ronald 34, 165
Reason Foundation 64
Red Interamericana de Democracia (Interamerican
    Network on Democracy) 204
Rees, Nina 64
regulation/deregulation 15-17, 26, 64, 71, 101,
    149-50, 153, 155-7, 161-81, 198
Renessen 87
Republika Srpska 208
research 26, 28-9, 32-8, 46, 50-1, 53, 56, 60-1,
    63, 65-7, 69, 70-2, 80-2, 85-8, 92-4, 96, 101-
    2, 111, 113, 116-24, 126, 129-41, 151-2, 157,
    161, 166, 169, 177-8, 186, 188-9, 194-5, 202,
    212, 227-9
Research Foundation for Science, Technology and
    Ecology 198
Rhine River 51
RhoBio 141
Rhone-Poulenc 49-50, 83-4, 106, 127, 133, 141;
    see also Aventis
Ribozyme Pharmaceuticals 132
rice 4, 6-9, 25, 38-9, 83, 85, 87, 118-22, 135-41,
    151-2, 198-9, 202, 207, 219, 230; Golden
    Rice 80, 122, 135-40
Richharia, R. H. 7

Rio Tinto Zinc 154
Roche 49-50
Rockefeller, John D. 195
Rockefeller, Winthrop 195
Rockefeller Foundation 5, 72, 107-9, 119, 122-5,
    136, 188, 212; International Programme on
    Rice Biotechnology 123
Romania 91, 161, 173, 176-9
RoundUp 31, 82, 86, 88, 91, 179, 198-9, 204,
    215-16, 218-20
Roussel-Uclaf 106
Ruckelshaus, William D. 167
Rulli, Jorge Eduardo 203
Rural Advancement Foundation International
    (RAFI) see ETC Group
Russia 127, 128, 176, 179

Sainsbury, Lord 133
Sainsbury family trusts 109, 134
Sainsbury Laboratory 134
Sakata 86
Sandoz 50-2, 82; see also Novartis
Santayana, George 226
Santer, Jacques 171
Sasakawa Africa Association (SAA) 194
Sasakawa, Rioichi 194-5
Sasakawa-Global 2000 Programme (SG 2000) 73,
    190, 194-5
Sasakawa Foundation 195
Save the Children 208
Savia 87-8
Scarlett, Lynn 64
Schering 83
Scheuplein, Robert J. 169
Schmeiser, Percy 31, 90, 137, 199
Schultze, Nikolaus 193
Science and Engineering Research Council
    (SERC) 133
Scotland 54
Scottish Enterprise 53
Scruton, Roger 66
Seminis 86-8, 108, 195; see also Asgrow
Senegal 196
Shapiro, Robert 56, 149
Shell 66, 154
Shiva, Vandana 55, 139, 198
Shonsey, Ed 54
SIBAT 189
Slovakia 174, 180
Slovenia 174, 176, 180-1
Smith, Frances B. 68-9
Smith, Steve 4
SmithKlineBeecham 133, 153, 172; see also
    GlaxoSmithKline
Smon tragedy 50-1
Socio-Ecologic Union 176
Sojaprotein 179
Solanum PEI 174
South Africa 59-61, 187, 194, 199, 210, 213
South America 24, 201, 229-30
South Korea 39, 92, 162
South Sea Company 22

Southern African Customs Union (SACU) 24, 213
Soviet Union (former) 127, 128, 161, 173, 230
soybeans 31-2, 73, 79, 85, 90, 95, 112, 173, 177-8, 184, 186-7, 203-6, 214-16
Spain 23
Sri Lanka 119, 162-3
Stanford University 37, 67
StarLink contamination episode 78, 83, 92, 96
Stott, Professor Philip 65, 68
structural adjustment programmes (SAPs) 16-17, 101, 130
Substantive Patent Law Treaty (SPLT) 36
Sudan 194
Suharto, General 57
Sumitomo 84, 106
Sustainable Development Network 55-6, 67
Swaminathan, M. S. 125
Swanson, Robert 37
Swaziland 210, 213
Swedish Environmental Institute 117
Swiss Federal Institute of Technology 135-6
Switzerland 37, 51, 124, 136, 153; Federal Office for Education and Science 136
Syngenta 18, 32-3, 38-9, 48, 58, 80-6, 93, 107-9, 116, 121-2, 124, 133-5, 137, 185, 191, 200, 202, 228; *see also* Novartis, Zeneca
Syngenta Foundation for Sustainable Agriculture 110, 185, 192-3
Syria 110

Taiwan 119-20
Takeda Chemical Industries 50
Tanzania 51, 194
Technical Barriers to Trade (TBT) Agreement 153
Technova Inc. 125
Terminator/Traitor technologies *see* genetic use restriction technologies (GURTs)
Tesco 174
Texas A&M University 88, 130
Thailand 91, 113, 125, 162, 190, 203, 214, 217
The Advancement of Sound Science Coalition (TASSC) 68
think tanks 62-4
tobacco industry 45, 55, 66, 68
Tobin Tax 28
Togo 194
Torrey Mesa Research Institute (TMRI) 39
Touchdown 83
trade liberalisation *see* free trade
Trade-related Intellectual Property Rights (TRIPs) 31, 34-5, 126, 148-9, 163, 227
traditional knowledge 130, 189, 193; *see also* local knowledge
Transatlantic Business Dialogue (TABD) 149-51
Treaty on Plant Genetic Resources 35, 114
Tuskegee University 70

UBINIG (Policy Research for Development Alternatives) 14, 129, 197-9, 230
Uganda 186, 190, 195, 212
Ukraine 127, 128, 174-5
Ukraine Green 175

Unilever 133-4, 174
Union Carbide Corporation 49, 57, 79
Union for the Protection of New Varieties of Plants (UPOV) 30, 104
United Kingdom (UK), academic training in 133-4; Advertising Standards Authority 3; Advisory Committee on Releases to the Environment (ACRE) 201; Agriculture and Environment Biotechnology Commission 98; BioIndustry Asociation (BIA) 61; and the Biosafety Protocol 158; biotech industry in 28, 102; in CGIAR 110; colonial history 21-3; conservation tillage in 218; corporations originate in 21-2; Council for Academic Autonomy 130-1; Council for Academic Freedom and Academic Standards 131; Department of Trade and Industry 133; GM contamination in 89, 92, 98; GM crops in 161, 210, 231; ISAAA in 125; Monsanto campaign in 2-3; Office of Science and Technology 133; patents in 134; regulatory regime in 161, 180; research spending in 188; Royal Society 201; seed corporations in 86; Terminator technology in 201; think tanks in 62-4; university–industry partnership in 130, 134; and the World Bank 103, 106-7
United Nations, Universal Declaration on the Eradication of Hunger and Malnutrition 1; Women's Conference (Beijing, 1995) 210; *see also* Food and Agriculture Organisation (FAO), World Food Conference (1974), World Food Summit (1996), etc.
United Nations Conference on Environment and Development (UNCED) 154; Earth Summit (1992) 154
United Nations Development Programme (UNDP) 110
United Nations Environment Programme (UNEP) 110, 125, 154
United States (US), African Growth and Opportunity Act (AGOA) 24, 212-13; Agricultural Cooperative Development International (ACDI/VOCA) 176; agricultural subsidies in 17; American Corn Growers Association 18; and the Biosafety Protocol 140, 153, 155-6, 158; biotech industry in 28, 102, 149, 227; BIO–USA 61; Chemical Manufacturers Association 49; in CGIAR 110; Committee on Public Information (CPI) 45; conservation tillage in 218; and the Convention on Biological Diversity (CBD) 154-5; corn crop in 112; corporate funding of universities 132; corporate public relations in 52, 58-9, 62; corporation history in 23; Croatia pressurised over GM products 178; Department of Agriculture (USDA) 1, 30, 38, 70, 95-6, 149, 166, 200-1, 208; Department of Commerce 53; Department of Energy 53; Environmental Protection Agency (EPA) 164-7; and the EU 149-51, 161, 172-3, 210, 213; Fairness and Accuracy In Reporting (FAIR) 63; food aid 1, 91, 95, 102, 176, 179, 207-12;

Food and Drug Administration (FDA) 55, 63, 67, 164-70; foundations in 122; gene banks in 112, 117; and genetic use restriction technologies (GURTs) 227; GM contamination in/by 81, 89-96, 210; GM food in 161-2, 164-5, 184, 187; growers' contracts in 199; Intellectual Property Committee 148; ISAAA in 125;in NAFTA 24, 149; National Academy of Sciences 166-7; National Center for Biotechnology Information (NCBI) 38; National Research Council (NRC) 166; oil crises (1973, 1979) and 15; patents in 31-2, 35-6, 90, 113, 132, 199-200, 213; pharmaceutical industry in 34; pharma-crops in 95-6, 175; plant breeding in 85; regulatory regime in 161-2, 164-70; research in 188; rice crop in 112, 121; and the rice genome 38-9, 121, 131, 151; Securities and Exchange Commission (SEC) 27; seed corporations in 86; and seed smuggling 91; think tanks in 62-4; and the Transatlantic Business Dialogue (TABD) 149-51; university–industry partnership in 130; war industry 13; wheat crop in 112; and the World Bank 103, 106-7; at the World Food Summit (2002) 2; at the World Summit for Sustainable Development (Johannesburg, 2002) 148; and the World Trade Organisation 147

United States Agency for International Development (USAID) 85, 102, 109, 125, 128, 176, 185, 190, 208, 211-12; Agricultural Initiative to Cut Hunger in Africa (AICHA) 211; Assessment of Biotechnology in Uganda (report) 212; Collaborative Agricultural Biotechnology Initiative (CABIO) 212

University of California 88, 93, 132
University of Colorado 132
University of Freiburg 136
University of Jerusalem 88
University of North Carolina 88
University of Panama 220
University of the Philippines 119
University of Wisconsin 73
Uruguay 155
US–Canada Free Trade Agreement 166

Veneman, Ann 64, 166
Venezuela 107
Videla, General Jorge Rafael 57
Vietnam 121, 125
Virmani, Sant S. 121

Wageningen University 88
Walt Disney 220
Wambugu, Dr Florence 126
Washington University 131-2
water 3, 6, 9-10, 130
Watson, Claire 163
Weaver, Warren 123
Wellcome 133; see also GlaxoSmithKline

Westfall, Don 88
wheat 4-5, 9, 17, 30, 34, 38, 72, 85, 87, 112-13, 134, 141, 175-6, 179, 203, 211
Williams, Alan 26
Winrock Foundation 122
Winrock International 195-6; On-Farm Agricultural Resources Management (ONFARM) 196
Winrock International Institute for Agricultural Development 195
Wolfensohn, James 107
women, in agriculture 6, 184-5, 196-8, 211, 230-1; and biodiversity 6, 198; in biotech industry rhetoric 185-6; in the CGIAR 110; and food aid 209; and micro-credit 185-6, 190, 196-9
World Bank 5, 7, 15-16, 23, 85, 101-10, 125-6, 185, 190, 203, 212; Initiative on Seed Supply in Sub-Saharan Africa (ISSSSA) 104-6, 212; International Centre for Settlement of Investment Disputes (ICSID) 102; International Development Association (IDA) 102; International Finance Corporation (IFC) 102; Multilateral Investment Guarantee Agency (MIGA) 102
World Business Council for Sustainable Development (WBCSD) 154
World Food and Farming Congress 74
World Food Conference (1974) 1
World Food Programme (WFP) 206, 208, 210-11
World Food Summit (1996) 1-2, 151; Five Years Later (2002) 2, 152, 212
World Health Organisation (WHO) 9, 66, 138, 152, 162, 164
World Intellectual Property Organisation 24, 35-6, 137
World Summit for Sustainable Development (Johannesburg, August 2002) 55, 109, 148, 155
World Trade Organisation (WTO) 17, 23-4, 31, 34, 96, 101, 130, 147-50, 152-3, 155, 158, 161-3, 178, 185, 227; Seattle Ministerial Conference (1999) 147, 155
WorldWatch Institute 12
WPP (Wire and Plastic Products) 46

Yeutter, Claydon K. 149
Young and Rubicam 46
Yugoslavia (Montenegro and Serbia) 161, 176, 178-9
Yugoslavia, former 176
Yunus, Muhammad 197-8

Zambia 60, 104, 127, 210-11
Zeneca 18, 62, 73, 80, 82, 84, 86, 88, 106, 122, 133-6, 153, 191, 200-1; see also Syngenta
Zia, Dr Shahid 163
Zimbabwe 60, 104, 107, 113, 125-6, 128, 210
Zoellick, Robert 162, 172, 213
Zyklon B 48